EAST–WEST RELATIONS

The international congress on *East–West Relations: Prospects for the 1980s*, organised by the Institute of European Studies 'Alcide De Gasperi' in Rome in the spring of 1980, was held at a time when the dramatic impact of the Afghan events and the ensuing US grain embargo and other counter-measures seemed to call for careful reconsideration of the benefits and disadvantages of closer interdependence between East and West. On the strictly economic plane, the slow recovery of Western economies from a sharp recession and the gradual slackening of Eastern growth rates seemed to lead to a revival of dangerous protectionist attitudes.

Many of the papers presented at the congress, analysing the basic political and economic issues of East–West relations and the prospects for trade and co-operation, are now collected in this volume.

Giuseppe Schiavone, the editor, is Professor of International Organisation in the Faculty of Political Science, University of Catania, Italy. He took his degree in political science at the University of Rome and subsequently became Professor of East European International Organisations at the Institute 'Alcide De Gasperi' of Postgraduate European Studies in Rome. His publications include *The Institutions of Comecon*.

EAST–WEST RELATIONS

Prospects for the 1980s

Edited by

Giuseppe Schiavone

WITHDRAWN

St. Martin's Press   New York

Library of Congress Cataloging in Publication Data

Main entry under title:

East–West relations.

    Includes index.
    1. International economic relations–Congresses.
2. World politics–Congresses.   I. Schiavone, Giuseppe.
HF1410.5.E16   1982   337   81-21433
ISBN 0–312–22496–6   AACR2

Contents

83/10/10

List of the Contributors

Silviu Brucan, University of Bucharest

Mario Guttieres, International Juridical Organisation, Rome

Joseph Hajda, Kansas State University

Philip Hanson, University of Birmingham

Alexej Kohout, CSSR Academy of Sciences, Prague

Yves Laulan, Société Générale, Paris

Jean Marczewski, University of Paris I, Panthéon-Sorbonne

Harriet Matejka, Graduate Institute for International Studies, Geneva

Tullio Morganti, Doctor of Law, Milan

Josef Mrázek, CSSR Academy of Sciences, Prague

József Nyilas, Karl Marx University, Budapest

Fred Parkinson, University College, London

Yoko Sazanami, Keio University, Tokyo

Giuseppe Schiavone, University of Catania, Italy

Georges Sokoloff, Groupe d'Etudes Prospectives Internationales, Paris

Foreword

The Institute of European Studies, founded in Rome by Adenauer, Schuman, Spaak and De Gasperi, the latter having served as its first Director, conducts scientific and teaching activities for the progress of studies concerning co-operation and integration in Europe.

Within the framework of its programme for the expansion of scientific relations with socialist countries, our Institute convened in Rome an international Congress on 'East-West Relations: Prospects for the 1980s'. The Congress, held on 22-25 April 1980, was organised by the Institute with the co-operation of the National Research Council of Italy and the Italian Office of the Commission of the European Communities, under the sponsorship of the President of the Italian Republic. The participants were experts and scholars specialised in East-West studies at universities and institutes mainly located in Europe - Austria, Belgium, Bulgaria, Czechoslovakia, Denmark, France, the FRG, the GDR, Hungary, Italy, Poland, Romania, Spain, Sweden, Switzerland, the United Kingdom and the USSR; they were joined by professors from Japan, Mexico and the USA.

The Congress was divided into working sessions, devoted to the following topics: (1) The Role of Western and Eastern Europe in the Global East-West Relationship; (2) Basic Issues of the East-West Dialogue and New Trends in the World Economy; (3) The Prospects for East-West Trade; (4) The EEC, the CMEA and All-European Co-operation; and (5) The Scope for East-West Co-operation. A good number of the papers presented at the Congress are now collected in this volume.

On conclusion of the Congress, the participants approved a resolution concerning the establishment in Rome of a Permanent Pan-European Secretariat for the Study of East-West Relations.

I think it is appropriate to repeat here my thanks to all those responsible for the planning and organisation of the Congress; in particular I wish to express my warm appreciation to Professor Giuseppe Schiavone, a member of our teaching staff since 1969, for his outstanding contribution to the success of the meeting, and to Dr Michele Formica, our Secretary-General. I also wish to acknowledge the co-operation of Dr Joseph Hajda, of Kansas State University, who assisted us in the revision of some of the papers.

Giovanni Zaccaria
Vice-President and Director of Studies
Institute of European Studies
'Alcide De Gasperi'

Preface

The East-West relationship has entered a phase of dramatic changes and it is difficult to tell at this moment whether the road will be smoother or even more rugged during the 1980s in a global environment that is itself far from clear. Western economies seem to be recovering only gradually from a sharp recession, while on the Eastern side growth rates appear to have slackened and are expected to remain well below average. The resort to protectionist measures and import restrictions on the part of many governments, the spreading activities of multinationals and the worldwide economic slowdown will dampen the growth of international and East-West trade. On the political plane, the Afghan crisis, the delicate situation in Eastern Europe and the recurring fears about new thrusts in the Gulf seem to increase the risks of a confrontation between the superpowers leading to a revival of highly dangerous cold-war attitudes. This will cause, inter alia, a much stronger growth in defence expenditures to the detriment of other sectors.

Within this rapidly changing context, the essays collected in this volume are intended to provide additional food for thought and to contribute to a deeper understanding of relevant issues concerning the East-West relationship.

The papers which follow may be roughly divided into three main groups: the first one deals with the basic political and economic issues of East-West relations while the two other groups are devoted to the prospects for trade and co-operation at both the bilateral and multilateral levels.

In the opening essay, M. Laulan discusses the nature and distribution of the benefits and disadvantages of closer interdependence between East and West; the author draws attention to some of the basic ambiguities, from the standpoint of Western security, of East-West economic exchanges and foresees a co-operation 'without illusions', largely stripped of ideological motivations and ultimately based on the short-term mercantile interest of the parties concerned.

Professor Brucan points out that political developments in Europe in the 1980s will depend largely on outside factors such as the power game between the USA and the USSR and the evolution of the world economic crisis. In forecasting future developments in both halves of the European continent, Professor Brucan considers four variables: (1) the pressure of technological interdependence; (2) power politics; (3) national self-assertion; and (4) social change.

Professor Marczewski for his part stresses that East-West co-operation is vital to the Eastern side but is also of considerable importance for Western countries especially as a means for over-coming world stagflation. However, the possibilities of expanding this co-operation will depend to a very large extent on the removal, on both sides, of a number of institutional and administrative restrictions and on the restoration of an acceptable degree of mutual confidence and respect.

The second group of papers deals with the prospects for East-West trade. Professor Matejka is directly concerned with payments' systems and the levels of trade and presents policy conclusions in terms of countertrade and compensation. In her view, compensation is a second-best policy which should be discouraged; it reduces the efficiency and volume of trade and its effects are even more damaging than those of clearing arrangements. First-best policy is a change in the exchange rate but this remains a long-term goal rather than an objective to be achieved in the short run.

The four papers which follow offer an insight into specific aspects of East-West trade. Dr Hajda examines four questions: (1) the heightened dependence of the USSR and other Eastern countries on grain imports from the West; (2) the effectiveness of the US grain embargo; (3) the Soviet efforts to contain the embargo campaign; and (4) the alternative futures constructed from different sets of assumptions.

The growing role of non-fuel commodities within the framework of East-West relations has become a matter of concern to many governments; the editor of this volume discusses in his contribution the exacerbated dependence of the USA and the EEC countries on the Soviet Union and South Africa as major suppliers of a number of vital minerals; attention is also drawn to the growing USSR reliance on outside sources for its non-fuel minerals supplies.

Professor Sokoloff has undertaken a survey to determine the reasons leading the Soviet Union to adopt more than two decades ago and subsequently to confirm the decision to open its economy to Western supplies of capital goods. His paper illustrates the main findings of the survey for the period 1959-79 and concludes that the USSR will pursue its import policy while refusing, on the other hand, really to link its interests with those of Western developed countries.

The role of Japan in the development of East-West trade relations is elucidated by Professor Sazanami. After a review of the development of trade relations between Japan and Eastern countries (including China) in the 1970s, the author underlines what, in her view, was the prime motive on the part of Japan in expanding these relations and makes an assessment of Japanese policy measures that can effectively contribute to the further promotion of East-West economic intercourse.

Several economic and legal aspects of East-West co-operation are dealt with in the third group, which comprises six papers. Professor Nyilas's paper investigates the current problems of all-European economic co-operation and presents the Eastern view on the basic issues. According to Professor Nyilas, the expansion of mutual co-operation is a timely necessity for both halves of Europe; with the levels of development coming closer, the benefits deriving from complementarity will gradually change into the advantages arising from economies of scale. Unfortunately, in the last half of the 1970s, factors of a mainly political nature along with cyclical and structural causes have contributed to curb the development of East-West relations, above all of joint co-operation ventures.

The establishment of an appropriate institutional framework is of paramount importance for the further development of East-West relations. This delicate matter is specifically examined in three papers and is also considered in other contributions.

The legal significance, functions and practice of the UN Economic Commission for Europe - traditional pivot of détente as well as centre of tensions - are analysed by Dr Parkinson. A detailed review of the past experience and many-sided activities of the Commission, including the implementation of the New Economic Order and the Helsinki Final Act, and speculations on the possibilities of extending its functions beyond its present routine, administrative and technical tasks into the executive field, are to be found in Dr Parkinson's paper.

Relations between the two integration groups in Europe, that is, the EEC and the CMEA, are discussed from a legal standpoint in the paper presented by Doctors Mrázek and Kohout. Taking into account the essential differences existing between the legal concepts and institutional structures of the two organisations, the authors show the many reasons in favour of the conclusion of an EEC-CMEA agreement on the basis of full equality and mutual advantage.

Dr Morganti, for his part, provides a definition of the basis on which an EEC-CMEA agreement could be signed and offers suggestions concerning the draft of a possible formal treaty between the two integration groups. In his view, the content of the proposed agreement should include the exchange of representatives and the establishment of a Joint Commission, the extension of the most-favoured-nation treatment, trade liberalisation, the concession of credits and the adoption of anti-dumping measures in the field of maritime transportation.

Dr Hanson concentrates on the fundamental influence of financial constraints with regard to Soviet-Western technological co-operation, and more precisely on the nature and importance of the limitations imposed by the USSR hard currency balance of payments. Despite the information gaps that make it hard to predict the future East-West aggregate trade flows, the author believes that a recovery in the rate of Soviet importation of Western machinery in the near future is feasible.

Finally, Dr Guttieres provides a detailed survey of the manifold aspects of East-West co-operation in the field of environmental policy and law. Pollution, particularly of air and water, knows no boundaries nor does it discriminate on the basis of ideologies or politics. After a discussion of the legal issues of liability, equal access and monitoring, the paper considers the prospects for the 1980s.

In summary, the authors of the contributions collected in this volume have explored the possibilities for the improvement and expansion of co-operation between East and West in a number of fields, from trade to science, technology and environmental protection. Although experts and scholars were inevitably influenced by the dramatic and largely unforeseen circumstances prevailing in the waning years of the 1970s, their analyses should make a valuable contribution to the clarification of some of the most controversial issues of the present decade.

February 1981   Giuseppe Schiavone

1 East–West Co-operation, Détente and Security

YVES LAULAN

Société Générale, Paris

Economic exchanges between East and West, in the broadest sense, that is including not only trade but also technological transfers and industrial co-operation, were conceived from the beginning both as a contribution to détente and as one of its most authentic manifestations. In other words, the strengthening of economic ties appeared as one of the results of the relaxation of tensions between the two blocs. But, conversely, the co-operation was also regarded as a powerful means of raising détente to a higher level. In brief, this co-operation, during the 1960s and even more in the early 1970s, was given a marked ideological meaning, sometimes professed in Messianic fashion, with trade being described as a carrier of freedom.

Looking back, it is now evident that the hopes reposed in the virtues of East-West economic co-operation have but very imperfectly responded to the expectations of its advocates. In terms of political relations, it is evident that the aftermath of Helsinki is characterised by a certain setback in détente. Thus, at the beginning of the 1980s, with the radical change in the world's political-strategic context and the proliferation of international crises, it is legitimate to ask whether the time has not come to take a new look at East-West co-operation, perhaps less in its substance than in its motivations and modes.

I CO-OPERATION AND SECURITY : AN AMBIGUOUS PAIR

It is not by chance that the Helsinki Conference, which has marked the apex of the efforts for a rapprochement between East and West, involves three 'baskets': economic, political and military. The conference's final declaration explicitly sets forth the objective pursued: 'The Participating Countries, convinced that their efforts to develop co-operation in the areas of commerce, industry, science, technology

1

and in other sectors of economic activity, contribute to the strengthening of peace and security in Europe and in the entire world ... acknowledge that co-operation in these areas would stimulate economic and social progress and the improvement of the standard of living ...' [1]

It would be inappropriate to go over again in detail all arguments put forward on this occasion. Three major ones, however, could be recalled. According to a formula sometimes used, 'better a fat Russian than a lean Russian', the first was that the raising of the standard of living in the Soviet Union was in itself a factor favourable to the détente between East and West. The reasoning was based here on the commonsense idea that, the more one has to lose, the less he is willing to lose it. A second notion, frequently advanced, was that it was useful to create a de facto economic solidarity between the two blocs, in order to create an interdependence between them. In other words, the multiplication of economic ties between the two partners would make it more difficult to sever them. Finally, a third concept has sometimes been proposed, particularly by Maurice Schumann, former French Minister of Foreign Affairs, that of the 'contagiousness of liberty'. According to this concept, the liberalisation of economic exchanges with the Eastern countries was likely to bring about, as by contagion, a spreading of liberal notions to the social whole. It is thus that we can, very roughly, sum up the political stake of East-West economic exchanges, as it could be defined at the end of the last decade.

Economic Co-operation : An Ambiguous Balance Sheet

It is undoubtedly too early and certainly difficult to draw up an overall balance sheet of East-West co-operation. One can, however, be content with observing that, on the strictly economic plane, the exchanges, after a very marked progress from 1970 to 1975, today tend to lag. Thus, while the share of the industrialised Western countries in the total imports of the USSR rose from 24 per cent in 1970 to 36 per cent in 1975, it fell back to less than 32 per cent in 1978. If we consider East-West exchanges as a whole, we find a similar pattern as regards exports by volume from CMEA countries to the Western countries. After a strong progress with rates of 21 per cent in 1972 and again in 1973, a fallback to 12 per cent occurred in 1974, followed by much lower growth rates in the order of 6 to 7 per cent, and as low as 1 per cent in 1977. Imports show the same trend.

The overall pattern is therefore clear-cut. There has been a marked progress, probably due to political thrusts, in the first half of the 1970s, peaking in 1975 and followed by a downturn. How to account for this evolution? Two types of explanations can be conceived.

On the economic plane, one must wonder whether the advocates of East-West co-operation have not to some degree underestimated the economic obstacles opposing a growth in exchanges.

In the first place, it is clear that in practice the exchanges are limited by the weakness of the possibilities, for instance of the USSR, which can only offer raw materials and semi-finished products, or of the other countries of the East, which can only contribute to trade products based on the use of low-cost labour.

The fact is, as shown by experience within the EEC or of trade across the Atlantic, that finished and technically advanced products are traded for other finished products of equivalent quality. Now, the difference in quality between East and West is such that, by nature, trade is subject to a definite ceiling.

Apart from this, one also cannot underestimate the considerable differences existing between the economic systems of the two areas (absence of convertibility of the currencies of the Eastern countries, centralisation of the economy, particularly as regards foreign trade, etc.) which interfere with the development of economic relations. Here again, the Helsinki negotiations have, perhaps somewhat irresponsibly, ignored this type of obstacle.

Taken all in all, if one considers the record of the period, it is evident that the essential prime mover of the exchanges was the strong increase in credits extended to the Eastern countries which, to tell the truth, does not constitute a very sound or balanced base for co-operation.

Exchanges and Security

Finally, one factor should be stressed which has been largely overlooked by the advocates of exchanges between East and West. This is the basic ambiguity, from the standpoint of security, of the purpose of these exchanges. In other terms, since the military purpose has always been, in the Soviet system, one of the primary uses of these exchanges, one can well wonder, conversely, whether Western security has been affected by their development.

Such a process could be explained by the very nature of the Soviet system, in which the military sector constitutes an absolute priority. In effect, the Soviet Union has been traditionally placing investment in heavy industry and in defence above and before consumption, which constitutes the residual element of the final demand. It is a known fact that the opposite is true in the market economies, where consumption is often given priority over other allocations of resources.

Two important consequences derive from this difference in treatment. In the first place, any increase in the available resources in the USSR yields a priority and immediate benefit to the national defence sector. As a corollary, any increase in available resources immediately translates itself into a lightening of the pressures exerted on consumption by the military demand. Being part of the system itself, these mechanisms operate in some way automatically and not deliberately.

In effect, it is permissible to consider that 'the Soviet economy produces weapons just as an apple tree produces apples'. This is thus an economy based, with priority, on the armament and military production effort. In other terms, the military-industrial complex is not superimposed on the economic structures as it is in the United States; it forms an integral part of the system or, better still, it is the system itself. [2]

The analysis of facts shows that this is actually the case. For example, during the whole period of the strengthening of détente which preceded the Helsinki Conference, it is significant that the growth rates of the Soviet military effort never dropped below 4 per cent a year, with a slight rise to 6 per cent in 1976. During these same years, the proportion of the Soviet GNP allocated to defence remained between 12 and 14 per cent. One will simply recall that it is precisely during this period, that of Nixon-Kissinger, that the US war effort, in real terms, declined, with the share of the GNP allocated to defence dropping from 6.5 to 5 per cent (it is now 4.5 per cent).

Once again, it is not a question of interpreting the divergence of these trends as a demonstration of Soviet duplicity or of American naivety, but simply as an almost mechanical consequence of the mode of operation of two radically different economic-political systems.

Whatever the case may be, it can legitimately be concluded that, when a Western country helps, by means of 'soft' loans or of exports permitted under privileged conditions, this or that sector of the Soviet economy, it helps the defence sector at the same time. This is why French historian Alain Besançon spoke of the double defence budget supported by the Western countries, meaning by this that, in addition to their own military effort, the Western countries, through the channel of international co-operation, were supporting part of the Soviet defence effort. Seen from this angle, economic co-operation works in some ways like a food, which nourishes both a patient and his disease.

This reasoning, of course, should not be taken to extremes. It should be considered that such an argument would generally be applicable to any economy whatever, in a period of military priority, for instance in a rearmament period. In other words, the effort of co-operation is to let the Soviet Union have guns, and a little butter as well.

This being the case, it is rather naive to attribute, as some do, a decisive historical role to the refusal of the US Congress to extend to the USSR the most-favoured-nation clause. In effect, the Soviet military choices were made long before that. In any event, this refusal, if it has had any influence, has done nothing but strengthen an armament effort pursued in a normal manner. In any event, it should be recognised that the facts seem to support this interpretation.

Actually, there is no lack of examples in the USSR of utilisation of Western technology for military purposes. For example, US enterprises have sold more than $1.5 billion[3] worth of equipment to the Soviets for the construction of a truck factory on the Kama. These trucks were intended for civilian uses. According to certain sources, it appears that the Red Army used the trucks made at the Kama plant in the invasion of Afghanistan. Another plant, also built with the help of US equipment, is reportedly making not only military trucks but also missile-launching ramps.

It is said that in 1978 the Soviets purchased from the US corporation, Litton Industries, some technology patents which are now used on board submarine-hunting aircraft and ships. The Gorki car plant, whose production depends on electronic material from US and Japanese sources, is now reportedly turning out civilian cars and trucks as well as amphibious assault vehicles and military trucks. Furthermore, it appears, in general, that US electronic equipment has been used for various purposes, such as guidance for the SS-18 missile, Backfire strategic bombers, air defence networks, etc.

Other sources claim that the USSR has purchased 140,000 tons of lead for use in productions which are officially civilian (car and truck storage batteries) but actually military. It is known that its titanium production capacity amounts to 45,000 tons. The USSR has discontinued its titanium sales: now, this metal is used in the building of submarines, missiles, nuclear power plants and in the aircraft industry. The USSR holds one-third of the world production of platinum and two-thirds of palladium; the sales of these metals have also been stopped.

Again, examples should be interpreted in a relative manner. After all the Soviets, for their part, could argue not unreasonably that the oil sold to the West can be found in the tanks of NATO armoured vehicles or aircraft. It should be stressed, however, that the key to the problem lies in the priorities followed in the allocation of resources. It is the priority systematically given to armament expenditures in the Soviet Union which makes up the whole difference from the system followed in market economies. This is where the necessarily ambiguous character of East-West co-operation comes from.

II CO-OPERATION AND SECURITY IN THE 1980s

The future appears to be characterised by a certain degree of reconsideration of East-West co-operation. This development is explained by reasons of fact, that is the general economic context. But it is also justified by political and strategic considerations. The Afghan affair, coming after that of Teheran, and the threats looming on the Persian Gulf, have changed profoundly the general psychological context of East-West relations.

The Context : A Slowing of Growth

This being the overall picture, the economic downturn in the West and the recrudescence of protectionistic pressures, which has been significant for several years, warrant the prediction of a certain retrenchment in world trade. For instance, the growth in world trade, which amounted to 9 per cent in 1972 and 12.5 per cent in 1973, has been ranging from 4 to 5 per cent a year since 1975. This factor alone would suffice to cause a decline in the growth of East-West exchanges.

As regards technology transfers and industrial co-operation, the Soviets now seem less interested in purchasing Western technology. Actually, they have become aware that such purchases did not constitute a cure-all. It is estimated that a $1 Western credit for the purchase of capital goods required $4 or $5 in domestic expenditures in the form of complementary investment for the actual implementation of the project. Furthermore, some items of Western equipment purchased in the past have proved ineffective, as Soviet productivity was too low to ensure an efficient working of the Western material. It is true that such considerations are applicable not only to the USSR but also, in a general way, to the less-developed countries. An excessively wide difference in productivity attributable to an overly different economic and social context is sufficient to reduce largely the economic interest of high-technology transplants. Besides, one finds that, since 1975, the Soviet orders for capital goods, which had increased by 70 per cent in 1971, 100 per cent in 1972 and 53 per cent in 1973, rose by only 29 per cent in 1979 and decreased by 37 per cent in 1977 and 27 per cent in 1978.

Another point is to be made as regards the indebtedness of the Eastern countries. While trade with Eastern European countries is encountering far fewer political difficulties than with the USSR, their increasing indebtedness is going to affect the possibilities of co-operation. The total indebtedness of the Eastern countries is now estimated at $74 billion, of which $17 billion is for the USSR alone. The service of the debts ranges from 17 per cent for the USSR to 30 per cent for Czechoslovakia, the GDR and Hungary and from 50 to 60 per cent for Bulgaria and Poland. These are in themselves very heavy rates, much higher than the average for the developing countries. But what is undoubtedly more important is the fact that to a purely economic risk, already considerable, is now added a political risk, with the reopening of a period of tensions which will weigh, like a sword of Damocles, on the repayment of these debts.

Finally, the comparative advantage of relatively cheap labour will be taken less and less into account by the West. On the one hand, the increasing unemployment in the industrialised countries will limit to a certain extent the need to import labour-intensive goods. On the other hand, the rise in the energy price pushes up the marginal cost of capital and therefore decreases the relative cost of labour in the industrialised countries. For this reason, during the coming years, a degree of substitution of labour for capital should take place, as is already evident in the United States and in Europe. This development will inevitably decrease the attractiveness of imports from the Eastern countries.

A Political Reappraisal

The reappraisal of East-West co-operation, however, is due essentially to political motivations. The Western countries have become aware of certain errors in judgement. The expansion of East-West trade was thus partly justified by political goals of improvement of détente and security in the world. Today, it would certainly be hard to find many people who would rate the Helsinki Conference an unqualified success. The repression of the dissidence movement in the USSR has abundantly proved, had this been necessary, that there is no evident connection between economics and human rights. Trade and freedom are not exchangeable. A certain illusion about détente has therefore disappeared.

Furthermore, the Afghanistan crisis has been an indicator of the evident military superiority of the USSR over the Western world, whether in conventional forces or even in strategic forces. Also, since the invasion of Afghanistan, the Western countries have become aware that East-West trade could, under certain circumstances, cause a weakening of their security. This accounts for President Carter's suspension of the granting of a certain number of US licences on high-technology items to the USSR. This embargo affects 20 to 30 per cent of the $700 million of US non-agricultural exports to the USSR.

Finally, the strategic stockpiling which will undoubtedly be progressively increasing could result in the USSR withholding supplies of available raw materials. The stockpiling for military purposes could result in some decrease of the volume of sale of some products by that country. Under these circumstances, one must see that other factors connected with the energy crisis are going to act in the opposite direction.

On the one hand, the considerable increase in international liquidities ($110 billion in 1980) will require an expansion of investment in the world. One has the right to think that an appreciable portion of these funds could finance additional credit to the Eastern countries.

On the other hand, the seeking of trade outlets by the Western countries is made more imperative by the rise in energy price. The need to offset the cost of oil imports will be a strong inducement for the industrialised countries, in particular Western European countries and Japan, to continue and even increase their exchanges with the Eastern countries. It should be noted in this connection that in 1980 the current deficit of the OECD area should rise to $50 billion.

This is why the continuation of the freeze in trade relations between the United States and the USSR is strongly feared by Western European countries, since 15 per cent of the natural gas used by West Germany comes from the Urals. This country has signed large contracts for capital goods with the USSR. Japan, for its part, is heavily involved in projects for the development of Siberia. Italy, finally, expects from its trade with the USSR the creation of tens of thousands of jobs.

In any event, allowance should be made for a certain inertia of the exchanges for certain countries, including France. Exchanges with the Eastern countries are very important to some sectors of industry: chemicals, fertilisers, transportation of energy products, oil exploration (pipelines and offshore well-drilling) and machine tools; 75 per cent of the Soviet fertiliser production uses Western equipment. Machine tool exports to Eastern countries account for 25 per cent of France's exports in this sector.

Many examples reflect the predominance of commercial interests over political considerations. Thus, in spite of US efforts to limit the trading by Western countries with the USSR, Montedison was awarded, at the end of March 1980, an $800 million contract for the construction of seven chemical plants in the USSR. Two French companies have signed a $125 million contract for the equipment of two yards for the construction of drilling platforms at Baku and Astrakhan. Four Japanese steelmakers are negotiating for the supply of 100,000 tons of steel pipe to the USSR. Also, some observers are happily pointing out that the number of US businessmen visiting Moscow has never been so large as after the Afghanistan affair.

III CONCLUSIONS

It follows from all this that East-West co-operation can very well survive détente, in so far as it responds to an economic need felt by both sides. All in all, it would be the first time in history that trading countries have subordinated their short-term mercantile interest to long-term strategic necessities. Thus, it would take a dramatic exacerbation of international tensions for these exchanges to be heavily curtailed or even stopped.

Certainly, it is clear that credits will become more difficult and costly. It is also evident that the industrialised countries of the West will be increasingly reluctant to give away their technological advantages. Co-operation will continue to forge ahead, at a pace perhaps slower but sustained. It is therefore towards a co-operation without illusions, without complacence or rhetoric, stripped in some way of its ideological content, that we are moving with a return to a certain mercantilism resting on sound bases. It is not evident that it will suffer from that.

NOTES

1. Conference on Security and Co-operation in Europe, Final Act, Cmnd 6198 (London: HMSO, 1975).
2. In this respect, there is an apparent paradox in maintaining that the USSR shows a quasi-Ricardian behaviour in specialising in the production for which it is best endowed. The amazing Soviet efficiency in the production of armaments contrasts with the remarkable inefficiency of this country's industry and, above all, agriculture. It could be argued, however, that the USSR limits itself to exploiting a natural advantage which enables it to maximise its benefits. Why try to sell cars of uncertain quality when there are so many markets for excellent T72 tanks or efficient Kalashnikov rifles? Why should it take great trouble to inject itself into international trade when the possession of the first war machine in the world makes it possible to obtain without having to give anything in return the best of trades within CMEA and even some East-West stakes? One finds here an economic rationality which is indeed impressive.
3. Reference throughout the book is always to 'US billions'.

APPENDIX

Table 1.1   Trends in the Volume Growth of East-West Trade
1966 to 1978 (annual changes, per cent)

Year	Exports from CMEA countries to Western countries		Imports by CMEA countries from Western countries	
	Total	USSR	Total	USSR
1966	17	12	14	15
1967	9	10	10	15
1968	10	20	6	4
1969	6	11	7	2
1970	7	5	-1	-8
1971	5	-2	6	1
1972	21	33	11	8
1973	21	22	11	24
1974	-12	-8	8	-4
1975	6	n.a.	21	n.a.
1976	7.4	n.a.	10	n.a.
1977	1	n.a.	-8	n.a.
1978 (9 months)	2	n.a.	8	n.a.

Sources: 1966 to 1973: United Nations Economic Bulletin for Europe, 28 (December 1976).

1974 to 1978: Economic Survey of Europe, 1978, United Nations Economic Commission for Europe.

Table 1.2   The Share of the Industrialised Western Countries
in the USSR's Trade (per cent)

	1960	1970	1975	1977	1978
Share in the total Soviet exports :					
- of industrialised Western countries	18.2	18.7	25.5	26.5	24.4
- of the EEC	10.7	10.5	13.6	15.3	14.7
Share in the imports :					
- of industrialised Western countries	19.8	24.0	36.4	33.0	31.8
- of the EEC	10.4	12.1	16.5	14.2	14.4

Table 1.3   East-West Trade, 1969 to 1977

As % of the total exports from each area of origin

Year	Share of the exports to Eastern countries :			
	Of the developed market-economy countries	Of the EEC	Of the USA	Of Japan
1969-71	3.1	3.6	1.0	2.0
1972-73	3.6	3.7	2.2	2.4
1974	3.9	4.3	1.4	3.1
1975	4.8	4.9	2.6	3.9
1976	4.6	4.3	3.1	4.2
1977	4.1	4.0	2.1	3.4

As % of the total imports of Eastern countries

Year	Share of the imports by Eastern countries from :			
	The developed market-economy countries	The EEC	The USA	Japan
1969-71	24.6	14.1	1.4	1.4
1972-73	28.4	15.1	2.9	1.8
1974	33.5	18.7	2.2	2.7
1975	33.8	17.6	3.4	2.7
1976	34.1	16.1	4.0	3.2
1977	31.0	15.9	2.6	2.8

Source: Handbook of International Trade and Development Statistics (UN, 1979).

Table 1.4   The Slowing Down of World Trade Growth Since 1974

Variations as % of the volume of world trade

| Annual average, 1960-70 | 1970 | 1971 | 1972 | 1973 | Variations over the preceding year | | | | | | (e) 1980 |
					1974	1975	1976	1977	1978	1979	
9.0	9.0	6.0	9.0	12.5	5.5	-5	12	5	5	7	3

Source: IMF Annual Reports.

Table 1.5   The Evolution of Soviet Orders for Capital Goods : Decreasing Since 1975

Year	Value (million $)	% Variation
1970	500	-
1971	850	70
1972	1700	100
1973	2600	53
1974	4300	65
1975	4650	8
1976	6000	29
1977	3807	-37
1978	2789	-27

Source: Joint Economic Committee, US Congress.

Table 1.6   The Military Sector : An Absolute Priority in the USSR

The evolution of military expenditures in the USSR and the USA

	Military expenditures in billion dollars				Military expenditures per capita, in dollars				% of the GNP			
	1973	1974	1975	1979	1973	1974	1975	1979	1973	1974	1975	1978
USSR	88-92	109-113	124	150	352-368	432-447	490	574	11	to	13	11 to 14
USA	78	86	89	114	372	405	417	520	6	6.1	5.9	5

Source: <u>The Military Balance 1976-77,</u> The International Institute for Strategic Studies (London).

2 Europe in the 1980s: Political Context

SILVIU BRUCAN

University of Bucharest

Although Europe no longer plays the predominant role in world affairs as in past centuries, it is still a continent of considerable importance in many respects. Its economic potential surpasses that of any other continent; with a population totalling one-fifth of the globe's, Europe produces roughly 47 per cent of the world's income and nearly 55 per cent of its industrial goods. Traditionally, Europe has led the way in international trade; today it accounts for 54 per cent of world exports. United Nations data show that nearly half of the world's scientists work in Europe.

It is in Western Europe that capitalism originated and it is in Eastern Europe that the Russian Revolution made the first crack in the capitalist system. Therefore, the stakes in Europe are very high and there are authors holding that it is here that the issue of 'where is our world going' will be decided. Small wonder that Europe is the last continent where the postwar bipolar structure of power with the USA and the USSR as protagonists has been stubbornly preserved. It is sharply divided into two military blocs and economic groupings and it shelters right in its middle the highest concentration of armed forces and weaponry on our planet, including nuclear warheads more than 100,000 times bigger than the Hiroshima bomb.

With the emergence of China as a world power and of Japan as an economic giant, Europe has become not only subject but also object in the big strategic game. Moscow is warning Western Europe not to sell modern weapons to China; on the world market Western Europe is fighting the USA and Japan, while Chinese leaders are urging Western Europe to get strong militarily so as to deter 'Soviet expansionism'.

I mention all these aspects to point out that future political developments in Europe will depend to a large extent on outside factors; therefore, Europe must be viewed in a global context, taking into account the host of factors that make world politics work these days.

I FROM COLD WAR TO DETENTE

Postwar political developments could be divided into two historical periods. The first one, starting in 1945 and extending till the end of the 1950s, marked the division of Europe along ideological lines into two hostile camps separated by the Iron Curtain. It all started with the revolutionary process stretching all over Eastern Europe under the Soviet military umbrella; the USA and its Western allies countered with the containment policy, the setting up of NATO, the Marshall Plan, the Truman doctrine and other measures. The class conflict and the ideology that goes with it was predominant: the cold war was the virulent expression of that state of affairs.

With the halting of the wind of change in Europe, its thrust shifted toward the underdeveloped continents. The West's economic boom reinforced this shift; capitalism seemed to have resolved its explosive social problems, enjoying a period of political stability. This basic reappraisal ushered in the transition from the cold war to the Development Decades, from confrontation to negotiation, from the doctrine of massive atomic retaliation to that of 'limited war' made to order for Third World conditions.

Hence, it was the redirection of the focus of conflict from the East-West to the North-South system that made détente possible. Against this background, the two superpowers discovered a common interest in maintaining their nuclear strategic lead and jointly drafted the two nuclear treaties (test-ban and non-proliferation); the de Gaulle rebellion against US domination in the West, the Sino-Soviet rift in the East, the thrust of national resurgence in the South - those are signs of the second period in which national interests and strategic rivalries override ideological considerations.

My contention is that during those two periods, political developments in Western and Eastern Europe have run parallel, displaying striking similarities.

During the cold war, both Western and Eastern nations were tightly lined up behind their respective leaders - the USA or the USSR. The position of the two was similar: undisputed authority, monopoly in the formulation of policy and strategy, complete subordination of Western and Eastern Europe to the goals set by the two big brothers. Once more, we saw that ideology is never pure in international relations; it is always mixed with power, and manipulated accordingly.

As they gained strength in the second period, both Western and Eastern nations began to assert themselves and promote their national aims, gradually demanding a say in the formulation of policies and strategies; and this has been going on to this day. In the West, France is resisting the US attempt to recapture the rudder of the Western world while advocating a distinct role for Western Europe in the conflictual situations not only in Afghanistan, but also in the Persian Gulf and the Middle East - a feeling increasingly shared by West Germany, Italy and the others. It is equally apparent that Eastern European nations are opposing in their own way a return to the cold war, trying hard to save what can be saved of détente.

Originating in the clashing ideological climate of the cold war, the North Atlantic Treaty Organisation and the Warsaw Treaty have survived the centrifugal force of nationalism through a stabilising system that is feeding its own dynamics as the institutional framework of the bipolar structure of power in Europe. At the heart of this system lies the mutual distrust inherited from the cold war which is continuously reinforced by the mutual fear that any 'lowering of the guard' may pose a challenge to the very basis of societies in both the West and the East.

Actually, military pacts with an ideological underpinning have two major functions: one, openly proclaimed, is directed outward; the other, not so well disguised, is directed inward. The former is meant to protect pact members against an external threat; the latter, to secure the system of relations inside the alliance, preserving its structure of power. Between the two functions, a self-adjustment mechanism is at work; when the external threat is imminent, the outward function becomes predominant, while the inward one recedes on a second plane. When the external threat diminishes, the inward function prevails and the outward one recedes into the background. In the latter case, the military pact is used to restore order inside, dealing with challenges to the system. The external threat is then only a pretext or a cover-up for the internal operation.

As for the economic background, to understand the complex nature of the East-West conflict one must go back to the historical conditions that allowed Western European nations to benefit fully from the Industrial Revolution and to acquire vast colonial empires, thus becoming highly developed and rich, whereas in Eastern Europe, peoples and nationalities (most of them still struggling for nationhood) remained predominantly agrarian with strong feudal structures lasting late into the twentieth century. Since the revolution started in backward Russia and later extended in less developed countries (except Czechoslovakia), they were all faced with the enormous task of becoming industrialised as rapidly as possible under very adverse conditions with capitalism holding a commanding position and dictating the rules on the world market. Even today, in spite of the tremendous achievements of Eastern Europe in industrialism, there is a great discrepancy in the structure of trade, financial potential, productivity and standard of living between the two parts of Europe. The share of manufactured goods in Eastern European exports is relatively small, whereas machinery imported from the West accounts for over 40 per cent of the West-East flow. This is compounded by the privileged position of Western currencies in financial transactions. As a result, the debts incurred by Eastern European nations with Western banks have reached an all-time high. These data inescapably lead to the conclusion that we are dealing here with a specific pattern of <u>disparity in development,</u> subjecting

Eastern Europe to the rules of unequal exchange, in what is a milder version of the North-South system. It is, therefore, my considered view that the major transformations in Eastern Europe can be described more accurately as a model of development strategy rather than one of socialism conceived by Marx for highly industrialised societies.

The significance of the Conference on Security and Co-operation in Europe has remained to this day highly controversial. The only safe assumption is that the thirty-five nations so different in size, power, culture and ideology were prompted to sign the Final Act by the hard military facts of the nuclear era, and particularly by the realisation that a military showdown in Europe would turn into a nuclear disaster.

II A SHORT-TERM SCENARIO

In forecasting future political developments, I am going to use an analytical model with four key variables: (1) the pressure of modern technology and interdependence, which is the current expression of productive forces operating in international relations; (2) power politics; (3) national self-assertion; and (4) social change. Briefly, the assumption is that the interplay between these four sets of variables eventually determines the course of international affairs.

Technological-interdependence pressure (TIP) constitutes the main driving force toward a smaller and shrinking world whose basic units (nation-states) are compelled to interact and regulate the increasing flow of information, people and ideas transcending national boundaries. TIP makes its impact felt both upon class relations inside societies pushing toward social change, and upon relations among nations under their two facets: power politics which today takes the dominant form of superpower competition, and its countervailing response from the small and poor nations - national self-assertion. I submit that this dialectical interaction makes the world work as a system.

Because of social conflicts inside societies and rivalries among nations the drive of modern technology does not operate as a one-directional sweep, but as a dual and contradictory motion. The effect is a dialectical interplay between the factors that make for division and conflict and those that make for cohesion and integration. The best illustration of this is the vagarious history of the EEC, where moments of elation for political union have been followed by discordant decisions of individual members threatening even the basic customs union.

In cases where TIP does not encounter resistance, the results are startling. Thus, in recent years, East-West trade in Europe has made a real jump with a 20 per cent annual increase. It is therefore safe to assume that economic intercourse will continue to be the prime mover of the European system. On the one hand, growing exports to the East are badly needed by Western economies beset by stagflation; on the other hand, the demand for modern technology in the East makes for an eager partner. Conservative projections show that by 1990 such intercourse in Europe may reach $60–80 billion annually.

At the start of the 1980s we are witnessing an outbreak of the traditional rivalry for spheres of influence and strategic positions between the superpowers, poisoning the whole political climate. Is détente dead and are we going back to the cold war? - that is the question troubling people around the world.

In retrospect, the Helsinki Conference now looks like the climax of the process of détente based on the common interest of the USA and the USSR in keeping the nuclear stategic monopoly in their hands while avoiding a direct confrontation. Its basic document - the 1972 Nixon-Brezhnev agreement - was a package deal in which military-security matters were lumped together with trade-technological commitments in a quid pro quo system built on a parity basis. But then the two amendments to the Trade Bill adopted by the US Congress (on Soviet emigration policy and on credits) were viewed in Moscow as cancelling the most attractive part of the deal (trade and technology) while Soviet actions in Angola and Ethiopia were viewed in Washington as cancelling the remaining part. The failure to ratify SALT II preceded by the fuss around the 'Soviet brigade' in Cuba was nothing but a first-class funeral of the whole deal. Thus when the Soviets decided to act in Afghanistan there was nothing left of détente.

What next? Clearly a new deal of that sort is not likely at a time when Washington is embroiled in presidential elections. Nor is it possible to bring back the structure and habits of the cold war. For one thing, the world is much more complex than the 'two camps' of the 1950s; the Iron Curtain between the East and the West is gone whilst ideological lines are cross-cutting and overlapping all three worlds. With more than 150 sovereign states scattered over all continents it is no longer possible to run the world from two centres or even to exercise effective control over allies or partners. Para-doxically, the unprecedented accumulation of power in Washington and Moscow coincides with the decentralisation of power in the international system. Under such conditions, the use of force has a very high price and is counter-productive.

What actually remains from all those years of détente is the idea that in the nuclear era there is no substitute for peaceful coexist-ence. This is even more true in Europe where Helsinki is and remains the right course to follow. Europeans will realise that the implemen-tation of the Final Act has been hindered by what happens in the bushes of Africa, the deserts of the Middle East, the oilfields of Iran and the mountains of Afghanistan, rather than by developments in Europe.

Hence in the 1980s we will see a stronger concern in both the Western and Eastern part of the continent for European issues, including an active participation in arms talks to halt the perilous course of nuclearisation (SS-20 versus Pershing II and Cruise missiles).

In Western Europe, since the economic crisis with high unemployment and inflation is likely to continue, a period of social change opens up. Whether the political forces of the left will be able to forge a solid alliance and turn these conditions into a real change of guard is still an open question; such a prospect is shaping up in France and Italy, perhaps in Spain. The challenge is formidable, for we are talking about a first crack in the developed world - the centre of the international system. Hence considerable forces will oppose such a change, including foreign powers. My forecast is that the advent to power of the new social forces will be easier than their consolidation of power.

In the East, the development strategy is approaching its limits as shown by the declining rates of growth. A change is now required in the political superstructure, for a complex industrial society getting ripe for socialism cannot properly function with the political institutions that were created to overcome underdevelopment.

Changes in both the West and the East will be affected in timing and depth by the big power game and the evolution of the economic crisis. A time of change will prevail all over Europe, generating a hot political ambiance with perilous moments of conflict and tension involving the superpowers.

3 World Stagflation and East–West Relations

JEAN MARCZEWSKI

University of Paris I, Panthéon-Sorbonne

I WORLD STAGFLATION AND ITS CAUSES

The main characteristics of world stagflation are the declining rates of production growth and the increasing rates of price rises in almost all countries of the world.

The declining rates of production growth result in a slowdown of imports and consequently of exports. This in turn slows down the growth of production in exporting countries and forces them to reduce their imports. The average annual rate of growth of world production fell from 5 per cent before 1973 to 1.3 per cent in the years 1974-75. It reached 4 and 3 per cent in 1978 and 1979 respectively. The average annual rate of growth of world trade, which approached 9 per cent for the years 1965-73, was reduced to 4 per cent during the years 1973-77. It recovered to 6 per cent in 1978 and 7 per cent in 1979, but it is expected to fall sharply in 1980 as a consequence of the latest oil price increases. The slow growth of production, combined with the growth of the working-age population, which is due to continue in most Western countries till the mid-1980s, leads to an increasing rate of unemployment. In Eastern countries a similar phenomenon exists but it results in a general decline of productivity growth rather than in unemployment.

Inflation

While the beginning of the production slack coincides with the first wave of massive oil price increases by OPEC in the years 1973 and 1974, the acceleration of inflation had already started in many countries before 1968. The main causes of inflation were then, at the internal level of most countries, the rising share of government expenses in GNP and cyclical jumps of investment combined with the Keynesian policy of stimulating the effective demand.[1] At the world

21

level the main inflationary pressure was coming from the cumulative deficit of the US balance of payments. Greatly enlarged by increasing outlays for the Vietnam war, the US balance of payments deficit contributed heavily to a tremendous increase in international liquidity. Easy international credit conditions on Eurodollar markets allowed internally unbalanced economies to expand their foreign trade deficits and consequently to tolerate a higher rate of domestic inflation.

In the aftermath of the 1968 social events, a new extremely powerful factor has in most countries reinforced domestic inflationary pressures, that is successful action by trade unions leading to wage increases larger than the feasible improvement in labour productivity or anticipating this improvement.[2] In many Western countries, such as France, this factor became by far the most important single cause of inflation and accounts for almost half of the total inflationary gap. [3]

But a sharp acceleration of inflation is not the only consequence of wage increases exceeding improvements in productivity. A normal reaction of a firm which is obliged to raise the wages of its employees by more than the possible improvement in productivity will be to increase its selling prices accordingly. However, in most cases this simple solution is not applicable, for example when the price-elasticity of demand is greater than one, when the competition of other domestic or foreign firms is strong or when the price is fixed by government. When a firm is unable to raise its prices proportionately to the increase of its labour costs, the only way in the long run to avoid failure is to make an investment capable of considerably improving the apparent productivity of the labour employed. The resulting production increment will involve a reduction in personnel unless the firm can expand its domestic or foreign outlets without significant price decreases. This, however, would imply an income-elastic demand and relatively little competition. Such favourable conditions are present only in firms producing new goods or selling to new markets. In fact, in Western countries, most of the industrial sectors which have intensified the amount of capital per employee (agriculture, energy, consumer-goods industries) have also considerably reduced the number of workers employed. The growing competition of the newly industrialised countries, like South Korea, Taiwan, Singapore and others, has appreciably reinforced this trend. Only the sectors which benefit from a rapidly growing demand, like investment-goods industries, intermediate industries and new expanding industries, have been able to avoid this restriction. Moreover, in most industrial countries, the new jobs created in the developing sectors did not fully compensate for the employment losses which occurred in ageing industries.

Decreasing capital profitability, observable in all industrial countries, is probably the main cause of this gap. Capital profitability has been decreasing since the 1960s for the following main reasons:

(i)   The reconstruction of the Second World War ravages is definitely finished in all countries.

(ii) Capital accumulation and consumption of industrial goods have reached a very high level in most industrial countries. Marginal efficiency of capital is low. It rises only in connection with the creation of new markets, new technologies or new products.

(iii) Most industrial countries which, after the Second World War, lagged considerably behind the US in technology, have now considerably narrowed or even closed the gap. Consequently, the average rate of technical progress incorporated in new investments has declined significantly. It will perhaps rise again with the 'third industrial revolution'[4] which begins to challenge the industrial structure of the most advanced countries, but this change has not yet attained a dimension which would markedly affect the rate of economic growth.

(iv) A rise in wages faster than the possible improvement in productivity results in lower profit expectations of investors and in the long run in the reduction of self-financing capacities of enterprises.

(v)   A relative retardation in economic development of Eastern countries and developing countries results in the impossibility of counterbalancing the rapidly rising prices of their imports from the West by an appropriate expansion of their exports. This in turn slows down the exports and activity of Western countries.

In spite of these negative trends, the world economy continued to expand rapidly until the end of 1973. But this growth was accompanied by an increasingly powerful inflation, both inside particular countries and at the international level. A few countries, such as West Germany, succeeded in mastering their domestic inflation but they had to protect themselves against imported inflation by a repeated re-evaluation of their currencies. Conversely almost all countries which were not able to maintain their internal and/or external economic equilibrium have been forced to accept a more or less marked depreciation of their exchange rates. The most important among these monetary adjustments were the successive devaluations of the dollar in 1971 and 1973, the suppression of the dollar convertibility into gold in 1971 and the official demonetisation of gold in 1976.

The 1973-74 Oil Price Increases

Under these circumstances the more than fourfold increase in oil prices by OPEC in 1973-74 has produced a dual effect:

(i)   Given the inelasticity of oil demand, it obliged the oil-importing countries consequently to expand their exports or reduce their imports or to accept an increase in their balance of payments deficit and in their foreign debt.

(ii) It added to the already existing inflationary pressure a new 'energy-cost inflation'. Combined with the principle of continually raising real wages, this cost increase resulted in general and spectacular accelerations of inflation in nearly all oil-importing countries. Only the nations which were able to dominate their domestic inflation could soften the inflationary impact of oil price increases through an appropriate re-evaluation of their money. This achievement reinforced the competitive position of these countries on foreign markets, especially in oil-producing countries which became practically the only dynamic factor of world trade.

Then the most important overall effect of oil price increases on the world economy was to change and widen considerably the economic differences between nations. From this point of view it may be useful to distinguish seven groups of nations:

(i) The oil-exporting countries able to invest into the domestic economy the totality of the surplus generated by oil price increases. These are countries such as Iran, Algeria, Mexico, Venezuela, Nigeria, China and the USSR.

(ii) The oil-producing countries unable to absorb entirely their oil surplus, like Saudi Arabia, Kuwait and Libya.

(iii) The oil-importing countries able to master their domestic inflation, such as West Germany, Austria, Switzerland and Japan.

(iv) Other oil-importing industrial countries except the USA.

(v) The USA which is at the same time an oil-importing and an oil-producing country and which moreover possesses a currency serving as a universal means of payment.

(vi) Low-income oil-importing developing countries.

(vii) Middle-income oil-importing developing countries, such as South Korea, Taiwan, Singapore and so on.

The surplus accruing to countries (i) and a part of the surplus accruing to countries (ii) is almost immediately spent on purchases of industrial goods. This sharp increase in demand benefits first all those countries capable of supplying the desired goods on the best terms. In this respect industrial countries (iii) are in a particularly favourable position since their production costs are more stable than those of their competitors. The rise of their exports to oil producers gives them a possibility of recovering at least a part of their additional expenses for oil. In order to attain this result they must expand the production of specific items demanded by oil-producing countries and the production of goods demanded by the earners of new incomes generated in these additional activities. But in so far as they succeed in doing without any wage increase, the deflationary effect of the additional expenditure on oil is offset by the inflationary effect of additional exports, while the inflationary effect of oil cost rises is compensated by a corresponding reduction of the consumers' purchasing power. In other words the fall in national productivity caused by the deterioration of terms of trade and expressed by the reduction in real wages is counterbalanced at the national level by an increase in employment.

This solution minimises the negative consequences of oil price increases. But its applicability depends on two necessary conditions: a sufficient elasticity of production (that is availability of labour and of productive capacities) and an implicit acceptance by trade unions of a real wage reduction corresponding to the price rises determined by oil price increases.

It would probably be excessive to pretend that this last solution represents exactly what has been achieved in all countries (iii). It is only a theoretical approximation made in order to throw light, by contrast, on the behaviour of countries (iv).

In the latter the inflationary impact of oil price increases is magnified by the inflationary rise in wages and other incomes. Accordingly the possibility of recovering part of the additional expenses on oil through an increase in exports is strongly reduced if not completely suppressed. A widening trade deficit forces the country to choose between a voluntary reduction of imports or a currency depreciation.

In the first case, the burden of the decrease in imports must be borne either directly by consumers who are deprived of the possibility of buying a number of foreign goods or by firms which are forced to slow down their activity with the consequent diminution of employment. The deflationary effect of additional expenses on oil is then expressed by the falling standard of living and increasing unemployment while the inflationary effect of oil cost increases is amplified by a reduced supply of certain goods and an accelerated wage rise.

In the second case, the increase in expenditure on imports may be partially offset, in the short run, by an increase of exports, as in the case of countries (iii). But as currency depreciation raises the prices of all imports - and not only the oil prices - and as wages are moving up at least as fast as prices, the inflationary effect of the exports expansion becomes cumulative. Sooner or later the country has to choose once again between a further depreciation of its money and a voluntary curtailment of imports. The deflationary effect of additional expenses on oil is magnified by the deflationary effect of the rise in the nominal value of imports, while the inflationary effect of rising oil costs is amplified by the inflationary effect of the rising cost of other imports and of rising exports and wages. Deflation takes the form of growing unemployment. Inflation expresses itself in an accelerated rise in prices. In other words, the fall in national productivity caused by the increase in oil prices is further deepened by a fall in productivity due to the depreciation of money. The purchasing power of wage earners being maintained by a steady rise in nominal wages, this loss of national productivity takes the form of a progressive increase in unemployment.

The case of the USA (v) is different. While the inflationary impact of the increased cost of oil input raises the level of domestic prices, the deflationary effect of additional expenditures on oil is offset by the fact that they are paid for in dollars. The USA is obliged neither to augment its exports nor to cut its imports in order to pay the additional oil bill. It suffices to extend the Federal Reserve credit facilities in response to an increased demand for dollars. Thus the international flow of petrodollars increases further, contributing to world inflation.

The position of semi-industrial, middle-income countries (vii), with a very low though rising wage level, is by and large similar to that of industrial countries (iii). They pay for the rising price of oil by harder work and expanded exports in so far at least as they are allowed for by the neo-protectionist attitude of developed countries.

This is unfortunately not the case of the majority of other developing countries (vi). Generally they have little chance of increasing their exports to oil-producing countries which do not buy large quantities of raw materials. On the other hand they are hit directly by the consequences of the slowing activity of industrial countries and the rising cost of imports both of oil and industrial products. Unable to master their growing trade deficit they are forced either to cut their imports with a consequent fall in activity or to increase heavily their foreign debt.

The above description of the consequences of oil price rises must, however, be further completed and complicated by the introduction into the world scenario of oil-producing countries (ii).

Unable to spend their surplus immediately and entirely, these countries try to manage it in the most secure and most profitable way. Consequently they are induced to invest a greater part of their net receipts in the USA and in other most developed countries. They may also finance some multinational enterprises in developing countries - (vi) or rather (vii) - which offer particularly favourable national resources or labour conditions and a satisfactory standard of security for their capital. In so far as the recipients of these investments show a deficit towards oil-exporting countries, this inflow of petrodollars helps them to maintain and to widen their trade deficit and consequently to tolerate a higher rate of domestic inflation.

However, most of the oil-importing countries and first of all most of the less developed countries (vi) do not receive any petrodollars investment (except for some public aid distributed by OPEC) and do not benefit by any increase of their exports. They are forced either to increase their debt or to reduce their imports and their activity. As the possibility of getting foreign credits is not unlimited a slowdown of imports and of production is inevitable. Transferred to the suppliers of the countries concerned, this production slack spreads gradually over the majority of other countries. The only nations which remain untouched by this growth slowdown are the oil-exporting countries and to a lesser degree the oil-importing countries (iii).

Given a lower rate of domestic inflation, these last countries are enabled to increase their share in world exports. But this is achieved at the expense of their competitors whose exports are consequently reduced.

Thus the economic recession which touched the majority of industrial countries during the second half of 1974 and the first half of 1975 was severely aggravated by the unprecedented rises in oil prices in 1973 and 1974.

The following period up to 1979 was a period of relative recovery. The prices of goods imported by oil-producing countries gradually and partially caught up with the prices of oil. The OPEC imports grew steadily. The oil surplus shrank from $64 billion in 1974 to less than $12 billion in 1978. But neither inflation nor deflation disappeared. Inflation continued because the causes which had existed before 1973 were not eliminated. Deflation was not completely set aside because all prices had not caught up with oil prices. In particular, this was not the case of many raw materials exported by oil-importing developing countries which had to pay higher prices for oil and for industrial products without receiving comparably increased prices for their exports. In many countries wages continued to rise faster than labour productivity. The profitability of investment was not completely re-established. Combined with the steady increase in the working-age population, the insufficiency of investment resulted in a continually rising rate of unemployment.

The 1978-79 Oil Price Increase

A new series of sharp oil price increases came during the years 1978, 1979 and at the beginning of 1980. On the whole the oil price reached in April 1980 a level more than 100 per cent higher than that at the end of 1978. The OPEC surplus rose to $44 billion in 1979 and will equal at least $85 billion in 1980. In real value it will be comparable to the surplus of the years 1974-75. An acceleration of both inflationary and deflationary pressures seems unavoidable. However, their intensity may be to some extent reduced if an appropriate action is undertaken at the international level. This is the point where East-West economic relations may play a decisive role.

The Situation of Eastern Europe and the USSR

With respect to the economic trends described the situation of Eastern Europe and the USSR does not differ substantially from the situation of Western countries. The marginal productivity of capital and the rate of economic growth are declining. Inflation is spreading over all Eastern countries. The apparent stability of administered prices only magnifies its negative economic and social effects.[5]

The USSR, the largest oil supplier of the region, every year raises the price of its supplies to other Eastern countries proportionally to the average OPEC price of the past five years. As in the West, the economic effect of these price rises is to operate a real transfer of resources from Eastern Europe to the USSR. This transfer is de-flationary in real terms in so far as it forces the countries concerned either to reduce their domestic consumption and investment or to increase their foreign debt. It is inflationary in monetary terms since the incomes generated in the production of additional goods trans-ferred to the USSR do not have any counterpart on domestic markets.

Conversely, oil price increases (and also gold price rises) strength-en considerably the economic position of the USSR which may in this way enlarge its imports from other CMEA countries and from the West without any additional effort. This fact makes it still more difficult to understand the rather poor performance of the Soviet economy during the last decade.[6] The bad weather conditions cannot explain a trend which has been observable for several years. Rising costs of exploiting natural resources and slower labour-force growth certainly are very important factors of a slowing economic growth and a declining investment. But some essential deficiencies in the system of centralised planning cannot be excluded.[7]

One of the most important among these deficiencies is the inability of the system to promote - except for some top priority branches - the introduction of technical progress into the process of pro-duction.[8] The seriousness of the technological gap between East and West which results from this inability cannot be measured merely by the differences between technologies used in similar industries on both sides. It has rather to be appreciated by the differences in the whole industrial structure of the countries compared. In view of the third industrial revolution which is nowadays completely changing the production pattern of Western countries, the industrial set up of the East appears as extremely backward. Consequently, intensive techni-cal co-operation with the West is particularly important for Eastern countries.

Another essential deficiency of the system is its low labour productivity and poor performance in agriculture (except for East Germany and Czechoslovakia). In this respect the position of Poland is especially worrying because of fundamental errors in the price and incomes policy and of social and economic discrimination against individual peasants who are not allowed to enlarge their micro-holdings to an economically rational dimension.[9] Taken as a whole, Eastern Europe and the USSR are not yet self-sufficient in food production. The imports of food and feed from the West are absol-utely indispensable.

Finally, the system seems to be unable to respond to the growing needs of consumers whose incomes have overpassed the line of bare necessities. The import from the West of numerous consumer goods became one of the necessary conditions of social satisfaction. In fact, between 1970 and 1978, Soviet imports from the West increased from $2.7 billion to $17 billion and the Soviet foreign debt reached an amount of about $20 billion. Other Eastern countries have also considerably expanded their imports from the West and their debt towards Western countries, proportionally to their capacities, is still higher than that of the USSR. On the whole, trade with the West represents about 30 per cent of the total foreign trade of Eastern countries and they owe to the West about $57 billion.

II   EAST-WEST ECONOMIC CO-OPERATION AS A MEANS OF OVERCOMING WORLD STAGFLATION

Absolutely vital from the Eastern point of view, East-West economic co-operation is also important for Western countries. Eastern Europe and the USSR constitute an important and extending market for Western agricultural and industrial products.[10]

Against the background of world stagflation the importance of this market is potentially still greater. The expansion of exports to the East may at least partially compensate the deflationary pressure of oil price increases and the declining marginal profitability of capital. The margin of unsatisfied consumers' needs in Eastern countries is still very large. The capital endowment of many fundamental activities (transportation, housing, consumer-goods industries, agriculture, handicrafts, services and so on) is extremely low. There are almost unlimited possibilities of joint investments in the exploitation of natural resources in Siberia. The manpower in Eastern countries is still very cheap as compared to that of the Western developed countries. Many Western manufacturing industries could be interested in joint ventures aiming at a mutually profitable combination of Western capital and know-how with Eastern labour and natural resources.

The problem of the reciprocal Eastern exports to the West is much more difficult. In the long run, Eastern countries do not possess any significant energy surplus. Other raw materials available mainly in Siberia will probably not suffice to counterbalance the value of extended imports from the West and the increasing amount of debt service to the West. Moreover, the inconvertibility of Eastern currencies - which is not to be removed[11] - and the consequent strictly bilateral character of East-West relations do not allow the use of the surplus realised by a Western country in trade with one of the East European countries for the payment of imports from the USSR.

That is why a really significant development of East-West trade relations is not to be expected without a far-reaching reform of the Soviet-type planning system, on the lines already partially adopted by Hungary, which would consist broadly in the restoration of market forces in economic relations inside and between Eastern countries.[12] Such a reform would not only make possible the multilateralisation of East-West trade, but it would also tremendously increase the adaptability of Eastern enterprises to the demand of Western countries. In this way it could be possible to expand Eastern exports sufficiently to counterbalance approximately the imports from and the debt service to the West. After all, the spectacular development of intra-EEC relations has been realised between countries which also originally had widely different economic potentials.

The efficiency of East-West trade expansion, as a means for overcoming world stagflation, may be greatly improved if it is accompanied by a similar action towards developing countries. Due allowance being made for the differences in the degree of economic development, the final repercussions of the oil price shock on the oil-importing Eastern countries are not substantially different from those which affect the oil-importing developing countries. Both are struck simultaneously by the rise in prices of oil and of imported industrial goods. Thus the deflationary impact of the oil surplus finally takes the form of an increasing balance of payments deficit in developing and Eastern oil-importing countries. Consequently the solution to world stagflation is to be found in the expansion of productive capacities both of Eastern Europe and of developing countries. Only the industrial countries of the West - with the help of the oil-surplus-producing countries - are capable of financing the huge investments and of providing the know-how necessary for achieving this objective.

But the possibility of extending this potentially mutually advantageous co-operation depends on two fundamental conditions:

(i)   The necessity of removing, on both sides, a great number of institutional and administrative restrictions[13] which hinder the development of a free, multilateral exchange of goods and services between the East and the West.

(ii) The necessity of preserving a high degree of mutual confidence and respect. This condition is all the more important as the development of East-West economic relations ineluctably implies the granting by the West to the East of huge long-term credits for financing investments which would considerably enhance the economic and consequently the military potential of the USSR.

Objectively speaking, it is impossible to deny that the Soviet invasion of Afghanistan has struck a terrible blow to all those in Western countries who were sincerely hoping for a peaceful and reciprocally advantageous development of East-West economic co-operation. There is only one means to restore a minimal confidence indispensable for once again taking up a constructive dialogue in this field: it is an immediate and complete withdrawal of Soviet troops from Afghanistan.

We do not claim that the probable unfulfilment of this last condition will completely stop the growth of East-West exchanges. The particular economic interests involved on both sides are much too strong to be neglected by the governments concerned. The number of Western businessmen visiting Moscow in search of new contracts has rather increased than decreased since the announcement of the last American embargo. But the break-through necessary for overcoming world stagflation will not be accomplished.

After all, from the Western point of view, the purchases of the East represent less than 4 per cent of the industrial countries' total exports. They can easily be replaced in their role of economic accelerator by a far-reaching development of investments in less developed countries and especially in China. The potential long-term capacity of this last country for absorbing highly productive investments is almost unlimited given the extremely low level of its consumption and capital accumulation, the high availability of natural resources and, last but not least, a billion of capable and industrious population.

NOTES

1. For the explanation of the inflationary impact of the Keynesian policy see J. Marczewski, Vaincre l'inflation et le chômage (Paris: Economica, 1978), p. 43.
2. See J. Marczewski, Inflation and Unemployment in France: A Quantitative Analysis (New York and London: Praeger, 1978), p. 193.
3. See J. Marczewski, Vaincre l'inflation, op. cit., p. 19.
4. It consists mainly in replacing mechanics by electronics.
5. See J. Marczewski, 'Inflation à l'Est', Banque, Paris (September 1977) and Problèmes Economiques, Paris (14 December 1977).
6. See UN Economic Commission for Europe, Economic Survey of Europe in 1979 (New York, 1980).
7. J. Marczewski, Crisis in Socialist Planning, Eastern Europe and the USSR (New York and London: Praeger, 1974 and 1976), p. 229.
8. Ibid., p. 235.
9. See J. Marczewski, 'The Problem of Consumption in Soviet-type Economics', Soviet Studies, No.1 (January 1979), 112-17.
10. See G. Schiavone, Gli Scambi Est-Ovest. Problemi e Prospettive (Padova: Cedam, 1971).
11. See J. Marczewski, 'La Convertibilité des Monnaies des Pays du CAEM' Revue d'Etudes Comparatives Est-Ouest, Paris (December 1979), 185-94.
12. See J. Marczewski, 'On Remodelling of the Polish Economic System: a Contribution', Soviet Studies, No.3 (July 1979), 434-40.
13. See G. Schiavone, op. cit., pp. 79, 128, 210 and 213.

APPENDIX

Table 3.1   World Exports

EXPORTING COUNTRIES	IMPORTING COUNTRIES (In % of the total)							
	Industri-alised		Developing		Centrally planned		Oil-exporting	
	1960	1978	1960	1978	1960	1978	1960	1978
Low-income	65	66	27	23	7	5	1	6
Middle-income	70	67	24	25	5	5	1	3
Industrialised	67	67	28	23	3	4	2	6
Centrally planned	21	n.a.	8	n.a.	70	n.a.	1	n.a.

Source: World Bank, World Development Report, 1980
(Washington, August 1980).

Table 3.2   World Exports of Manufactured Goods

EXPORTING COUNTRIES	IMPORTING COUNTRIES (In % of the total)							
	Industri-alised		Developing		Centrally planned		Oil-exporting	
	1963	1977	1963	1977	1963	1977	1963	1977
Low-income	n.a.	51	n.a.	27	n.a.	12	n.a.	10
Middle-income	n.a.	58	n.a.	30	n.a.	6	n.a.	6
Industrialised	65	65	31	25	3	4	1	6
Centrally planned	n.a.	18	n.a.	18	n.a.	64	n.a.	4

Source: as for Table 3.1

4 Convertibility, Compensation and East–West Trade

HARRIET MATEJKA

Graduate Institute for International Studies, Geneva

I INTRODUCTION

This paper is concerned with payments' systems and the level of trade. It thus seems appropriate to begin with a brief reminder both of the methods available to a country wishing to control and adjust its external payments, and of their implications. It brings out the fact that compensation, when policy-induced, is a means of financing international transactions which is associated with inconvertibility.

There are two methods by which a central authority can control and correct its external payments. The first is indirect, that is resorting to price-mechanism devices such as exchange rates, tariffs, import surtaxes, advance import deposits and export subsidies. The second is direct, that is resorting to measures such as quantitative restrictions, exchange controls and plan directives, which do not operate through the price mechanism, but administratively limit or determine the volume or value of trade. In practice, the two methods are often combined.

The first method is compatible with currency convertibility. This consists in the unrestricted purchase and sale of a country's currency at a single exchange rate for current transactions,[1] where 'unrestricted' signifies only that the purchases and sales of the currency are not subject to direct limitation. It should not be understood, as it often is, to imply free trade for, historically, convertibility has always been associated with protection exercised through price-mechanism devices, that is essentially tariffs. The second method excludes convertibility.[2] As central authorities normally combine both methods, convertibility in practice is rarely perfect.[3]

Convertibility implies the multilateral balancing of payments. But inconvertibility need not exclude it. A country with an inconvertible currency which trades with a number of countries with convertible currencies can use its favourable balance with one country to offset its unfavourable balance with another and thus balance its payments multilaterally with this group of trading partners.[4] Countries with inconvertible currencies can also form a payments union and balance their payments multilaterally while maintaining restrictions incompatible with convertibility.[5] In the absence of a payments' union, however, the flows of payment between two countries with inconvertible currencies must be equal, that is bilaterally balanced.

The adjustment, or correction, of a country's payments will differ according as to whether the indirect or the direct method is used. In the first case, the central authority will have two options. If its exchange rate is fixed, it will resort to import and export taxes or subsidies, or to a monetary, fiscal or incomes policy. If its exchange rate is flexible, the variations of the rate itself will correct the payments' disequilibrium leaving the other instruments, that is taxes and subsidies on international transactions, monetary, fiscal and incomes policy, to be trained on other objectives. In the second case, the central authority will correct a disequilibrium by introducing quantitative restrictions or exchange control, or by issuing restrictive or expansionary plan directives.

The means of financing a deficit, on the other hand, will generally be the same whichever of the two methods is used. They will consist essentially of international credits and the use of national reserves. A country whose currency is inconvertible, however, is one which suffers from a chronic payments' imbalance which is only held in check by direct restriction. Constantly short of foreign exchange, its authorities will therefore encourage the linking of imports to exports, that is compensation or countertrade.[6]

In the following discussion, the evolution, policy response to, and present and predicted importance of countertrade in East-West exchanges will be presented first. It will then be shown that countertrade tends to reduce the volume of trade. In so doing, the distinction will be drawn between autonomous arrangements, that is those not undertaken for balance of payments' purposes and which do not reduce trade, and accommodating arrangements, that is those that are undertaken for balance of payments' reasons and which do reduce trade. It will incidentally be suggested that the term 'countertrade' be reserved for the first type of transaction and 'compensation' for the second. In closing, the policy implications of the discussion will be drawn and the recommendation made that compensation should, whenever possible, be replaced by other forms of financing and that measures of adjustment be taken which would move the Eastern European currencies in the direction of convertibility.

II COUNTERTRADE IN EAST-WEST EXCHANGES

Countertrade may be defined as any type of bilateral balancing arrangement between enterprises or industries. It includes barter, that is the simultaneous exchange of products; counterpurchase, that is the simultaneous conclusion of two separate contracts for the compensating sale and purchase; and buy-back agreements, that is the sale of equipment and technology and the return purchase of products produced with the equipment and technology.[7]

Countertrade has always been a feature of East-West trade. Before 1971 and the emergence of a substantial East European debt in convertible currencies, however, it was occasional. Since then the demands for full or partial compensation have become systematic.[8] They have been sustained by major policy declarations,[9] and accompanied by the statements of Eastern European officials contending that countertrade constituted a technically advanced form of financing. Moreover, they have met with greater Western response than was the case previously for, it would seem, two reasons. First, since 1973, Western Europe has sought new sources of energy and has been willing to conclude countertrade agreements to secure them. Second, since the middle of the 1970s, enterprises hit by recession have sought new outlets in order to maintain output and employment, and have accepted countertrade agreements as a means to this end.

The greater emphasis on compensatory arrangements between East and West has so far elicited little policy response or institutional change, however. In Eastern Europe, these are unnecessary, for countertrade corresponds to the trading tradition of the centrally planned economies. Exchanges between the Eastern European countries take the form of international bilateral balancing, that is countertrade at the national level. Balance of payments difficulties in a number of socialist countries have been met by requiring each industrial ministry to balance its own payments, that is by countertrade at the industrial level. In addition, the joint development projects of the Council for Mutual Economic Assistance (CMEA) involve contributions of equipment, engineers and labour by co-operating countries in return for resulting products, so these too are countertrade arrangements.

Furthermore, Eastern European foreign trade corporations are equipped to handle countertrade. They are often responsible for both the import and export of a range of products and can thus deal with compensatory flows within their sector. More appropriately still, all the Eastern European countries have long had foreign trade corporations specialising in compensation and switch-trading. Thus the only recent measures adopted with respect to countertrade have been some decrees promoting compensation arrangements,[10] a few institutional modifications,[11] and some joint marketing enterprises created with Western firms.[12]

In the market economies of the West, by contrast, independent purchases and sales and the multilateral balancing of imports and exports through the intermediation of money are the tradition. Countertrade, though practised not only with the Eastern European countries, is alien. The necessary adjustment to the recent emphasis on East-West compensatory transactions seems thus to have been more considerable than in Eastern Europe, but has been made essentially by the market. New trading houses have been specially created to handle the imports shipped as a consequence of counter-trade, and which Western export producers are not generally equipped to sell. Trade associations in the FRG and Belgium are also making information available to their members. The role of Western central authorities, meanwhile, has been limited to the issue of advice and information.[13]

The modest policy response suggests that, although it may have been increasing, the share of compensatory arrangements in East-West trade nevertheless remains small. But figures differ widely. In 1978, for instance, countertrade was variously estimated to account for 30 per cent of East-West transactions,[14] 40 per cent of total East-West trade, and 25 per cent of East-West trade in industrial products.[15] Estimates for individual countries are more sober. A survey conducted in the FRG the same year indicated that approximately 15 per cent of its imports from the Soviet Union could be attributed to countertrade, while the corresponding figure for imports from other Eastern European countries was less than 10 per cent.[16] Soviet calculations show that the share of trade conducted under large-scale compensation agreements between the USSR and developed market economies rose from 9 per cent in 1976 to 17 per cent in 1978. Czechoslovak, Hungarian and Polish economists, finally, estimate the share of compensation in their exports to the West to be some 5 per cent of the total.[17]

The figures indicating the importance of countertrade in total East-West exchanges would thus appear to be exaggerated, while in the Western trade of, or with, the USSR, the share of compensation would seem to be as much as three times as high as in the Western trade of, or with, the other Eastern European countries. However, if there is some uncertainty as to the share of countertrade in East-West trade recently, there is general agreement about its continued existence in the future and, depending on the study consulted, probable or certain increase.[18] This being so, an examination of the impact of compensation on East-West exchanges becomes necessary.

III THE EFFECT OF COUNTERTRADE ON EAST-WEST EXCHANGES

Compensation is a form of bilateral balancing, that is a method of doing trade without money. This is clear in the case of barter. But it is equally the case in other forms of bilateral balancing whether at the enterprise, industry or national level. For although these may include the extension of credit from one partner to the other or, as counterpurchasing often does, the money payment of matching trans-actions, the outcome is to offset a flow of trade in one direction by a return flow of trade so as to eliminate or, at least, minimise the net money outflow in that direction.

Bilateral balancing means that imports have to be bought from the supplier who is willing to accept exports. This normally leads to a loss of efficiency. For the supplier who is willing to accept exports is not necessarily the cheapest source of imports. Nor is he necessarily prepared to pay the highest possible price for the compensating exports. As a result, the volume of trade under bilateral balancing will normally be reduced below the level achieved within a multi-lateral framework. This may be understood by examining a simple example and may be demonstrated more formally.

Consider a case of countertrade which is an extreme but real one. An Eastern European importer sought to buy machinery from a Western producer and to pay for it in baby food which the Western producer had no use for. The Western exporter could respond in two ways. He could either refuse the deal, or increase the price of his machinery to include a mark-up designed to cover the costs of finding a trader who would accept and dispose of the baby food. The result of proposing baby food in payment for machinery was, therefore, either to cancel a possible trade flow, to reduce the quantity of machinery which could be imported in exchange for the original quantity of baby food or, conversely, to increase the quantity of baby food required to pay for the original quantity of machinery, and so to reduce the baby food available to finance other imports. Trade thus tended to be reduced below the level which would have been achieved had the Eastern European trader been in a position to sell his baby food to the highest bidder and used the proceeds to buy machinery.

A More Formal Treatment

More formally, if bilateral balancing is pursued, every export will generally have a number of different prices depending on the market in which it is exchanged. Thus if X denotes one unit of an export and M_r (r = 1,2, ..., n), the quantity of an import for which it is exchanged in n markets, then the M_r may be so ordered that:

$$\frac{X}{M_1} > \frac{X}{M_2} > ... > \frac{X}{M_k} = \frac{X}{M_{k+1}} > ... > \frac{X}{M_n} \, .$$

It follows that the volume of trade could be increased if X were shifted from markets in which the price of X is lowest (the price ratios largest) to those in which it is highest (the price ratios smallest) and the proceeds used to buy M. In other words, trade would be increased if trade were balanced multilaterally through the intermediation of money, instead of bilaterally.

The reduction of trade under bilateral balancing can also be shown with the help of the simple model presented in the Appendix. This is a trade model designed to analyse the international allocation of resources. It isolates price as the independent variable since it is differences in price which determine trade and the international division of labour. But the word 'price' has no institutional conno-tation. In particular, the symbol P does not stand for 'market price' but for 'indicator of relative scarcity' and is therefore as relevant to producers and consumers in a market economy as it is to planners in a centrally planned one.

There are three countries producing and consuming three products. Each country exports a different product and imports the two others. X_{ij} and x_{ij} denote, respectively, the production and consumption of the ith good in the jth country. P_i stands for the price of the ith good. ES_{ij} is $X_{ij}-x_{ij}$, that is the domestic excess supply of the ith good in the jth country. If ES_{ij} is positive, the ith good is exported; if negative, the ith good is imported. ES_{ij} is divided between the country's two partners so that:

$$(X_{ij} - x_{ij}) = (x_{ih} - X_{ih}) + (x_{ik} - X_{ik})$$

$$i, j, h, k = 1, 2, 3$$

$$j \neq h \neq k \neq j.$$

$x_{ih}-X_{ih}$, the import of the ith good into the hth country, is the export of the ith good from the jth country to the hth country, and $x_{ik}-X_{ik}$, the import of the ith good into the kth country, is the export of the ith good from the jth country to the kth country.

Given the initial trade and payments situation, the balance of trade conditions for the three countries are as follows:

$$P_1 ES_{11} = P_2 (-ES_{21}) + P_3 (-ES_{31}) \tag{1}$$

where $\quad P_1 (-ES_{12}) > P_2 (-ES_{21})$

and $\quad P_1 (-ES_{13}) < P_3 (-ES_{31})$

$$P_2 ES_{22} = P_1 (-ES_{12}) + P_3 (-ES_{32}) \tag{2}$$

where $\quad P_2 (-ES_{21}) < P_1 (-ES_{12})$

and $\quad P_2 (-ES_{23}) > P_3 (-ES_{32})$

$$P_3 ES_{33} = P_1 (-ES_{13}) + P_2 (-ES_{23}) \tag{3}$$

where $\quad P_3 (-ES_{31}) > P_1 (-ES_{13})$

and $\quad P_3 (-ES_{32}) < P_2 (-ES_{23}).$ [19]

Trade is multilaterally balanced. Moreover, domestic and foreign prices are equal.

Given this equilibrium, bilateral balancing is then imposed. The trade flows between any two countries must then be cut back to the smallest of the two flows between them. For, at constant prices, any other solution would require an increase in the export of at least one product and this could not take place without an increase in its price. The balance of trade conditions thus become:

$$P_1 (-ES_{12}) = P_2 (-ES_{21}) \qquad\qquad (4)$$

where $-ES_{12}$ is reduced so that $P_1 (-ES_{12})$ is equal to the value of country 1's imports from country 2.

$$P_2 (-ES_{23}) = P_3 (-ES_{32}) \qquad\qquad (5)$$

where $-ES_{23}$ is reduced so that $P_2 (-ES_{23})$ is equal to the value of country 2's imports from country 3.

$$P_3 (-ES_{31}) = P_1 (-ES_{13}) \qquad\qquad (6)$$

where $-ES_{31}$ is reduced so that $P_3 (-ES_{31})$ is equal to the value of country 3's imports from country 1.

The restriction of trade under bilateral balancing will, however, create an excess supply of product 1 in country 1, of product 2 in country 2, of product 3 in country 3, and an excess demand of product 1 in country 2, of product 2 in country 3 and of product 3 in country 1. The price of product 1 will thus be reduced, by the market mechanism or the planner in country 1, and raised in country 2, the price of product 2 will be reduced in country 2 and raised in country 3, and the price of product 3 will be reduced in country 3 and raised in country 1. New opportunities for trade will thus be created. But, although additional trade will flow between the three countries, the volume attained must remain below the multilateral level. For, as additional trade begins to flow between them, so prices will increase, or be increased in the exporting countries. In order that the multilateral level of exports be achieved, however, so the prices consistent with that level would have to be attained. But at those prices, bilateral trade would be unbalanced. In other words, trade would have to be multilaterally balanced whereas it is constrained to bilateral equilibrium. The volume of exports and imports must therefore remain below the level achieved given multilateral balancing.

Addenda

The formal discussion has considered bilateral balancing in general, although the initial example related to a compensation agreement. It should be noted, however, that countertrade, that is interenterprise bilateral balancing, is more restrictive than bilateral balancing between countries, or international bilateral balancing. For whereas in the latter, countries can match the whole range of their exportable production and so find tradeable goods for their reciprocal consumption, this is not true of interenterprise compensation. The risk of no trade, or of costs being increased because of the need of one partner to re-export the goods he receives, is thus much greater in interenterprise than in international compensation. More formally, in international bilateral balancing the prices of any export differ only as between countries. In interenterprise bilateral balancing they also differ as between enterprises in a given country. To go back to the inequalities on page 37, therefore, there are likely to be more prices for a given export with interenterprise than with international bilateral balancing and, hence, more opportunities of trade foregone with the first than with the second.

It should also be noted that while the volume of trade will be lower under bilateral than under multilateral balancing, certain countries may nevertheless benefit under bilateral balancing. For the bilateral framework will restrict competition from other potential buyers and sellers and enable the stronger partner to exert its price-making power and thus to achieve terms of trade which are better than the terms of trade that it would have obtained in the multilateral framework. By the same token, however, the weaker partner must suffer a terms of trade deterioration as compared to the multilateral situation. In East-West countertrade at the moment, there is no doubt that it is the Eastern European raw material producers and the Western producers of advanced technology which have price-making power, and which are in a position to turn the terms of trade in their favour in compensation agreements.

A Qualification

Finally, a qualification must be entered to allow for the fact excluded from the discussion of the model, which is that while bilateral balancing tends to reduce the volume of trade below the multilateral level, it does not necessarily do so. To go back to the example of the Western producer of machinery who was offered baby food in payment of his machines, it is clear that the volume of trade would not be reduced if the Western producer were simultaneously a general trader who dealt in baby food and if the Eastern seller of the product were the cheapest source of supply. Similarly, to go back to the inequalities on page 37, there would be no loss in efficiency and in the volume of trade if the price of X were the same in all r markets, and if the exporter of X bilaterally balanced his trade in all r markets by choice in order to diversify his supply of product X. In other words, countries may balance their trade bilaterally while buying their imports from the cheapest suppliers and selling their exports to the clients willing to pay the highest prices. Some compensation may be 'natural', that is not imposed for balance of payments' reasons. Certain agreements involving Western purchases of Eastern European raw materials and certain buy-back contracts which are the result of a Western reallocation of production to Eastern Europe may constitute 'natural' countertrade agreements of this sort at present.[20]

The identification of 'natural' countertrade suggests the transposition to bilateral balancing of a distinction commonly drawn in the case of multilateral payments.[21] This is the distinction between autonomous and accommodating transactions, where autonomous transactions are defined as those which are not undertaken for balancing purposes, and accommodating payments as those which are. Applying this to countertrade yields an economically significant classification of arrangements into autonomous, or 'natural' ones, on the one hand, and accommodating ones, on the other. This, in turn, suggests a modification of present terminology which would reserve the term 'countertrade' for autonomous or 'natural' bilateral balancing arrangements, and the term 'compensation' for accommodating agreements, that is for those concluded for balance of payments' reasons.

IV   POLICY CONCLUSIONS

The policy conclusions which follow from the discussion may, in closing, be drawn in terms of countertrade and compensation as just defined. Countertrade, which takes place for economic reasons in the absence of balance of payments restrictions, and does not reduce the efficiency or the volume of trade, needs neither encouragement nor restriction. On the other hand, certain buy-back arrangements, which may constitute autonomous agreements, are at present creating difficulties for Western producers owing to the large quantities of resulting products which are entering Western markets, and there is some call for central intervention on this account. But the cause of these problems is the reallocation of production between East and West which, in turn, is part of the present worldwide structural adaptation of both production and trade. This is shifting the manufacture of standard technology products to the newly industrialised countries in Eastern Europe and elsewhere, and is imposing a reallocation of resources in favour of the advanced technology industries in the advanced industrial countries. To the extent that central intervention is required therefore, it should be trained on the objective of structural adjustment and not on the countertrade agreements which are but one of the many channels through which it is occurring.

Compensation, however, which reduces the efficiency and volume of trade, is a second-best policy[22] which should be discouraged. While recognising that the Eastern European countries may have no other alternative than to finance their external disequilibria by means of compensatory arrangements in the very short run, preference should be given whenever possible to other forms of financing. These could include the creation of banks such as the Central-European International Bank (CIB), the creation of other joint ventures, or membership of the International Monetary Fund (IMF) or the World Bank. Beyond this, as the means available to finance an imbalance are limited, measures should be taken to correct the payments' disequilibria from which the Eastern European countries are suffering. First-best policy for this purpose is a change in the exchange rate. But since the devaluations required could seriously disrupt production, they could be associated with independent domestic price adjustments. In other words, the Eastern European authorities could pursue the progressive exchange rate and price adjustments which they have been undertaking since the mid-1960s. These would enable them to restore the multilateral balancing of their exchanges with the West and, for those relying sufficiently on price-mechanism devices, to move towards currency convertibility. This would remain a long-term goal rather than an objective to be achieved in the short run, however. For convertibility requires not only the fulfilment of the formal conditions indicated in the introduction to this paper, but also the creation of a policy apparatus capable of maintaining internal and external balance in the absence of extensive direct controls on international transactions.

In sum, compensation should be discouraged, and there would seem to be no justification for the intervention of central and other authorities in favour of interenterprise bilateral balancing. At the national level, additional Western governments will certainly issue information on the subject, particularly as China is now also requesting such agreements. But to go beyond this and attempt to generalise compensation, as certain Eastern European decrees seem to advocate, would impose a network of bilateral balancing arrangements on East-West trade more damaging than the international clearing agreements which governed it until 1958. This would affect the smaller European countries whose dependence on East-West trade is relatively greatest particularly seriously and, among them especially, the smaller Eastern European countries whose price-making power within bilateral balancing agreements is the smallest. At the international level, productive alternatives to a preoccupation with countertrade and compensation would be the identification of the obstacles impeding the channelling of Western funds to the East, and the collection and issue of precise and complete information on the export potential of the Eastern European economies.

NOTES

1. For countries which are members of the General Agreement on Tariffs and Trade (GATT) and the International Monetary Fund (IMF), convertibility thus means meeting the requirements of Article XI of the General Agreement, which prescribes the general elimination of quantitative restrictions on trade, and of Article 8 of the Charter of the IMF, which prescribes the abandonment of exchange controls on current payments and the use of the single exchange rate.
2. Or at least it does so in practice. In theory, one can conceive of the central authority in a planned economy so issuing directives as to allow the holder of the country's currency to buy and sell it at a single exchange rate for current transactions subject to no administrative restriction.
3. For a discussion of the modern concept of convertibility and of the imperfections acceptable in practice, see Robert Triffin, Gold and the Dollar Crisis, The Future of Convertibility, revised edition (London and New Haven: Yale University Press, 1961), pp. 22-6.

4. The USSR, for instance, balanced its trade multilaterally during the 1920s and 1930s and, since the return of the major Western European currencies to convertibility in 1958, the Eastern European countries have cleared their trade multilaterally with the Western developed economies.

5. As the Western European countries did in the European Payments Union from 1950-58.

6. For the equivalence of the two terms in present discussion, see United Nations Economic Commission for Europe (ECE), 'Countertrade Practices in the ECE Region', Committee on the Development of Trade, 9 November 1979, p. 10.

7. Jenelle Matheson, Paul McCarthy and Steven Flanders, 'Countertrade Practices in Eastern Europe', in East European Economies Post-Helsinki, A Compendium of Papers submitted to the Joint Economic Committee, Congress of the United States (Washington: US Government Printing Office, 1977), pp. 1279-83.

8. The initiative for compensation came from the Eastern partner in more than 90 per cent of the cases, according to a survey conducted in the Federal Republic of Germany (FRG) in 1978, and in 80 per cent of the cases according to a Swiss study. See F.-L. Altman and H. Clement, Die Kompensation als Instrument im Ost-West Handel, Gegenwartsfragen des Ost-Wirtschafts, Band 10 (München: Olzog-Verlag, 1979), p.70 and C.J. Gmür, Barter, Compensation and Co-operation (Zürich: Crédit Suisse special publications, vol. 47, 1978), p.20.

9. 'Another important subject is the development of new forms of economic links with foreign countries, links which go beyond the framework of ordinary trade operations, considerably expand our possibilities and, in principle, produce the most significant results. I am thinking in particular of compensatory agreements, under which new enterprises owned entirely by our State are constructed in co-operation with foreign enterprises. We receive credits, equipment and licences, and pay for them with part of the output of these enterprises or of other enterprises.' Extract from the report of the Central Committee of the Communist Party of the USSR presented by L.I. Brezhnev at the twenty-fifth Party Congress, Materialy XXV S'ezda KPSS (Moscow, 1976), p.5.

10. 'Payments between the parties shall be effected in full or in part by means of goods and services mutually supplied or by means of goods derived from the execution of the agreement.' Decree No. 1196 of 12 June 1974 of the Council of State of the People's Republic of Bulgaria on Economic, Industrial and Technical Co-operation with Foreign Natural and Juridical Persons, article 2, Recueil des législations des pays socialistes européens sur la coopération économique (Geneva: Graduate Institute of International Studies, 1974), BG.4, p.3.
'Foreign trade enterprises and services shall pursue export,

import and international economic co-operation activities and trade transactions with a view to obtaining foreign exchange earnings and, wherever possible, shall organise appropriate service activities and ensure that the required goods for exchange are available in accordance with the purpose of the activity established by this Decree.

In pursuit of this activity, care shall be taken, under the terms of the law, to promote exports and international economic co-operation and, on this basis, to achieve a balance between imports and exports, especially through the conclusion of long-term counter-purchase contracts.

Imports of plant, machinery, tools and components shall be made in particular within the framework of co-operation and export activities in exchange for products of the machine-building sector.' Decree No. 276 of 21 July 1979 of the Council of State of the Socialist Republic of Romania, article 2, ECE, op. cit., p.40.

11. In the USSR, the Department of Economic Co-operation òf the Plan Commission and the Compensation Project Department of the Ministry of Trade were created. ECE, op. cit., p. 46.

12. Marie Lavigne, Les relations économiques est-ouest (Paris: Presses universitaires de France, 1979), p. 242, who cites the creation of Technocar by Technip, a French group, and Balkancar, Bulgaria, for the marketing of Balkancar's fork-lift carts accepted in payment of the delivery by Technip of a low-density polyethylene plant to Bulgaria.

13. See ECE, 'Institutional Arrangements at the National Level for Counter-Trade in Selected Western Countries', Committee on the Development of Trade, 16 October 1979, which lists the following recent measures:
    (i)   the information sheets provided by the United Kingdom and United States governments;
    (ii) the semi-official, advisory Austrian Evidenzbüro für Aussenhandelsgeschäfte, founded in 1968, and the French Association pour la compensation des échanges commerciaux (ACECO), founded in 1977;
    (iii) the advisory and intermediary services department being set up by Sweden's Export Council.

14. Marie Lavigne, op. cit., p. 241.

15. Figures cited by ECE officials.

16. Altman and Clement, op. cit., p. 62.

17. For both the Soviet and Czechoslovak, Hungarian and Polish estimates, see ECE, op. cit., p. 29.

18. Matheson, McCarthy and Flanders, op. cit., p. 1303; Marie Lavigne, op.cit., p. 248; ECE, op. cit., p. 66.

19. The left-hand terms of the inequalities denote the imports of the ith good into the hth and kth countries, that is, as explained above, the export of the ith good by the jth country to its

' partner, the hth and k^{th} countries.

20. Nevertheless, one wonders whether, in the case of undertakings such as the Ust-Ilimsk project, it would not be more economical for the USSR, reserves of gold and convertible currency permitting, to buy equipment and hire technicians and labour from the cheapest source and sell its cellulose independently to the highest bidder, instead of buying equipment and hiring technicians and labour from the future consumers of cellulose.

21. James E. Meade, The Theory of International Economic Policy, vol. II, The Balance of Payments (London: Oxford University Press, 1951), pp. 11-13.

22. In the general sense of 'suboptimal'. It is clear that compensation creates more than one by-product distortion and is probably much worse than second-best in the strict sense.

APPENDIX

Let x_{ij} and X_{ij} be, respectively, consumption and production of the ith good in the jth country. For simplicity's sake, assume that there are only three countries and three plus one commodities, commodity 0 serving as numéraire. Let P_i stand for the price of the ith good. Then:

$$x_{ij} = x_{ij}(P_i) \qquad \begin{array}{l} i = 1, 2, 3 \\ j = 1, 2, 3 \end{array} \qquad (1)$$

Demand for the ith good in the jth country is a decreasing function of the price of the ith good expressed in terms of the numéraire, commodity 0.

$$X_{ij} = X_{ij}(P_i) \qquad \begin{array}{l} i = 0, 1, 2, 3 \\ j = 1, 2, 3 \end{array} \qquad (2)$$

Supply of the ith good in the jth country is an increasing function of the price of the ith good. A supply function for the numéraire commodity is included in this set of relationships although it is not under (1). The reason for this is that the demand for numéraire, commodity 0, can be derived from relations (1). On the other hand, the supply of 0 cannot be derived from (2).

In a closed economy which, because it is autonomous, can be considered as a world in its own right, equilibrium would require that:

$$x_{ij} = X_{ij}$$

for every commodity produced. Any individual within the economy could produce more than he consumed or consume more than he produced but, for the economy as a whole, the production of any good would have to equal consumption.

In the world system described above, economies take the place of individuals and exchange goods and services with each other. The individual economies are characterised by the production, consumption and exchange of a variety of goods. As they are traders, their production can exceed or fall short of their consumption in any one of the commodities they deal in, so that for each individual product market, it will be true that:

$$X_{ij} - x_{ij} \gtreqless 0 \qquad\qquad \begin{matrix} i = 1, 2, 3 \\ j = 1, 2, 3 \end{matrix} \qquad\qquad (3)$$

Let ES_{ij} denote $X_{ij}-x_{ij}$, that is the domestic excess supply of the ith good in the jth country. When for a given P_i, ES_{ij} is positive, the good in question will be exported. When negative, it will be imported.

World equilibrium, however, like the general equilibrium of the closed economy, will require that the production and consumption of every individual good be in balance, so that:

$$\sum_{j=1}^{3} (X_{ij}-x_{ij}) = 0 \qquad\qquad i = 1, 2, 3 \qquad\qquad (4)$$

5 The Outlook for East–West Agricultural Trade

JOSEPH HAJDA

Kansas State University

Agricultural trade figures prominently on the current list of East-West issues of immediate relevancy and concern. But during the 1970s, agricultural trade was frequently viewed as a less important aspect of East-West interactions, and in many scholarly discussions it was a forgotten issue. The vast majority of specialists misperceived the evolution of the 'systemic' realities and, as a result, underestimated the possibilities for agricultural trade expansion. Looking at the food and agricultural policy trends and developments of the early 1970s, and taking into account past 'systemic' differences, scholars usually expressed doubts whether East-West agricultural trade could soon grow to very large dimensions.

Only a handful of seasoned watchers of East-West relations, who keep a constant close check on vital signs of policy trends and developments, can boast about their trade projections based on an accurate perception of the evolution of the 'systemic' realities.

By the end of 1979, it was difficult to dispute the evidence showing that agricultural trade and its infrastructure were an important aspect of East-West interactions. The trade dimensions reflected the acceptance by the trading partners on both sides of the notion that agricultural trade should be conducted on the basis of mutual satisfaction and reciprocal benefits. In the broadest terms, agricultural trade was perceived as contributing to the trading partners' development, promoting their national economic growth and creating conditions conducive to the general well-being on both sides. The recognition of beneficial effects of agricultural trade strengthened the propensity to trade, with definite consequences for the pattern of trade, the modalities of trade relations and the configuration of the infrastructure's component parts.

The great importance attached by the United States to agricultural exports derived from the concern about the dynamic evolution of the

47

American agricultural economy, the aggregate farm income, the shape of the infrastructure and the balance of payments. Due to their key role in East-West agricultural trade, grain exports not only figured prominently in public policy deliberations, but also contributed to fashioning an operational environment in which the intensity of the motivations for continued East-West agricultural trade reached a very high level. Given the tenuous shape of the national economy, it was generally expected that expanding grain exports to the Soviet Union and the grain-deficit countries of Eastern Europe would be strongly supported in the 1980s. These expectations were reinforced by comparative appraisals of the 'systemic' realities, pointing out that the centrally-planned economies were in an even more tenuous shape, and that they could not soon achieve grain self-supply.

During the 1970s, for the Soviet Union and the grain-deficit countries of Eastern Europe grain imports from the United States, Canada and other Western nations were not just a stop-gap measure to remedy a short-lived problem, but a necessity to meet the needs periodically created by dismal harvests. A most significant manifestation of this necessity was the action taken on 20 October 1975, when the Soviet Union signed a grain agreement with the United States, providing for a Soviet commitment to buy six to eight million tons of wheat and corn in equal amounts annually for five years starting in October 1976. The agreement also committed the USSR to consult with the United States if it wanted to buy more than eight million tons in a given year.

Table 5.1   USSR: Grain Production, Trade and Utilisation, 1972/73-1979/80   (million metric tons)

Year	Pro- duction	Trade (July/June) Imports	Trade (July/June) Exports	Net imports	Imports from the US	Util- isation
1972/73	168	22.8	1.8	21.0	13.7	187
1973/74	223	11.3	6.1	5.2	7.9	214
1974/75	196	5.7	5.3	0.4	2.3	206
1975/76	140	26.1	0.7	25.4	13.8	180
1976/77	224	11.0	3.3	7.7	7.5	221
1977/78	196	18.9	2.3	16.6	12.5	228
1978/79	237	15.6	2.8	12.8	10.5	231
1979/80	179	30.5a	0.8b	29.7	15.4c	222b

a   US Department of Agriculture estimate of grain imports from all foreign sources, 10 March 1980.

b   US Department of Agriculture forecast, published in Foreign Agriculture, February 1980, p.26.

c   US Department of Agriculture projection as of 18 March 1980.

The extent of Soviet dependence on Western grain supplies can be seen by examining the data concerning the USSR's grain production, trade and utilisation in 1972/73-1979/80 (see Table 5.1). The data show that grain production fluctuates widely. Still, average annual production increased from 182 million tons in the first four years to 209 million tons in the next four years - nearly one-fifth of world grain production.[1] Assuming that the 1979/80 estimates are fairly accurate, one can see that grain import data show considerable fluctuation, and that imports averaged 16.5 million tons in the first four years and 19 million tons in the next four years. Net import averages were 13 million tons and 16.7 million tons, respectively. It should be noted that the US share of grain imports reached 67 per cent in the 1976/77-1978/79 period.

Comparing production, utilisation and import data for the whole eight-year period provides additional insights regarding the extent of Soviet dependence on Western grain supplies. While grain imports amounted to 142 million tons, domestic production totalled 1563 million tons, or eleven times the volume of imports; 8.5 per cent of the Soviet grain utilisation depended on world trade.

By the end of the 1970s, the Soviet Union was a major and expanding market for Western grain traders, especially American traders, who viewed the Soviet market as an important economic entity in the world food system. The USSR was reported to be the largest single-country importer of grains in 1979/80, accounting for over one-sixth of the total world grain trade. It was generally expected that the Soviet Union would buy up to 25 million tons of grains from the United States in the fourth year (1 October 1979-30 September 1980) of the five-year grain agreement - nearly one-fourth of total US grain export sales.[2] The prevailing view was that the USSR, the world's current largest grain importer, and the United States, the world's largest grain exporter, would not curtail their economically beneficial trade relationship.

The extent of East Europe's dependence on US grain supplies can be seen by examining the data concerning US grain exports in 1971-78, and the projections for the 1979/80 marketing year (see Tables 5.2 and 5.3). US exports to the six countries grew from an average 2.2 million tons in 1971-74 to 5.3 million tons in 1975-78, and to 10 million tons projected for 1979/80. Corresponding export figures for the four principal destinations include (in million tons): Poland - 2.1, 2.4 and 4.3; East Germany - 0.9, 2.1 and 2.5; Czechoslovakia - 0.1, 0.4 and 2.5; and Romania - 0.3, 0.5 and 1.1.

Grain trade projections put the 1979/80 Soviet and East European imports from all origins at 46.4 million tons. The combined imports are expected to be more than one-fourth of the world grain trade.

The expectations along economic lines were complemented by expectations along political lines. Parallel to the general assumption that East-West agricultural trade expansion in the 1980s would provide economic benefits to all participating nations was the

Table 5.2 United States Grain Exports to Eastern Europe,
1971-78 (in thousand metric tons)

	1971	1972	1973	1974	1975	1976	1977	1978
Bulgaria	-	-	-	64	115	246	3	226
Czechoslovakia	259	98	120	5	10	912	81	426
East Germany	403	702	1160	1175	1961	2877	1332	1314
Hungary	-	-	24	-	-	-	112	107
Poland	459	448	1745	896	1973	2799	2133	2683
Romania	366	212	121	512	620	666	413	327
Total	1487	1460	3170	2652	4679	7500	4074	5083

Source: Eastern Europe Agricultural Situation, US Department of
Agriculture, May 1979, p.18. The volume of exports includes tranship-
ments through Belgium, Canada, the Netherlands and West Germany.

Table 5.3 Eastern Europe: Grain Imports, 1 July 1979-30 June 1980
(in thousand metric tons)

	Total	From the US
Bulgaria	300	100
Czechoslovakia	2500	2000
East Germany	3600	2500
Hungary	100	-
Poland	8000	4300
Romania	1500	1100
Total	15900	10000

Source: US Department of Agriculture projections as of 18 March 1980.

assumption that agricultural trade would remain a significant part of efforts for greater stability in East-West relations, and that trade expansion would contribute to a decrease of international tensions and insecurities. Agricultural trade was looked upon as transmitting not merely goods and capital but also ideas: ideas about marketing and management, agricultural science and technology, farming systems and infrastructures, standards of living and ways of life, and institutional designs and arrangements. Given the critical importance of food issues in public-agenda building, the total gain from East-West agricultural trade appeared to be both immense and incalculable.

It was generally agreed that the establishment of lasting and extensive ties in the sphere of agricultural trade was an issue of special concern. Envisaged as a means to foster an orderly development of trade relations while avoiding abrupt fluctuations, intergovernmental agreements offered a framework for creating an array of institutional and personal ties and linking intergovernmental relations with the other parts of the infrastructure, such as scientific and other research, education and training, commerce and banking, and related activities.

The general view was that the maintenance of these ties would have to be based on a stable and favourable political atmosphere, that is on a comprehensive approach to the problem of political security and co-operation. The expectation of agricultural trade expansion was based on the assumption that East-West interactions would reinforce the process of reducing tensions in international relations.

At the same time, it was impossible to overlook the influence of political forces advocating a different approach to East-West relations. In the United States, some leading advocates of a different approach argued that the West should forge an effective political weapon from the limitation of economic links with the East. Their plea for a policy of blocking East-West economic interactions, or restricting East-West trade ties, included the proposition concerning the use of the 'food weapon'.

Focusing on the possibility of a US embargo on grain exports to the Soviet Union, the discussion took into account three criteria of effectiveness. First, the target country must not be able to obtain needed grains from any other source. Second, the target country must not be able to achieve significant adjustment of internal consumption resulting in diminished grain import needs. Third, the political climate of the embargo-initiating country must be conducive to accepting the economic and political costs associated with reduced grain exports.

The critics of the 'food weapon' approach pointed out that the potential use of US grain exports as a flexible and reliable 'weapon' for dealing with the Soviet Union would be very limited. They warned about unrealistic expectations concerning the possibilities of curtailing the Soviet access to alternative sources of grain supplies; they stressed the USSR's capability to control and conceal its 'needs'; and they called attention to the possibility of increased Soviet grain production. Moreover, they anticipated serious complications stemming from the US domestic political and economic considerations. In short, the critics felt that the 'weapon' would have little impact, poor reliability and considerable threat of backfiring.[3]

The events of late 1979 and early 1980 led to discarding the expectation of East-West agricultural trade expansion in the foreseeable future. The general assumption that the short-term prospects were for Soviet-West trade decline rather than expansion resulted from the US launching of economic sanctions in response to military actions by the Soviet Union in Afghanistan. With the United States pressing for the disruption of Soviet grain import patterns, it became apparent in early 1980 that grain shipments to the Soviet Union had become a major controversial issue in the diplomatic arena.

Soviet military intervention in Afghanistan triggered major shifts in American foreign policy. In his address to the nation on 4 January 1980, President Carter announced the forms of 'punishment' to be administered to the Soviet Union for its invasion of Afghanistan, and called on other nations 'committed to world peace and stability' not to continue to do business as usual with the Soviet Union. Shortly after launching the campaign of economic and other sanctions, he vowed to stick to the campaign, gloomily forecasting that 'under even the best of circumstances, normal trade will not be resumed with the Soviet Union'.

Announcing that trade with the Soviet Union would be severely restricted, President Carter stated that he had decided to halt or reduce exports to the USSR in three areas: high technology or other strategic items, fishing privileges in United States waters, and grain. The most controversial decision was his pronouncement concerning grain exports:

> The 17 million tons of grain ordered by the Soviet Union in excess of that amount which we are committed to sell will not be delivered. This grain was not intended for human consumption but was to be used for building up Soviet livestock herds ... After consultation with other principal grain-exporting nations, I am confident that they will not replace these quantities of grain by additional shipments on their part to the Soviet Union.

Several questions can be raised in the context of President Carter's campaign to disrupt regular grain trade patterns with the Soviet Union.

The first concerns the heightened economic dependence of the Soviet Union and some of its allies on grain imports from the West. Can they decrease their dependence on Western grain supplies so that they can feed themselves without importing large quantities of grain from the West?

Political authorities in the Soviet Union (and in the countries of Eastern Europe) recognise that political survival depends on securing adequate food supplies to meet the needs of society. In this day and generation, no set of leaders can take lightly the main thrust of the mood of rising expectations, that is, improved standards of living and, in particular, providing the population with more satisfactory diets.

But the analysis of grain output, trade and utilisation in the 1970s clearly shows that the Soviet Union cannot feed itself in the foreseeable future. Indeed, the inability of the Soviet domestic grain production to meet the demand for improved diets in that country continues to place the USSR in a position where sustained grain imports are necessary.[4] According to the US Department of Agriculture projections made four months before the embargo campaign, total Soviet grain imports from all origins from July 1979 to June 1980 were likely to reach an all-time record of 32.5 million tons. To meet sustained demand for better diets, Soviet grain imports will have to stay at a high level in the years to come. In addition, the dependence of East Germany and Poland on Western grain supplies is no minor matter. If the weather-related problems are like the 1979 problems, the combined Soviet and other East European grain import requirements could reach 55 million tons in the mid-1980s.

This view is based on the assumption that no fundamental changes will take place in the USSR's current policies and in the policies of its allies. The assumption is that improved performance of the farm sector will remain a major concern of public policy, that large amounts of capital will be channelled into agriculture, and that agricultural producers' prices and incomes will again be improved.

The problem is that the rising monetary incomes of the population will continue to exert considerable pressure on the food sector, and that ways provided in the existing sets of policies will be unable to solve the problem of agricultural productivity and cost efficiency. A dispassionate appraisal of the incentive system, along with the assessment of the shortage of industrial inputs in the farm sector, and the very serious shortcomings in the infrastructure, leads to the conclusion that inefficiencies will persist, and that the high capital cost of the existing agricultural enterprises is unlikely to pay off economically.[5]

Because the reality of contemporary food and agricultural conditions in the European East is complex, multifaceted and multi-layered, and because weather-related problems are unquestionably important in assessing agricultural performance, one should not assume that the built-in obstacles to greater efficiency and quality of work are the same everywhere.[6] For example, the impact of the deep-rooted inertia is especially visible in the Soviet Union: inertia in planning, inertia in economic management and, perhaps most important, inertia in economic thinking. Therefore, no viable strategy for coping with the Soviet food predicament can succeed unless the deep-rooted inertia is somehow drastically reduced.

Assuming that a major goal of policies in the countries of the European East will be to improve their populations' diets by increasing consumption of meat, eggs and milk, a steady increase in feed grain and other feedstuff supplies will be necessary. Since average harvests will be inadequate to meet grain requirements, large quantities of grain will need to be imported by the Soviet Union; likewise, grain import needs of Poland and East Germany are unlikely to decrease in the coming years.

The second question deals with the effectiveness of US countermeasures chosen to 'punish' the Soviet Union for its military action in Afghanistan. Some observers felt that putting a partial and temporary embargo on grain shipments can be looked upon as an understandable measure under the circumstances. But many seasoned watchers of East-West relations were disturbed by the use of food as a 'weapon'. While President Carter pointed out the embargoed grains were to be used for building up Soviet livestock herds, and were not intended for human consumption, he did not add that his move could lead to cuts in meat consumption by the mass of Soviet people.

There was no close consultation with the allied and associated countries before the announcement of unilateral US economic sanctions against the Soviet Union, so it came as no great surprise that the consultation with other principal grain-exporting countries after the grain embargo campaign was launched produced less than enthusiastic support. Not all countries that took part in the consultation responded in identical ways to the US request to limit grain exports to the USSR to prevent taking over the trade that the US gave up. While most major exporting countries pledged not to sell the Soviet Union more grain than normal, Argentina did not make the pledge.

Several weeks after President Carter's address, it became apparent that many countries would not join the embargo, and that countries that pledged their support of the embargo action would not be able to enforce it effectively - primarily because of third-party sales.

Critics of President Carter's embargo of grain sales to the Soviet Union pointed out that the move would do as much harm to the US as to the intended target. Some critics even felt that the action would hurt the American farmers and taxpayers more than the Soviet Union. According to a study released on 11 March 1980, by the Kansas City-based Farmland Industries, the direct impact of the embargo on farm sales is likely to be considerably greater than the government predicted. Based on estimates of farm sales before and after the embargo, the study said that grain farmers are likely to lose more than $4 billion in gross sales in 1980 because of the embargo and more than $4.6 billion in 1981, with corn farmers bearing the brunt of the impact.

To overcome the effect of the embargo on farmers, the US Department of Agriculture has announced several steps, including government takeover of Soviet grain contracts, purchases of corn and wheat from farmers and country elevators and boosts in grain prices guaranteed under government programmes. It is estimated that these steps will cost the taxpayers at least $2.8 billion.

While it is possible that farm sales will not decline by the amounts estimated in the Farmland Industries study - and rising demand for livestock feed has been pushing US corn exports to levels near those expected before the embargo action - it is quite obvious that the action 'will require some sacrifice on the part of all Americans', as President Carter put it.

Finally, some critics were disturbed by the President's statement that the US would use some of the grain shipments withheld from the Soviet Union to 'increase amounts of grain devoted to the alleviation of hunger in poor countries'. The critics felt that it is cynical to tell the poor countries that if Soviet military action makes grain sales to the USSR unwise, then the US will make such grain available to needy nations.

The third question deals with the Soviet Union's efforts to contain the US grain embargo campaign. Assuming that the USSR could be faced with tight feed supplies that might put pressure on the Soviet livestock industry, one should not overlook the possibility of reduced meat consumption in the coming years. However, such a policy shift would involve considerable political risks. In 1975-78, the USSR's meat consumption stagnated at the not very impressive 56-57 kg per capita level. If the feed grain and other feedstuff situation remains tight over a long period, the supply of meat could be short enough to lead to serious political consequences.

Because the political import of demand for meat is enormous, it is essential for the Soviet Union to deal with the loss of the 17 million tons of grain ordered from the US by a combination of measures: additional shipments from other origins, less grain feeding and a drawdown of available resources.

According to the US Department of Agriculture estimates of 10 March 1980, the USSR's grain imports from all foreign sources in the current marketing year ending 30 June 1980 are expected to be about 30.5 million tons. This estimate is only two million tons less than the estimate issued in September 1979 - several months before the embargo announcement. It is clear that the embargo action cannot and will not be airtight in the months to come.

While the Agriculture Department expects the impact of the embargo to be more pronounced after the current marketing year (ending 30 June 1980), it is safe to assume that the Soviet Union will make every effort to make additional headway in finding the required quantities of grains in world markets for shipment to the USSR. Argentina, Brazil, Thailand and other countries have already been mentioned in press reports as being willing to make additional sales to the Soviet Union. Even if Canada and Australia do not repudiate their pledge, they will not be able to enforce it effectively. Nor is it certain that no grain can be found in the European Community to offset part of the embargo.

Furthermore, the embargo is directed solely at the Soviet Union, not at its allied and associated countries. It is generally expected that Soviet allies will be able to increase grain imports from Western countries - especially feed grains and other feedstuffs - for transhipment to the USSR. They may also have to get by without grain imports from the Soviet Union. (USSR's grain exports averaged 2.8 million tons in 1976/77-1978/79.)

Press reports indicate that the six European countries allied with the Soviet Union hope that their own commercial exchanges with the United States will not be affected by the latter's economic reprisals against the USSR for its Afghanistan action. Keeping in mind that American grain exports to Eastern Europe - especially to East Germany and Poland - have increased substantially in the last few years, one can see that their hope is motivated by both economic and political reasons. US Department of Agriculture reports indicate an increased volume of US grain exports to Eastern Europe in 1979-80.

The fourth and final question deals with East-West grain trade projections beyond 1980. If one assumes that East-West agricultural trade has entered genuinely uncharted waters, and that it will be impossible for some time to maintain US-Soviet trade relations at pre-embargo levels, one can conclude that trend analysis would not be a very helpful approach to estimating the future volume of grain shipments to the Soviet Union. Because one does not want to have one's fingers burned by putting forward quantitative projections beyond 1980, it is preferable to look ahead by making use of the scenario approach, which attempts to describe alternative futures from different sets of assumptions.

Assessing continuity and change plausibly associated with the potentialities of the present, one can envisage two general scenarios for the early 1980s. Scenario I assumes for the coming years effective management and containment of East-West tensions and insecurities. The scenario visualises President Carter's grain embargo campaign as a stop-gap measure crafted primarily for domestic consumption and to express his Administration's anger over the Soviet military actions in Afghanistan. Hence, the United States in due time should abandon its headlong rush into an economic trap - a self-inflicted denial of a major export market.

Scenario II assumes circumstances not conducive to effective management and containment of East-West tensions and insecurities. The scenario visualises the hardening of US countermeasures into firm and sustained responses to Soviet military actions. Hence, the United States makes the grain embargo a regular feature of US-Soviet relations, and undertakes a concerted effort to make the economic sanctions more effective by curtailing further the Soviet access to alternative sources of grain supplies.

Keeping in mind the dual motivation - economic and political - these scenarios can be extended and refined to sketch more sophisticated alternative futures for East-West agricultural trade. Assuming that they are well integrated with reality, the scenarios are valuable not so much for predicting what will happen as for helping us to clarify possibilities and options as well as uncertainties about the future - helping us understand what can happen under alternative sets of conditions.

What will be practical - that is, possible - will depend on the prevailing scale of priorities of the principal East-West actors - their attitudes and beliefs about which things should come first. One can only hope that their choices will be conducive to preventing a recurrence of excessive tensions.

It is noteworthy that despite the rise in East-West tensions, the principal actors on both sides found it desirable to hold the 'Scientific Forum' in Hamburg, 18 February to 3 March 1980, in accordance with the provisions of the Final Act of the Conference on Security and Co-operation in Europe. Agricultural issues figured prominently on the Forum's agenda as one of four major topics of discussion. Participants agreed to promote expansion of contacts, communications and the exchange of information between scientific institutions and among scientists in the field of food production - as well as in the other scientific fields represented at the Forum - bilaterally and multi-laterally through intergovernmental and other agreements, inter-national programmes and co-operative projects.

While it is only a part of the infrastructure of East-West agricul-tural trade, scientific co-operation is no minor matter. It could motivate further East-West interactions affecting other parts of the infrastructure.

These reflections suggest that the fate of East-West agricultural trade depends on whether the principal East-West actors will prove to be adequate to the task of managing and containing world tensions.

NOTES

1. The US Department of Agriculture estimated on 12 March 1980 that world grain production in 1979-80 would be more than 1.151 billion tons.
2. The US Department of Agriculture estimated on 12 March 1980 that world grain trade in 1979-80 would be 181.8 million tons (up from the 160.8 million tons traded in 1978-79), and that the United States would export some 108.4 million tons of grain. According to the estimate, the USSR would be in 1979-80 the largest grain-importing country, followed by Japan with 24 million tons. China is expected to import 10.5 million tons. Increases are also anticipated for Western and Eastern Europe.
3. For a discussion of the US use of food in dealing with the USSR see Joseph W. Willett and Sharon B. Webster, ' "Food Power": Food in International Politics', in Joseph Hajda et al. (eds), Political Aspects of World Food Problems (Manhattan: Kansas State University, 1978).

4. For a more detailed analysis see Roy D. Laird, Joseph Hajda and Betty A. Laird (eds), The Future of Agriculture in the Soviet Union and Eastern Europe: The 1976-80 Five Year Plans (Boulder: Westview press, 1977).
5. See Karl-Eugen Wädekin, Sozialistische Agrarpolitik in Osteuropa; II. Entwicklung und Probleme 1960-1976 (Giessen: Justus Liebig Universität, 1978).
6. For a comparative assessment see Joseph Hajda, 'The Impact of Current Policies on Modernizing Agriculture in Eastern Europe', in Ronald A. Francisco, Betty A. Laird and Roy D. Laird (eds), Agricultural Policies in the USSR and Eastern Europe (Boulder: Westview Press, 1980).

6 Non-Fuel Minerals and East–West Interdependence

GIUSEPPE SCHIAVONE

University of Catania, Italy

I THE GROWING ROLE OF MINERAL RESOURCES AND EAST-WEST RELATIONS

The world demand for non-renewable commodities has risen significantly over the last few years and several countries now face potentially serious problems in view of their exacerbated reliance on outside sources of essential materials. The overwhelming attention given to oil and gas has made it relatively easy to overlook the vital importance to industrialised countries of strategic minerals and metals for a considerable number of which there seems to be essentially no substitute.

Given the fact that a disproportionately large share of the world's reserves of key minerals and metals is concentrated in a limited number of countries - most of which are located in the Southern hemisphere - little diversification would be possible with regard to sources of supply should the production of some mineral-rich areas be halted or severely reduced by internal political troubles or external attacks. Abrupt stoppages of supplies of an essential commodity from a major producer would force industrialised countries of both the West and the East into intense competition, aggravating basic tensions and conflicts of interest. The developing countries themselves are competing in the world markets for the purchase of mineral raw materials.

In a world of fast-moving events, changing power relationships and eroding alliances, it is the accessibility to energy and mineral resources, not the constant threat of price manipulation, which is becoming in fact an increasingly crucial concern for many governments and an expanding part of international foreign policy.

The dependence on imports of essential raw materials is all the more disturbing since it has grown to such an extent that it may well place considerable strain upon long-established alliances on the one hand and eventually lead to a 'resource war' between East and West on the other hand. The greater the rate of rise in demand, the more likely is it that the competition for securing adequate supplies of critical·commodities will play a significant role in the shifting of the balance of power.

Although scores of countries trade in industrial raw materials, a handful of nations - the US, the Soviet Union, Canada, South Africa and Australia - supply the bulk of the increasing quantities of non-fuel minerals which are indispensable in the development of advanced technology, especially in the metallurgical and chemical fields. These minerals, for which few or no substitutes are presently available, are normally required in the primary production stages, a circumstance which enhances their strategic importance for both the military and civil sectors. It is therefore possible that a major supplier of a given mineral might use the threat of a suspension or reduction of deliveries to achieve important political goals. Serious political or economic instability in other mining countries, with the consequence of massive cost escalations or substantial curtailments, might further increase the potential that trade holds to help promoting the attainment of foreign policy objectives. This factor has underlain much of the discussion and comments by several Western analysts who stress the predominant importance that the USSR - being the most self-sufficient industrialised country in the world with regard to domestic mineral reserves - would easily gain vis-à-vis its Western counterparts should supplies from some leading producer located in Central and Southern Africa become unavailable. In fact, the Western countries' marked dependence on oil and gas imports appears to be only the most publicised aspect of a much wider minerals crisis concerning several essential resources.

The lack of a NATO-wide policy for strategically critical minerals and the apparent inadequacy of existing national stockpiles might result - in the event of serious disturbances in Third World and especially African mineral-exporting countries - in heavy political and economic strains, encouraging individual members of the Atlantic Alliance to take independent and potentially conflicting moves to ensure resource security. Despite the growing awareness of these issues and the mounting interest of the Soviet Union and other CMEA members in mineral-rich developing countries, only sparse efforts are being made by Western nations gradually to decrease dependence on potentially unstable suppliers, to establish stocks and to develop new sources and technologies leading to a more economical use of critical materials.

The eroded credibility and prestige of the American leadership and the waywardness of its foreign policy since the mid-1970s have had a far-reaching and unsettling impact on Western European countries that increasingly see their political - and especially their economic - interests as neatly distinct from, if not sometimes opposed to, those of the US. Moreover, the growing tendency of individual EEC members to make direct deals for essential commodities with Eastern or Third World producer countries is likely to greatly impair the functions of the EEC itself. Although it may well be the case that government-to-government deals bring substantial benefits to all parties involved, the failure to achieve an enhanced level of co-operation at the EEC scale cannot but cause serious concern. Quite apart from political motives, Western European countries have increasingly strong economic reasons of their own for adopting common postures on major foreign policy and resource issues.

The long-term political effects of the substantial trade and financial ties between the EEC countries and the Soviet Union are difficult to predict. Yet there seems to be little doubt that the USSR is gaining greater leverage within Europe and that the prospects for the establishment of a coherent Western minerals policy are more doubtful than ever. The Soviet Union has now firmly established itself as a major supplier of oil and gas to Western Europe while the overall importance of CMEA markets and industrial raw materials to the EEC economic systems is increasing.

Western European dependence and vulnerability are even greater for supplies of non-fuel minerals which are increasingly costly and, in some cases, of uncertain availability. Most major European countries depend heavily on either the USSR or Southern Africa or both for deliveries of several strategic minerals and are by no means in a position readily to modify the geographical pattern of their imports.

The United States - although remarkably well-endowed with mineral resources and far less deficient than Western Europe or Japan as regards strategic raw materials - depends on outside sources for more than 90 per cent of several critical minerals.[1]

The USSR, traditionally self-sufficient in most key industrial materials, has gradually become a substantial net importer of various critical metals and non-metallic minerals. For at least some of these commodities, a considerable proportion of Soviet domestic requirements are met by other socialist countries.

One of the ongoing concerns in the USSR has been the improvement of the efficiency of mineral resource exploitation - onshore and offshore - through an extensive influx of advanced technology and other assistance from the West. In this connection it should be stressed that the pressure to expand production stems not only from the Soviet interest to secure full self-sufficiency whenever possible in the face of a growing domestic demand but also from the intention of maintaining an adequate level of mineral exports as a major source of much-needed hard currency earnings.[2] In other words, mineral exports to the Western countries are used, at least to some extent, as a mechanism to balance the USSR trade deficit.[3] Yet Soviet sales to the West of some critical minerals have dropped sharply over the last few years.

Growing efforts are presently being made in mineral-rich areas of the Eastern countries for a major expansion of processing plants and the development of new mines. This CMEA-wide attempt might eventually result in a sizeable increase in the output of specific commodities despite the unsatisfactory progress made in the introduction of advanced technology, the persistently low recovery rates and the huge difficulties connected with the exploration and development of new reserves far from the main consumer areas and, in most cases, located in climatically hostile regions.

However, in speculating on the future prospects for East-West interdependence as regards critical non-fuel minerals, it cannot be overemphasised that a full knowledge of the points at issue and detailed information about the geographical distribution and magnitude of the world mineral trade are extremely difficult to obtain. On the whole, it seems that the availability and security of supplies of strategically important minerals is not as pressing a concern to the USSR - which holds plentiful reserves of a wide range of products - as it is to the increasingly mineral-deficient US and particularly to Western European economies that rely heavily, if not entirely, on outside sources to cover their requirements.

Actually, a host of factors may substantially influence international trade in minerals, such as impending threats of nationalisation and expropriation without compensation of mining companies in the Third World, increased state control in industrial countries, cartel-like activities on the part of the producers, soaring energy prices (especially in the case of energy-intensive minerals and minerals from low-grade deposits), strained labour relations and widespread concern about the protection of the environment in both developed and developing areas.

International commodity agreements do not generally have a significant impact on world trade of non-fuel minerals; a far more important role is played by several governments' strategic stockpiling programmes, notably those of the US which date back to the early 1940s. Other Western countries have generally been reluctant to take any steps substantively to encourage or speed up stockpiling by public or private agencies. While it is without question that the Soviet Union maintains its own stockpiles of minerals of strategic importance, little or no information is available as to the size of stocks, the materials included and Soviet long-term policy in the area.

According to recent predictions of an overall decline in the growth of production and also because of an expanding domestic consumption, the Soviet Union will become increasingly dependent on outside sources of non-fuel minerals as well as oil after the mid-1980s and will face major problems in supplying its traditional East European customers. Nonetheless, the inability to find substitutes for critical non-renewable resources in the short term enhances the dominant role of the USSR and South Africa as major suppliers of a number of vital metals and non-metallic minerals. Moreover, the levels of the US strategic stockpile are far below the planned national goals with respect both to quantity and grade, while France and Federal Germany are building up limited stocks of their own. In any case, very serious difficulties are involved in establishing, maintaining and regularly updating stocks.

In a situation of extensive price fluctuations and periodic shortages of raw materials - attributable to political and social developments rather than to physical scarcity - the necessity of reducing instability in world markets has been clearly felt by several international economic organisations, but very little progress has been made thus far.

Within the framework of the UNCTAD integrated commodity programme, after four years of negotiations an agreement has been reached by over 100 countries in June 1980 for the creation and management of a Common Fund. The integrated programme, based on traditional market-sharing mechanisms and buffer-stock arrangements, includes 18 commodities amongst which are copper, tin, bauxite, iron, manganese and phosphates.[4] On the other hand, the successful negotiation of international agreements on individual mineral commodities proves to be considerably harder than expected because of the uncertainty in determining what makes a balanced price level.

A more effective - though limited - approach is probably represented by the second Lomé Convention signed by the EEC and 58 African-Caribbean-Pacific (ACP) countries in October 1979. The convention provides a new version of the EEC's export income stabilisation scheme applicable to selected mineral commodities (copper, cobalt, phosphates, manganese, bauxite and aluminium, tin, iron ores). The EEC is also ready to provide the capital and expertise needed by the ACP countries for the adequate exploitation of their mineral resources.

As a matter of fact, decreasing investments by Western countries in mining operations in the Third World and the ensuing production shortfalls are a cause of major concern.[5] The attitude of the governments of several producer countries toward foreign investment and the development of local natural resources has changed remarkably during recent years making the participation of foreign concerns more and more difficult. In this connection, it is worth re-emphasising that high costs and capital formation problems are a major barrier to the rapid development of raw materials.

Apart from investment questions, however, the most recent developments in world commodity trade suggest that a larger role, not only diplomatic, by Western Europe is needed if resource security is to be ensured. Neither national stockpiles nor substitution would compensate for the persistent unreliability of sources of supply. Nevertheless, several EEC governments still seem to prefer in practice an approach based on an assessment of their particular interest in individual commodities much to the detriment of Europe's long-term interests and needs. This attitude is of paramount importance in terms of Western policy implications since it is connected with the Western European countries' increasing unwillingness to align more closely with US political, economic or military positions and might bring about a further shift in the balance of power in favour of the USSR.

II THE EEC DEPENDENCE ON OUTSIDE SOURCES

The outside dependence of EEC member countries as regards non-fuel minerals is extremely high and in a number of cases virtually total. Although they are needed in comparatively small quantities and do not immediately appear as essential as oil, imported non-fuel minerals are virtually irreplaceable in many specialised uses in industry. In fact they are critical to the development of advanced technology and ultimately to the maintenance of the present standard of living and economic system of Western Europe.

Not only the EEC area but Western Europe as a whole is very poorly endowed with non-fuel minerals; as a matter of fact, a huge share of the reserves of the industrialised countries is located outside Europe (US, Canada, Australia and South Africa).

In particular, the EEC relies on imports for all or nearly all its supplies of antimony, asbestos, cadmium, chrome, cobalt, germanium, manganese, molybdenum, nickel, niobium, phosphate, platinum group metals, selenium, tantalum, titanium, vanadium and zirconium. The EEC dependence is more or less heavy as regards aluminium, copper, iron ore, lead, sulphur, tin, tungsten and zinc. This dependence may become extremely dangerous when a very small number of countries cover a substantial proportion of EEC consumption and no other sources would readily be available should a major supplier abruptly reduce or suspend its deliveries.

The risks involved in the acute dependence of the EEC on very few foreign sources loom even greater when the major supplier is politically unstable because of internal and external pressures and conflicts (as may be the case with mineral-rich countries of Africa south of the Sahara) and the major alternative supplier belongs to a different economic and social system (as is the case with the USSR) or vice versa.

Among the essential non-fuel minerals, where both Sub-Sahara Africa and the Soviet Union have critical importance as present and/or future suppliers, are the following: asbestos, chrome, cobalt, manganese, platinum group metals, titanium and vanadium.

With respect to asbestos, the EEC is entirely dependent on South African supplies for two important types, amosite and crocidolite, whose production is practically confined to that country. The EEC relies for a substantial proportion of other types of asbestos on the USSR which alone accounts for virtually half of total world output.[6] Canada, the world's second largest producer, delivers a large share of its output to the US.

The demand for asbestos - despite widespread concern over health and environmental risks and various efforts aimed at the elimination of inessential uses in consumer products - will probably grow in some EEC countries,[7] while Soviet sales are expected to drop because of a rising domestic demand. Large housing and industrial projects in Third World countries will also substantially strengthen the asbestos demand.

The production and reserves of chrome are highly concentrated in South Africa and Zimbabwe. These two countries together account for about 90 per cent of the world's known reserves of chrome ore (chromite) and supply nearly 40 per cent of the world's ferrochrome production. South Africa at present produces some 3.5 million short tons of chromite per year while the USSR - only a few years ago the world's leading producer - is facing the depletion of its reserves with an estimated output of 2.5 million short tons.[8] Increasing amounts of chrome are exported by South Africa in the form of ferrochrome to the EEC countries which are heavily dependent on South African producers. The EEC relies for about 20 per cent of its chromite needs on Soviet sales. The USSR will probably continue its exports to the West though at a lower level partly because of an expanding domestic and East European demand.

Chrome is of critical importance in the production of high-grade stainless steel and for at least some important applications no substitutes are currently available. The EEC could gradually reduce its dependence by limiting the uses of stainless steel but its vulnerability would remain very high.

The continuity of supplies of cobalt is a matter of deep concern not merely to the EEC and the other Western nations but also to the East. A strategic supply source is Zaire where roughly half of the world cobalt production originates. Zambia is the second largest producer (around 10 per cent of the world total) followed by the USSR. The stability of the two leading suppliers is therefore of paramount importance. Events that could restrict or cut off the flow of African - and especially Zairean - cobalt would pose a very serious threat to the EEC and to the West as a whole.

After two unsuccessful attempts by rebels in the late 1970s to take over the mineral-rich province of Shaba (formerly Katanga), the political situation in Zaire has apparently stabilised and there seem to be fewer worries from the military security standpoint.[9] Increased stability in Zaire and Zambia and in neighbouring countries such as Angola and Zimbabwe with the ensuing restoration of reliable supply lines and an improved climate for the influx of foreign financial assistance and technicians could boost cobalt production in the next few years.

Since its domestic output is insufficient to meet its requirements for immediate use or stockpiling, the Soviet Union imports cobalt from both socialist (mainly Cuba) and non-socialist sources.

Manganese is another mineral of vital importance to the steel industry where South Africa has a critical role to play as present and future supplier of the EEC and other Western markets. The two leading producers of manganese ore are the USSR - whose output currently accounts for nearly 40 per cent of the world total - and South Africa, whose present share of 22 per cent is expected to increase sharply. The importance of South Africa is destined to grow considerably as its share of manganese ore reserves amounts to practically half the world total while the Soviet share is about 37 per cent.[10]

Despite an expanding domestic demand the USSR remains the only major industrialised country self-sufficient in this mineral but Soviet sales have gradually dropped since the mid-1970s and are mainly directed to Eastern Europe.[11] The EEC countries depend heavily on imports from South Africa for their ore and ferromanganese requirements.

Over 90 per cent of the world output of platinum group metals is supplied - in roughly equal proportions - by South Africa and the Soviet Union.[12] Here too the role of South Africa is destined to become even greater since estimates put its share at around 70 per cent of the total world reserves, with the USSR accounting for most of the balance. South Africa is quite naturally the major supplier of platinum and associated metals (such as palladium and rhodium) to the EEC and other Western countries. Deliveries of platinum group metals from the Soviet Union cover about one-fourth of the Western needs. Despite the upward price trend and the importance of platinum sales as a major foreign currency earner, no substantial increase of Soviet exports is apparently expected in the short term. As a matter of fact, the USSR is a large consumer of platinum; other CMEA members depend on outside supplies mainly from the West.

Apart from speculative activity and the jewellery industry, platinum group metals are irreplaceable in several conventional uses - such as glass fibre manufacture, oil refining and control of automobile emissions - and a significant reduction of supply would pose very serious problems.

The combination of a surge in demand from both the civilian and military sectors and a substantial decline of Soviet exports contributed to create widespread worries in the West over titanium supplies. The source of titanium for sponge production in Western countries is rutile; titanium sponge is then turned into ingots. The USSR reportedly uses ilmenite which, for this purpose, is converted to a high-grade titanium slag. Major resources of both rutile and ilmenite occur in several countries, among them South Africa and the Soviet Union. The world's largest titanium mine, located in South Africa, is expected to reach full production soon.

The UK is the only sponge producer among the EEC countries and accounts for about 3 per cent of current world sponge capacity. The USSR's share is around 50 per cent, while the US accounts for nearly 30 per cent. Several EEC countries were heavily dependent on Soviet deliveries of titanium sponge but the USSR has severely reduced exports since mid-1978. Moreover, the Soviet Union is reported to have bought large quantities of titanium on the spot market for immediate use and for stockpiling. According to some sources the USSR is using titanium for making deep-water high-speed submarines. Western demand for titanium has been booming because of the large orders placed by commercial aircraft manufacturers, military pro-grammes and increased use of titanium tubing for nuclear power condensers and desalination units. For aircraft and space uses there is essentially no substitute for titanium which has become strategically crucial to the EEC. Several analysts believe that the USSR will not fully resume exports until the mid-1980s.

Vanadium is another essential alloying element which has been increasingly used in the manufacture of high-strength low-alloy steels, particularly for missile and aeroplane engines and frames and for large-diameter pipeline applications. The EEC countries depend on imports for all their supplies. South Africa has a dominant position since it accounts for over 45 per cent of world production and nearly half of world reserves. The Soviet Union is a large producer and consumer itself and covers - at least to some extent - Eastern European requirements.[13] A remarkable drop in Soviet sales of vanadium slag to the West took place in the last few years while Soviet exports of ferrovanadium apparently showed no significant variation.

In view of its existing capacity and enormous reserves, South Africa would be extremely hard to replace as a supplier of this strategic metal to the EEC and other Western countries. On the other hand, the role of the USSR is expected to grow sharply because its share of world vanadium reserves is estimated at around 45 per cent and therefore is considerably larger than its present share of output.

III   US MINERAL SUPPLIES AND STOCKPILE POLICY

The maintenance of mineral availability from potentially unstable or hostile sources has become a growing concern in the US, despite America's substantial and varied ore reserves. While alternative energy resources may be successfully developed by the US to meet increasing domestic requirements, very few substitutes, if any, are available as specifically regards non-fuel minerals. As a matter of fact, the US has experienced a dramatic shift from a non-fuel minerals balance-of-trade surplus to a deficit which has reached an all-time high of about $9 billion. Some estimates put the US non-fuel minerals deficit at around $65 billion by the end of the century.

To cover its growing industrial requirements, the US is at present dependent on external sources in excess of 75 per cent of its needs for aluminium, antimony, asbestos, chrome, cobalt, columbium, fluorspar, manganese, mica, niobium, platinum group metals, strontium, tantalum, tin and titanium.[14] The US also relies on outside sources for cadmium, mercury, nickel, potash, selenium, tungsten and zinc for a proportion roughly between 50 and 75 per cent of its domestic requirements.

The massive reliance of the US on imported critical non-fuel commodities especially from Central and Southern Africa has been raising important questions on the maintenance of mineral availability in view, <u>inter alia</u>, of the present lack of a comprehensive minerals access plan taking national security exigencies into adequate consideration. The interruption of deliveries of indispensable items in consequence of grave operational problems - both internal and external - or political embargoes could greatly impair the operation of several sectors which are vital to the American industrial economy.

Chrome, cobalt, manganese, platinum group metals and titanium apparently pose the most serious risks in the short term. Compounding the problem are the fact that the USSR represents - more often than not - the only identifiable alternative to African supplies and the strong tendency of some major producer countries to use non-renewable commodities as a foreign policy instrument.

Although it was established about forty years ago for the specific purpose of serving 'the interest of national defense', the US stockpile of strategic and critical materials seems to be lacking in both quantity and quality. Current levels of several basic stockpile materials are far below the established national goals and could hardly cover both military and civil requirements in the event of an extended conventional war.[15] Over the years the stockpile has been remarkably affected by major changes in the US foreign and domestic policy and its management has been inspired not infrequently by political and economic rather than strategic reasons.[16]

IV   ESTIMATED SOVIET DEPENDENCE ON OUTSIDE SOURCES

Because of their inherently secretive nature, the Eastern countries do not disclose the bulk of information concerning the output, import and export of mineral commodities. It is thus far from easy to predict how the Soviet and Eastern European dependence on outside sources for non-fuel minerals supplies will evolve during the 1980s. Generally speaking, the needs of the USSR and Eastern Europe should increase as a result of expanding domestic requirements in the industrial sector and stockpiling for strategic or speculative reasons. This raises an important issue apropos the policies that will be pursued by the Soviet Union to ensure resource security as well as about the possible role of Eastern Europe in the creation and maintenance of additional stockpiles.

For some highly critical minerals - such as platinum group metals, manganese, chrome and vanadium - the USSR will apparently be able fully to cover its own and Eastern European needs while at the same time a somewhat large surplus ought to be available for sale to the

West. Since the latter half of the 1970s, however, there has been a significant slump in Soviet sales of the above mentioned minerals. On the other hand, the decline in ore exports could be at least partially offset by increased Soviet deliveries of more sophisticated products, such as ferromanganese and ferrochrome.[17] Given their continuing need of convertible currency, in view, inter alia, of the exploration and development of mineral resources in Siberia,[18] it does not seem likely that the Soviets will halt these lucrative exports. In addition, an end to mineral exports would weaken to some extent the political influence of the USSR over its 'clients'.

A handful of metals and non-metallic minerals represent a notable exception in the overall picture of Soviet self-sufficiency with respect to mineral commodities. The USSR apparently depends on outside sources for at least one-quarter of its requirements of alumina and bauxite, cobalt, molybdenum, tungsten, fluorspar, barite and tin. Soviet dependence is likely to remain heavy or even to rise in the next few years in the case of bauxite,[19] barite, fluorspar and tin, while a decrease is expected for cobalt, molybdenum and tungsten. For a number of these commodities, that is to say for barite, fluorspar, cobalt and molybdenum, the USSR relies to a considerable extent on deliveries from other socialist sources and such reliance will probably increase in the medium term when large plants in Cuba and Mongolia come on stream. The Soviets purchase tin from Bolivia while they compete with Western buyers on the world market for bauxite and alumina.

Soviet dependence appears to be gradually falling with regard to antimony and possibly mica; for both commodities imports represent about 10 per cent of present domestic requirements. In the case of lead, zinc and certain non-metallic minerals such as phosphates and sulphur Soviet dependence on foreign supplies seems to be rather slight, even though it is not expected to decline in the next few years.

In order to secure adequate supplies of the most important commodities, long-term bilateral agreements have been concluded by the USSR with a number of Third World countries such as Guinea for bauxite and Morocco for phosphates.[20] Yet, even if more such agreements were signed, the share of resources imported by the Soviet Union would still be too small to allow it to challenge the market power of Western countries.

The significant fall in Soviet exports of several vital non-fuel minerals has further increased the importance of South Africa as the principal alternative supplier. As a matter of fact, South Africa holds a leading position both in reserves and output of many kinds of raw materials and is now the world's largest exporter of non-fuel minerals. Moreover, South Africa is moving increasingly into the manufacture and export of metal alloys and especially of high-speed, high-strength and high-temperature special steels. The interruption of deliveries from South Africa and other mineral-rich African countries would directly disrupt strategic and non-strategic sectors of the economy in Western Europe, the US and Japan. From this standpoint and despite its recent metamorphosis into a net importer of some metals and non-metallic minerals, the USSR enjoys on the whole an enviable position.[21] However, should the 'worst case' scenario of a 'resource war' occur, it appears far from certain that the Soviet Union and its allies would reap substantial benefits from the resulting economic turmoil. This does not mean that Western governments have no reason for being concerned about the accessibility to critical non-fuel minerals. Nor would it be safe to ignore the correlation between events in Southern Africa and the Horn of Africa on the one hand and the Middle East and Afghanistan[22] on the other hand.

But, as is already the case for energy, it may not be in the ultimate interest of either the USSR or the US to deny each other and each other's allies access to important and strategic minerals. On a long-term basis and within the global context of East-West interdependence, co-operation - as long as it does not compromise vital security interests - might still be the safest path to follow.

NOTES

1. Sub-Sahara Africa: Its Role in Critical Mineral Needs of the Western World, A Report by the Subcommittee on Mines and Mining, US House of Representatives, July 1980 (Washington: US Government Printing Office, 1980).
2. M.I. Goldman, 'The Changing Role of Raw Material Exports and Soviet Foreign Trade', in Soviet Economy in a Time of Change, Joint Economic Committee, US Congress (Washington: US Government Printing Office, 1979) pp. 177-95.
3. As a matter of fact, 'since it is unable to pay for this (Western) technology with highly fabricated goods, in all likelihood the Soviet Union will have to continue to rely on the exportation of relatively primitive raw materials and semifabricated products' (M.I. Goldman, 'The Changing Role ...', op.cit., p.195).
4. Tungsten, though not formally included in the list of the integrated programme, is another mineral commodity to which UNCTAD has been giving special attention.
5. According to recent estimates, developing countries account for just one-third of the total world's reserves of non-fuel minerals; industrialised countries account for 44 per cent and socialist countries for 23 per cent. It should be stressed that China is gradually emerging as an important exporter of strategic minerals and should therefore play in a not too distant future a significant role as an alternative supplier. China's known commercial deposits of tungsten, titanium, molybdenum and vanadium are of outstanding importance. Foreign help is obviously needed to mine and process these metals.

6. A major CMEA multilateral project, the Kiembai asbestos complex in the Orenburg region (USSR) with a planned capacity of 500,000 tons per year, is under way. The Eastern European members of CMEA are participating in this project along with the USSR.
7. Greece, a full member of the EEC since 1 January 1981, should soon be able to export asbestos to its partners.
8. According to estimates, Soviet output constitutes about 25 per cent of total world production. In 1980 the USSR bought 20,000 short tons of high-grade chromite from Iran - a deal which caused some concern in Western circles.
9. However, the possibility of a third attempt by rebels - apparently enjoying East German and Cuban support - cannot altogether be ruled out.
10. With respect to ocean nodules - which should provide substantial reserves of manganese, copper, cobalt and nickel - it is widely believed that their actual exploitation is far from imminent.
11. Hungary apparently is the only Eastern European country self-sufficient with regard to manganese.
12. The production of South Africa consists of about 60 per cent platinum, 25 per cent palladium and 15 per cent other platinoids; Soviet production apparently follows the same pattern though the proportion of palladium may be somewhat larger.
13. The remaining needs are apparently satisfied by Eastern European countries from domestic production and imports from the West.
14. The US dependency apparently is very high with regard to rutile and less than 40 per cent as regards ilmenite.
15. For example, the stockpile goal for chrome is 20,000 tons, while the stockpile level is 3763 tons; for cobalt the respective quantities are 85.4 and 40.8 million pounds; for chromite 3.2 and 1.9 million dried tons; for titanium sponge 195,000 and 32,231 tons; for platinum 1.3 million troy ounces and 439,597 troy ounces. Moreover, some stockpiled commodities meet only in part current quality standards. See T. Velocci, 'Minerals: The Resource Gap', Nation's Business (October 1980), 37.
16. See: 'What Stalled the Non-fuel Minerals Policy', Business Week (27 October 1980), 74.
17. Through joint efforts of the European members of CMEA, additional production capacities are being created in the USSR with regard to ferro-alloys - ferromanganese, ferrochrome, ferrosilicone and others. The project is based on the large ore deposits of the Kursk Magnetic Anomaly and of the Krivoi Rog mining basin. Another important project is carried out by CMEA European members in co-operation with Cuba for the development of nickel production. The nickel-cobalt plant, located in Cuba, will have the capacity to produce about 130,000 tons of nickel - roughly one-quarter of total world production. These projects, like the one concerning the Kiembai asbestos complex previously mentioned,

are included in the 'Coordinated Plan of Multilateral Integration Measures for 1976-80', approved by the CMEA Assembly in June 1975. See G. Schiavone, The Institutions of Comecon (London: Macmillan, 1981), pp.41-3.

18. The acquisition of Western advanced technology and equipment is destined to play a dominant role in the Soviet effort to increase the efficiency of mineral resource exploitation in remote areas. This applies not only to critical non-fuel minerals but also to offshore oil and gas reserves. Actually, development of Siberian resources is being carried out at a slower pace than expected due to rising costs and technological problems.

19. Despite its rising dependence on imported bauxite and alumina, the Soviet Union is developing its capacity to produce and export primary aluminium to other socialist and Third World countries.

20. Direct deliveries from China were apparently resumed at the end of the 1970s.

21. The picture is far less bright for Eastern Europe, whose minerals balance is deteriorating further with the ensuing necessity to buy badly needed commodities elsewhere than from the USSR.

22. Apart from its well-known coal, oil and natural gas reserves, Afghanistan appears to be well-endowed with high-grade iron ore and chromite, asbestos, copper, bauxite, barite, fluorspar, beryl, lead, zinc, lithium, tantalum and niobium.

7 Western Participation in Soviet Development, 1959–79

GEORGES SOKOLOFF

Groupe d'Etudes Prospectives Internationales, Paris

The Soviet Union has purchased some $40 billion worth of machinery and equipment from the industrialised West, since its first major imports in 1959.[1] According to the recent official declaration of a Soviet expert, the USSR's hard currency indebtedness amounts to $20 billion. To meet its short-term payments needs, the Soviet Union has sold some 5000 tons of gold on the world market - or twice the reserves of the Bank of France. Though these amounts may seem modest on a world scale, they nevertheless reflect operations of considerable economic significance. Between 1973-78 alone, Soviet capital goods imports from the West were comparable to annual equipment investments in France, double the annual Italian level.[2]

Though an economic event, the reopening of the Soviet Union to Western capital imports immediately gave rise to a political debate. The famous declaration attributed by the New York Times in 1955 to N.S. Khrushchev: 'we appreciate trade for political rather than economic reasons' in a way coincided with the opinion of such influential American experts as Bernard Baruch, George Kennan and Zbigniew Brzezinski.

Since the discussion remains open, a detailed survey has been undertaken by the author to determine the reasons leading the Soviet Union to adopt, and subsequently confirm, its decision to open its economy to Western suppliers of capital goods. The reasons have been sought by examining the results of this move inside the USSR. The examination of these 'material indices' of Soviet intentions can be fairly detailed for the period 1959-75: but necessary statistical data are lacking for the preceding period and, more curiously, for succeeding years. Despite this however, it has seemed useful to update the examination in the second part of this study. Indeed, if the last years of the 1950s clearly mark the policy of opening towards the West, another historical milestone may have operated in the second half of the 1970s. East-West relations have certainly had their ups and downs in the past: in 1970, and above all, in 1965. Although the present political crisis has not yet affected trade, it does appear to be especially alarming: beyond certain periodic recessions, are we now on the threshold of the end of a vast historic cycle of 'westernisation' of the Soviet Union?

I MAIN FINDINGS OF THE SURVEY

On 12 November 1958, a plenum of the Central Committee of the Communist Party of the Soviet Union approved Khrushchev's theses on the seven-year plan for 1959-65.[3] This programme, he said, would 'open major prospects' for Soviet foreign trade. 'The Soviet Union' he added, 'is ready to develop its trade and economic relations with all countries.'[4]

This announcement was followed by major developments, but also set off much speculation about the true intentions of Soviet leaders. Were they not masters of a hostile power, a competing social system, a country reputedly closed to world trends?

The Triple Paradox of the New Policy

Efforts to interpret this new policy of opening towards the West reflect these concerns. 'We do not need war, we need peace', Khrushchev said,[5] even though conflicts which took place at the end of the Stalin era, as well as events in Eastern Europe in 1956, were still fresh in everyone's minds. The peaceful declarations of Khrushchev were greeted with great suspicion in the West. His 'chemicalisation of the economy' was analysed, by several Western official milieus, as a military programme. The grave crises which followed in succeeding years led to a generalisation of the American embargo legislation. For supporters of this law, trade with the USSR was, and remains today, 'trade with the enemy' at its blindest.

The policy of opening towards the West also created an area of interference between social systems which until then were reputed to be parallel. Khrushchev and his successors lavished rhetoric on justifying this twist to Socialist orthodoxy. From the rather confused corpus of doctrine on 'peaceful coexistence' there emerged a second interpretation of economic relations with the West: a stratagem allowing the USSR to control imperialist States while history dragged them down to their demise.

While Soviet leaders boasted about steering their country 'against the current', they seem to have taken an abnormally banal decision in authorising major purchases of Western products. But is this surprising laisser-faire more understandable under conditions of extreme urgency? This would seem to be the feeling of those who interpret the new policy as an irrepressible need for technology - the sole reason forcing the USSR to buy modern Western capital goods incorporating this precious 'substance of development'.

The Limited Explanations Inherent in Leading Interpretations

None of the interpretations arising from this or that 'paradox' of the new policy is devoid of interest. But they throw light only on very partial reasons for this policy.

Are imports influenced above all by military considerations? This thesis can be retained only, it seems, either in a too precise or a too general fashion. Doubtless, engineers can cite numerous concrete examples of Western capital goods which can find military applications in the USSR.[6] But statistically observable data are not accurate enough to prove such an idea. Looking at the problem on a much higher level, it is also possible that arms programmes weighed so heavily on domestic investments that they are the indirect origin of Soviet needs for foreign civilian capital goods. This still amounts to saying that the USSR does not import goods for its arms programme, but investments.

A similar observation can be made on the Soviet thesis of 'trade for peace'. Foreign policy considerations probably led the Soviet government to correct the distribution of Western suppliers, so as to encourage some of them, all other things being equal. But this does not go far enough to explain all of the opening to the West by a will to 'peaceful coexistence'. Moreover, it is very likely that this doctrine contains a highly important message. While insisting on the 'economic competition between systems', the doctrine also implied that the USSR wished to exercise world influence as an economic pole, and not just as a military power. This part of the doctrine of coexistence thus offered a true explanation - not just an ideological justification to the new policy. But it did not attract sufficient attention.

The explanation of the new policy by 'technological starvation' has certain merits, even though it finds supporters amongst those fearing Soviet belligerence. This approach re-establishes the necessary link between imports and internal economic concerns. More precisely, it can indicate how the 'transfer of technology' helps loosen a bottle-neck highly damaging to the development of modern activities. But the technological aspect is not the only obstacle in the way of such economic development. Nor is it the only problem which Western capital goods could solve.

Imports as Instruments of 'Progress' Investments

An analysis of the Soviet investment cycle shows that imports present a solution to the specific problems posed by each phase of this cycle. First of all, the choice of the investment is a decision involving risks, especially when information needed for feasibility studies is as sparse as it is in planned economies. Such economies also do not provide the framework in which to define the production strategy to adopt - a point underscored by all the research works carried out on 'technological starvation'. Also, the manufacture of capital goods needed for investments is an essential operation which Soviet civil contractors seem little suited to achieving within target delivery dates, or in the quantities and according to the quality norms required.[7] Finally, the assembly and start-up of installations often produce surprises when original designs and manufacture are deficient.

Of course, these investment difficulties are greatest in areas in which Soviet enterprises have the least experience: really new industries on the world scale - or more traditional processes requiring extensive modernisation. Thus, left on its own, or when foreign assistance is insufficient, Soviet investment policy quickly falls into cautious routine. This inclination to industrial conservatism was particularly marked during the Stalin era: especially when the Soviet economy once again lost its Western source of inspiration and supply (while devoting the bulk of its meagre resources to rearmament).

By welcoming back these suppliers, post-Stalin USSR conferred a fairly precise function on its import policy - the stimulation of the internal investment policy. There has been a prevailing view in both Soviet economic doctrine[8] and certain Western theories,[9] that economic growth depends to a large extent on structural modifications of investment in favour of modern sectors, since they exercise a powerful pull effect on the growth of GNP. Imported Western capital goods are thus focal points for progress, since they destabilise[10] Soviet industrial structures otherwise threatened with inertia.

In order to play this role, imports of Western capital goods clearly had to be the instrument of a sectoral policy. Statistical analyses carried out on this confirm it strongly. In several economic sectors, it can be clearly seen how total capital goods imports, stimulated by the Western 'hard core', respond to sectoral investment plans. Also, there is a striking coincidence between general 'modernisation' and the Westernisation of Soviet industrial investment.[11]

The 'dose' of imported Western capital goods had to be sufficiently large in volume to make this kind of structural impact possible. The financial result of capital goods purchases from the West, the visible trace they have imprinted in the form of a Soviet 'accumulation' on the whole far more dependent on abroad than could have been supposed, show that this condition was fulfilled.

These conclusions derive from demonstration procedures, which are not only statistical. Thus writings by Soviet authors (especially in the early 1970s) give very interesting pointers. This is especially the case in their very useful comments on blockages in the investment cycle,[12] on the need to call on the 'richer experience' of Western countries so as to modify structural aspects of growth,[13] on the use of Western capital goods in new Soviet industries[14] and on their importance in the achievement of investment programmes.[15]

Also, the study of institutions in charge of Soviet import policy has proved quite fruitful, especially when it reveals the functions of the Gosplan in this policy. This confirms that imports of Western capital goods are part of Soviet economic policy. Gosplan is not just one economic administration amongst others. It is the arbiter, at the highest level, of all Soviet industrial strategy. This characteristic no doubt explains better why imports of Western capital goods seem to have been part of high-level economic restructuring programmes, with visible sectoral objectives, rather than just the result of diffused micro-industrial needs.

The Banality of Soviet Import Policy

The role assigned to Soviet import policy in the restructuring of entire parts of the productive system is an original feature. However, the banality of this policy at first sight is striking. The importing behaviour of the USSR does not seem to have been all that different from that of developing countries, especially those which are now called the 'Newly Industrialised Countries'. The analogy was perhaps exaggerated by the managements of the Western firms concerned. Company leaders, dedicated to selling comparable products around the world using the same technico-commercial arguments and similar financing agreements, spread the image of a homogeneous world - where Arab countries, Latin America, the Far East and 'Eastern countries' resemble each other, in so far as they constitute alternative markets. This is a subjective view: nevertheless major international markets for capital goods evolve under the influence of universal economic factors, and first of all the need for new investments.

Also, the parallel drawn between the USSR and other countries importing capital goods from the West seemed less daring when the exclusive hold of central Soviet administrations over imports seemed to loosen, as imports multiplied. Western representatives started meeting other people, from institutions with purely domestic jurisdictions, with new purchasing needs conceived along specific criteria. Imports no longer seemed to obey only positive signals regularly issued by the political authority. There was the impression that Soviet imports had become part of a self-sustained economic process, as in other countries.

Also, the main slogans used in the USSR to legitimise the economic opening to the West possessed little originality. Amongst them, the 'time-saving' aspect attracts attention. It implied a justification for imports adapted to the various types of theories held by various Soviet circles. In academic language, it expressed the benefits of the international division of labour. For managers of major projects, it presented possibilities for shortening completion schedules. For planners, it recalled the principle that the most profitable investment was the one with the shortest payback time. For political leaders, finally, it provided a haughty defence against accusations of Westernisation. Leaders such as Khrushchev and Brezhnev had to win time, since Stalin had lost too much. Moreover, this time was won with a view to achieving the final goal: the victory in the race against capitalism, by making use of it. To sum up, while remaining concrete, the expression did not go against the theories of the leading strategists of socialism.

But the 'time-saving' idea is by no means new. Lenin had been attracted by it ('the rope to hang them with'), and before him, Count Witte in his notes to the Tsar.[16] Nearly all the leaders of developing countries took it up, so as to explain present dependence on imperialism by the promise it implies of future national power. And 'time-saving' is also the most general expression possible for the theory of comparative advantage: any beginner uses it frequently to entrust a job to someone more qualified, without losing face. It is its universality which doubtless makes the 'time-saving' argument not only a slogan for internal use, but also a more generally acceptable explanation of Soviet import policy.

The 'Autonomy' of Soviet Behaviour

The banality of the policy of opening towards the West is due to the lack of economic development in the Soviet Union. But this is not only characterised by a modest level of GNP per inhabitant. Its world ambitions, as well as the unique features of its social system, are also key characteristics. Even if they do not explain why the USSR turned to the West for capital goods, they do contribute to understanding how this policy was carried out.[17] From this point of view, Soviet behaviour seems to be 'autonomous'.

First, imports of capital goods respond to the obvious urgent need to complete the productive capital stock to meet the broadest range of internal needs. It is a systematic 'inward-looking' strategy rather than an 'import substitution' policy. A major drawback of this attitude is the absence of an efficient exporting sector in the USSR - a drawback belatedly and uncertainly countered by the promotion of compensation deals. Furthermore, the USSR, though a more open economy than it was, is hardly much more integrated into the world system than it was in the past.

Secondly, the opening up of the Soviet economy often seems to be precarious. Export problems (that is external balance in hard currency) mentioned earlier are part of this, as well as the continuing nervousness characterising Soviet-Western relations. But moreover, Soviet leaders are boxed into ideological theories which hardly make a clear line of behaviour possible. The 'Peace programme' of the XXIV Congress of the CPSU assures the West of the USSR's intentions of permanent co-operation, but does not abrogate the 'Communist' programme of the XXII Congress. If the latter were to be respected, the USSR would by now produce five times the volume of the United States' machinery production, and would have nothing to expect from a system it had completely outstripped.[18] But, though their real impact should not be exaggerated, ideological constraints have maintained an atmosphere which is hardly propitious to a firm association with world economic events.

Also, it may be reassuring that Soviet leaders accepted the opening towards the West so as to be able to catch up on the 'objective' backwardness of many sectors of the Soviet economy. But the appreciation of the results of this policy can be very subjective. Does one measure progress achieved by the aid of the 'structural norms' referred to earlier? From the point of view of accounting structures, the Soviet productive apparatus seems to have developed a good deal more than in fact it has. This optical illusion can lead authorities to suspend the restructuring mission bestowed on imports of Western capital goods. [19]

Obviously, decision-makers have other elements of appreciation of the Soviet economy, which on the contrary reveal the continuing aggravation of growth conditions and certainly would not justify any kind of premature optimism. But instead of concluding that the Western contribution is insufficient - or, as would be fairer - that its efficiency is reduced by the 'autonomism' it encounters in the USSR, the government may decide that it is ineffective.

Finally, the problem posed by the central monopoly of the interpretation of collective needs has even more worrying aspects. As stated earlier, the post-Stalin USSR wanted to found its capacity for world influence on an economic base strengthened by Western contributions. But as it is now quite clear that the economic situation of the USSR will remain very mediocre throughout the 1980s, [20] it may be feared that leaders have decided to pursue their goals of world influence, by the 'introduction of other means'. Recent Soviet penetration in the Third World would seem to reveal a fundamental change of tactics, where military intimidation takes over from the failure of economic seduction.

II RECENT DEVELOPMENTS

The import of Western capital goods should permit, according to one Soviet author, 'the acceleration of the building of Communism in our country, thus gaining time in the contest with the most developed capitalist countries.' [21]

While Soviet behaviour of recent years comprises the two aspects implied in the typical formulation - recognition of economic imperatives and the call for Socialist authenticity - there seems to be a different balance between the two.

The Permanence of Flows of Purchases

In 1975, Western supplies to the Soviet Union seemed to reach a record level of $5 billion - or 40 per cent of total Soviet purchases. Contrary to what could have been expected at the start of a five-year plan, these figures were however exceeded in 1976, with over $5.7 billion and a Western share of 41.5 per cent. In the same year, the speech of Leonid Brezhnev to the XXV Congress of the CPSU celebrated the 'materialisation of détente'. During the next two years, Soviet imports of Western capital goods remained at a very high level: $6 billion in 1977 and $7 billion in 1978.

Admittedly, some less favourable signs appeared at the same time - the West's market share dropping from 38.6 per cent in 1977 to 32 per cent in 1978. Also, the examination of Soviet orders in the West, which usually precede deliveries by about a year on average, pointed to a sharper drop.[22] These American forecasts are confirmed by the more recent information of the French Embassy in Moscow on orders up to the end of 1979 placed with the six main suppliers of the USSR, that is the United States, France, Great Britain, Italy, Japan and Federal Germany. Taking into account their share in total orders, and the usual relationship between these and amounts subsequently imported, forecast purchases in 1979 and 1980 would reach $5.5 and $4.5 billion respectively. Amongst various possible explanations, this slowdown would seem to confirm the difficulties of Soviet exporters in the face of dropping Western demand, despite the strong card of oil sales.

No presently observable statistical indicators, however, point to a 'closure' of the Soviet economy to Western capital goods. If the curve for Soviet purchases during the X plan is fairly unusual, this is principally due to the importance of orders in 1974-75 and purchases in 1975-76, followed by very little acceleration. The discernible drop for 1979-80 is relatively in line with what happened under the VII and VIII plans.

Bad Signs

This overall impression remains questionable, since it is no longer possible to observe with the precision desired the relationship linking the import of capital goods to investments in the USSR. Statistical annuals issued after 1975 do not give details on final output from the point of view of expenditures - data necessary to the study of this relationship. For some time, it seemed that this omission was based on security reasons, but censorship of economic statistics has spread since then, to include data of apparently no strategic significance.[23] This extension of the area of secrecy can be interpreted as one of the signs of a general withdrawal by the USSR on to itself.

Another sign: Soviet personalities and institutions (especially the State Committee for Science and Technology), which have been in the vanguard of co-operation with the West, have been quite harshly attacked in private conversations by members of the traditional administrations. In 1978, the Deputy Chairman of the said Committee, D. Gvishiani, published an article on technology presented, surprisingly for him, as a phenomenon which could only flourish in a socialist regime.[24] Chairman Kirillin recently left his various appointments. The campaign of 'de-Westernisation' which one seems to see here also surfaced a year earlier, in the form of an anti-American attack. This is highly significant, for it is American firms which have sufficient size to carry out direct investments abroad. And despite ideological counter-indications, this form of co-operation could be efficiently adapted to Eastern countries: for it is less costly than purchases of capital goods on credit, also permits a better trans-mission of industrial know-how, and is associated with major gains on export markets. The Soviet Union certainly realises these advantages, since it appears that discussions on a possible opening to foreign investments went on for two years, before coming to an unproductive end. [25]

These indications of a relative disengagement from the West are accompanied by signs of an economic recentring of the USSR around the CMEA and domestic supply potential.

In the former case, the operation has become virtually essential due to the rise in the price of Soviet energy and raw materials in exchange for which East European countries must step up deliveries of capital goods. As for the emphasis on domestic supply potential, this is reflected in recently adopted measures of industrial policy. [26]

A Relaunching of Soviet Conquests

In parallel, there has been a sharp revival of Soviet penetration in the Third World, often based on violent action and perhaps reflecting a reformulation of Soviet world strategy.

In the ten years before 1975, Soviet positions in the Third World undoubtedly weakened: success in South Yemen (1969) against three failures in Indonesia (1969), Sudan (1971) and Egypt (1972). Since then, the balance sheet has changed: some negative elements emerged with the situation in Guinea (1975), then from 1977 to 1979, in Somalia, Iraq and Equatorial Guinea. But they were largely counterbalanced by gains which the Soviet Union made, directly, or through allies, in Angola, Laos and South Vietnam (1975), Ethiopia and Mozambique (1977), Afghanistan (1978) and Cambodia (1979). Direct military intervention of the USSR in Afghanistan can be a new illustration of this development, underlining the role of the use of force.

The Fundamental Ambiguity of the Soviet Position

From these recent developments, it can be concluded that the USSR has pursued its import policy, while energetically refusing really to link its interests with those of Western developed countries. Without being totally unbalanced, the trend seems to be toward 'autonomism'. Most recent Soviet analyses on co-operation with the West indicate that it will return to its essentially European framework and could even completely cease if all its adversaries achieve their aims. [27]

Westerners tend to see in these indications a crucial struggle inside the Soviet state between two political schools of thought. The first would still want to transform the Soviet Union into a major modern and 'civilised' power (in all senses of the word) with a marked

Westernising leaning. The second wants to dig into a system of values comprising isolationism, militarism, autocracy and the socialist way of life (by resignation if not by innocence): and this 'hard' faction would seem to be carrying the day.

Even supposing such schools of thought can explicitly express themselves in the USSR, it remains highly dubious that the outcome of the battle can be easily foreseen for at least three reasons:

(i)   The economic cost of the separatist solution is fairly easily measurable and could be very high. Can one seriously contemplate squeezing investment - the almost exclusive source of growth in the next ten years - between even greater armaments production and the shutting out of Western suppliers, already strongly entrenched in a number of industries? The economic advantages of the alternative solution cannot be directly demonstrated. But if it is considered necessary to continue purchases from the West, there is need for a more efficient solution to the only real problem of the USSR's external equilibrium - the creation of adequate export markets. From this point of view, the 'Westernisers' are the only ones to propose a coherent approach.

(ii) Soviet authorities are supposed to be endowed with a supernatural gift for multicriteria cost-benefit analysis: could the supposed political advantages of the separatist situation exceed the economic costs? A precise answer to this seems quite impossible. However, it is easy to imagine that a break with the West would be accompanied in the USSR by a return to a very high level of autocracy to limit needs artificially, suppress prerogatives acquired by the bureaucracy in contacts with the West and impose on the entire Soviet society extra-rational decision criteria. It is far from certain that this kind of situation implies major political advantages.

(iii) The role of central power doubtless does not consist in being carried away by this or that momentarily dominating trend, but in managing and maintaining a situation of ambiguity. This is deeply rooted in the 'Socialist public', with its conflicting impulses towards tradition and modernity, Russia and the West, 'London and Asia' as Trotsky said. In order to last, power maintains ambiguity, placing the individual between fearful Westernisation and hard-headed individuality.

This is done by applying certain balancing formulas including both a sense of universal progress on the one hand, and active idiosyncrasy on the other.[28] If the second element seems stronger today, this is doubtless due mainly to the Western crisis. The West no longer plays the role of 'external compass' of the USSR as well as it used to.

But the West - even including its problems and redeployments - remains the only concrete model for the Soviet leadership as well as constituting a source of a certain internal social equilibrium. According to their 'capitalism experts',[29] present and future leaders could also hold to an intermediate goal involving a perfecting of the 'material bases' of society: a continuing 'saving of time', even in relation to their own uncertainty about the long-term future of the country.

NOTES

1. Calculated according to data from <u>Vneshniaia Torgovlia SSSR v . . . g</u> expressed in US$ on the basis of an annual average conversion rate for the foreign-exchange ruble supplied by the monthly <u>Bulletin of Statistics</u> of the UN.
2. According to the OECD National Accounts for 1977.
3. <u>Preds'ezdovskoe obsuzhdenie tezisov doklada tovarishcha N.S. Khrushcheva; kontrol'nye tsifry razvitiia narodnogo khoziaistva SSR na 1959-1965 gg.</u>, 3 volumes (Moscow, 1959).
4. Ibid., vol.1, p.46.
5. 14 November 1958, speech to the military academy graduation classes, ibid. p.131.
6. See G. Double, 'Utilisations possibles des produits fabriqués dans les usines chimiques vendues clef en mains par la France à l'URSS', <u>Revue d'études comparatives Est-Ouest</u>, <u>CNRS</u>, 10 (1979), No.4, 153-6.
7. One of the most recent and virulent attacks on this endemic problem is contained in the speech of L. Brezhnev to the <u>plenum</u> of the Central Committee of the CPSU of November 1979. See <u>Sotsialisticheskaia industriia</u>, 28 November 1979.
8. See especially A. Efimov, <u>Sovetskaia industriia</u> (Moscow, 1967). The author was the Director of the economic research institute of the Gosplan and one of the leading personalities in the mixed Franco-Soviet group on reciprocal economic information.
9. F. Perroux's work is characteristic of this school of thought. See especially his contribution: 'Les industries motrices et la planification de la croissance d'une économie nationale', in <u>On Political Economy and Econometrics, Essays in Honour of Oskar Lange</u> (Warsaw, 1964), pp. 463-99.
10. The Russian 'strukturnye zdvigi' expresses the notion better.
11. This point concerns the relation observed between variations in:
    (i) the cumulative share of investments in machine-building and chemicals within total industrial investments;
    (ii) the share of Western imports in total production investments in machinery and equipment.
12. V. Krasovskii, 'Investitsionnyi protsess i ego sovershenstvovanie', <u>EKO</u>, 1975-1, pp.16-31.
13. <u>Problemy razvitiia ekonomicheskikh otnoshenii mezhdu sotsialisticheskimi i kapitalisticheskimi stranami</u> (Moscow, 1974), p.26.

14. Ekonomicheskie sviazi Vostok-Zapad, problemy i vozmozhnosti (Moscow, 1976), p.291.
15. Ibid., p.286.
16. 'Why (he writes of the Western countries) do they create an even more terrible rival with their own hands? It seems obvious to me that by offering us capital, foreign countries are committing a political mistake, and my only wish is that their blindness will last as long as possible.' Quoted by A. Nove, An Economic History of the USSR (London: Allen Lane, 1970), p.18.
17. Cf. J. Bognar, 'The role of East-West economic relations in promoting European Cooperation', Acta Oeconomica, 6, No.1-2 (1971), 5-25. This outstanding study has many indications about the weight of 'structural' concerns in the foreign trade of Soviet-type planned economies.
18. Cf. S. Strumilin, Nash mir cherez 20 let (Moscow, 1964).
19. There remains of course the hardly flattering pattern of trade with the West. But the weaknesses this reveals can be concealed, in the presentation of overall results, thanks to a more active orientation of trade with the Third World. Cf. J. Bognar, op.cit., pp.17-18.
20. G. Sokoloff, 'Sources of Soviet Power: Economy, Population, Resources', in Prospects of Soviet Power in the 1980s - Part 1, Adelphi Papers, No.151, The International Institute for Strategic Studies, 1979.
21. D. Fokin, Vneshniaia torgovlia SSR, 1946-1963 gg. (Moscow, 1964), pp.186-7.
22. P. Erickson and R. Miller, 'Soviet Foreign Economic Behaviour: A Balance of Payments Perspective', in Soviet Economy in a Time of Change, Joint Economic Committee, Congress of the United States (Washington: Government Printing Office, 1979), Vol.2, p.229, give the following histogram for Soviet orders to the West, in a moving quarterly average and in millions of dollars:

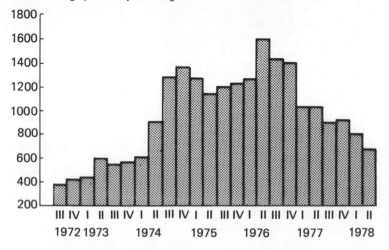

23. CEDUCEE, L'information statistique en Union Soviétique, 1980.
24. D. Gvishiani, 'Nauchno-tekhnicheskaia revoliutsiia, obshchestvo i chelovek', Pravda, 23 June 1978.
25. I. Ivanov, at the Franco-Soviet Colloquium on 'Bilateral Franco-Soviet relations', University of Paris I, Centre d'économie internationale des Pays Socialistes, Paris, 22-24 October 1979. The Soviet decision on this question can be linked to conservatory measures, taken in July 1979, to reorganise industry and construction (cf. CEPII, The reorganization of the Soviet economic mechanism, Paris, September, 1979).
26. Notably the decree of the Central Committee of the CPSU and of the Council of Ministers of the USSR: 'O dal'neishem razvitii mashinostroeniia v 1978-1980 gg.', Pravda, 5 August 1978.
27. N. Shmelev, 'Material'naia tkan'razriadki', Pravda, 25 February 1980. Referring to CMEA countries, the author writes: 'Their own growth potential, their fraternal co-operation, the advantages of Socialist economic integration, their overall economic potential represent a sure guarantee of the economic and technical independence of fraternal Socialist states, whatever changes take place in the international situation.'
28. G. Sokoloff, 'Malentendus entre l'Est et l'Ouest', Politique internationale (1979), No.3, 85-98.
29. Cf. the various opinions of N. Inozemtsev, outlined in the 'closing words' of the first Soviet debate on the energy crisis: N. Inozemtsev, 'Zakliuchitel'noe slovo', Mirovaia ekonomika i mezhdunarodnye otnosheniia (1974), No.3.

8 Japan and the Development of East–West Trade

YOKO SAZANAMI

Keio University, Tokyo

The importance of Eastern countries in Japanese trade increased in the 1970s. Among the factors that contributed to the increase were: the recession in the industrial countries after the oil crisis, the Japanese efforts to diversify natural resource supply by promoting co-operation projects with the USSR, and the changes in Chinese trade policy from the former autarky to a more outward-looking attitude. But, towards the end of the 1970s, there were signs that widening trade deficits in Eastern countries, not only with Japan but also with the other Western countries, might impede the future expansion of East-West trade.

The purpose of the present paper is to review the development of trade relations between Japan and Eastern countries in the 1970s, to see what was the prime motive on the part of Japan in promoting trade with Eastern countries, and to assess Japanese policy measures that can contribute to the future expansion of East-West trade.

In the first section, Japanese trade in the 1970s, particularly the impact of the oil crisis and its aftermath, will be analysed. Japan being so poorly endowed with natural resources and so heavily dependent on foreign oil, the expected rises in oil price will make the oil bill soar and will influence trade as well as trade policy. This paper tries to evaluate the importance of Eastern countries to Japan in the light of the future trade problems that the Japanese economy will face, the energy problem being the greatest. The overall development of trade between Eastern countries and Japan is reviewed in Section II, followed in Section III by suggestions of possible policy measures to promote trade between the two. The Eastern countries were divided into the USSR, Eastern European countries and China. Since each country or group of countries has different obstacles that have to be removed in order to expand trade with Japan, it seems preferable that policy prescriptions for trade promotions be written separately.

I JAPANESE TRADE IN THE 1970s

By the end of the 1960s, Japan was able to shift its comparative advantage from labour-intensive light manufactures to more capital-intensive goods. At the beginning of the 1970s, exports of iron and steel and machinery including transport equipment accounted for 67 per cent of total exports. The exports of capital-intensive goods continued to grow, as the expansion of the domestic market as well as exports made possible the establishment of large-scale plants that embodied the latest technology. The expansion of the world market and the relatively stable prices of primary commodities that continued until the late 1960s had helped the Japanese economy as well as trade to grow.

Especially, the abundant supply of primary commodities on international markets at low prices was a prerequisite for production in Japan. Since major exports from Japan were not only capital-intensive but also natural-resource-intensive, the Japanese economy became increasingly dependent on imports of raw materials. Indeed, Japan was becoming a major importer of natural resources in the world market toward the end of the 1960s. Japan's share in the international commodities market rose to over 30 per cent in the case of iron ore and lumber, and over 20 per cent in the case of wool, copper and coal by the mid-1970s.

The rise in primary commodity prices in the 1960s and the outbreak of the oil crisis in 1973 were tremendous blows to the Japanese economy which was becoming more and more dependent on foreign supply of raw materials. High oil prices increased the import bill to create a $10 billion deficit in the balance of payments in 1973. The increased oil prices not only contributed to worsening the balance of payments situation but had a severe impact on the whole economy. The rise in oil price in late 1973 occurred at the very time when the Japanese economy was becoming increasingly inflationary and accelerated the price rise still further.   The wholesale price index rose from 115.8 in 1973 to 152.2 in 1974 when 1972 is taken as a base year. Steep rises in prices curtailed consumer's spending and a strong restrictive policy to stop the price rises brought an abrupt business downturn.   The rate of economic growth which had averaged 10 per cent in the preceding decade showed minus 0.5 per cent in 1974.

The businessmen found their plants operating at appreciably below their full capacity level, only 75 to 80 per cent of the total capacity being utilised in 1975. They also found that their profits had been curtailed by rises in raw material prices and by the increased capital cost of carrying excess capacity. They tried hard to rationalise their production process to reduce costs and seek markets elsewhere to maintain production. Indeed, the changes in the balance of payments situation, which showed a $2.9 billion surplus in 1976 and another $7.7

billion surplus in 1977, reflected the reduction in raw material imports as industries needed less and an expansion of exports far exceeding the rate of increase in other Western industrial countries. Growth of manufactured exports, in real terms, only fell by 2 points from 13.6 per cent per annum in 1965 to 1972, the period just preceding the oil crisis, to an average of 11.7 per cent in 1973 to 1977. The rate of increase in Japanese exports was substantially higher than the growth of world trade in manufactured goods which averaged 5.2 per cent after the oil crisis.

As most of the Western industrial countries were suffering from a similar kind of recession, Japanese exports were directed more and more to the Middle Eastern countries enriched by oil revenues and to the Eastern countries relatively immune to business cycles. The proportion of exports to Middle Eastern countries in the total rose from 3.6 per cent in the period preceding the oil crisis to 9 per cent in the mid-1970s. The increase in the exports share was rather modest in the case of Eastern countries, but it rose from 5 per cent of total Japanese exports to 6.9 per cent in the same period.

It is quite evident that Japan will have to continue to pay the huge oil bill which presently accounts for almost one-third of the total payments for imports. Although efforts are being made to adjust production processes and consumption habits to high energy prices, and these have brought about substantial savings in energy consumption, Japan still imports 90 per cent of its total energy supply and 80 per cent of the crude oil is imported from the Middle East. Recent estimates made by the Agency of Natural Resources and Energy predict that 366 million bbl. of crude oil imports will be needed in 1985, despite the wishful assumption that the proportion of imports of petroleum on total energy supply will be reduced from 74.5 per cent in 1977 to 62.9 per cent. An increase in the supply of coal and nuclear energy is expected to contribute to the reduction in excessive dependence on imported oil.[1] But still the fact remains that Japan will have to rely heavily on imports for energy supply.

Another problem that confronts Japanese trade is the heavy dependence on the Middle East for the sources of energy supply. Any political as well as economic instabilities in the region upset the Japanese energy supply. Therefore, efforts will be made to participate in the co-operation projects for the development of natural resources in other regions including Eastern countries to assure the supply of end-products. There are already cases in which industries which consume a lot of energy are moving into energy-rich countries, in form of joint ventures.[2] Such a development will contribute to the transfer of technology and capital from Japan to the partner countries and will also promote trade relations between the two.

It will be necessary for Japan to continue its export of manufactured goods to pay for the increased import bills. It will become more important on the part of Japan to diversify product lines and to shift to more technology-intensive products. It will not be of interest to Japanese industry to resort to protectionist measures when faced with an increase in imports of manufactured goods. The experiences of the 1970s have taught that when industrialisation proceeds in the developing countries, a large demand for capital goods is generated to carry out such processes. This was the case with the expansion of Japanese trade with Korea and with ASEAN countries in the 1970s. For example, imports of manufactured goods from newly industrialising countries to Japan rose from $1.7 billion in 1973 to $2.4 billion in 1977. Whereas exports from Japan to these countries rose from $6.5 billion to $12.8 billion during the same period.[3]

There will be more room for Japan to expand its exports, if new lines of products can be developed and if factors of production, especially labour, can be moved into industries that produce these new products. The industrialisation in the countries that have not fully exploited their growth potentials will provide ample opportunities for exports of capital goods incorporating new technology. Also, there will be more capital needed in these countries. By transferring the technologies and by exporting capital equipment to countries that are about to grow further into industrialised countries, such as China, Japan can contribute to the expansion of trade in the 1980s. In view of the emergence of countries taking off and accelerating growth in the 1970s, the importance of Japanese trade with the developing countries is expected to increase in the future.

As for trade with industrialised countries that export mainly manufactured goods, including the countries in Eastern Europe, the lowering of the Japanese trade barriers in the 1970s and in the recent Multilateral Trade Negotiations (MTN) agreement will promote the exchange of goods that are differentiated according to types, designs or brands. The rise in income of the Japanese people will undoubtedly diversify their demand and leave more room for imports of sophisticated consumer goods. There may be an increase in imports of products in other areas than consumer goods, if joint ventures by Japan and other industrialised countries can be increased in various parts of the world, filling the information gap that may have existed in the past.

II TRADE WITH EASTERN COUNTRIES

The relative importance of Japanese trade[4] with Eastern countries[5] is somewhat greater than the average of OECD countries.[6] The proportion of trade with Eastern countries to total trade ranged between 5 to 6 per cent in Japan while it was between 3 to 4 per cent in OECD countries. The regional distribution of trade among Eastern countries in Japan differs from the distribution in other Western countries. For Japan, trade with Eastern countries means trade with the USSR and China. In fact, the trade with these two countries accounts for almost 90 per cent of trade with Eastern countries. For OECD countries, exports to Eastern European countries[7] weigh nearly as much as exports to the USSR. The importance of China as a trading partner is much greater to Japan than to OECD countries, taking 2 per cent of the total trade. The difference in regional distribution of trade with Eastern countries becomes even greater when we compare Japan and the EEC. Both the EEC and Japan had developed a highly industrialised economy, holding comparative advantages in capital and technology-intensive goods, by the end of the 1970s. But they exported these products to different regions in the East. While the EEC exported $8399 million to Eastern European countries in 1977, exports to China only totalled $901 million, almost one-tenth of exports to the former. In the same year, Japanese exports to Eastern European countries were $736 million and those to China $1935 million, about twice as much as exports from the EEC to China.

Development of trade between Japan and Eastern countries from 1968 to 1978 meant substantial expansion of exports from Japan to Eastern countries. Japanese exports expanded by 11 times while imports rose by only 4.6 times. The stagnation in imports from Eastern countries was particularly pronounced in the cases of the USSR and the Eastern European countries. Imports from both regions actually fell in 1975 and 1976. In contrast to such sluggish imports, Japanese exports to both regions expanded at a high rate for three successive years following the oil crisis in 1973.

The rapid expansion of Japanese exports basically reflected the strong demand for plant and equipment and also iron and steel in both regions. In the 1970s, technological progress and the resulting rise in productivity had strengthened Japanese competitiveness in these fields and Japan was starting to emerge as a leading supplier of capital goods among Western industrial countries. In addition to these fundamental factors, one cannot deny that after the oil crisis, there was a strong pressure at work to promote exports from Japan. The Japanese businessmen, faced with a stagnant domestic demand, had to seek markets abroad. When Western industrial countries were suffering from severe recession, the centrally planned economies with a relatively limited business downswing were viewed as a promising market to keep the level of production. In 1975, exports to Eastern countries took as much as 8 per cent of the total exports from Japan, appreciably more than the average 5 per cent in the preceding years.

On the other hand, the stagnant domestic demand following the oil crisis eventually reduced the import demand for industrial raw materials. While other Western industrial countries import substantial amounts of oil and natural gas from the USSR, Japanese imports from the USSR mainly consist of wood, timber and raw cotton. Thus, when other Western countries experienced a rise in imports from the USSR, reflecting the rise in prices of crude oil and gas, Japanese imports from the USSR fell sharply in 1975 and 1976 as industries that use timber and raw cotton were most severely hit by the recession.

These divergent movements between Japanese exports and imports left a large deficit on the part of Eastern countries. Until 1974, Japan had actually run a trade deficit with the USSR. But in 1976 it was reversed to show a $903 million surplus and though this surplus was halved in the following year, preliminary estimates for 1978 give another $883 million surplus for Japan. The trade balance between Japan and Eastern European countries also showed an increased surplus on the part of Japan after the oil crisis. The surplus almost doubled from $142 million in 1973 to $246 million in 1974 and presently it averages about $300 million a year. Compared to trade with other regions, exports grew at almost a similar rate to imports in the case of Japanese trade with China. But reflecting the strong demand for capital goods to build social infrastructures and to promote industrialisation, the trade deficit of China increased in 1974, 1975 and again in 1978. In 1978, the total Japanese trade surplus with Eastern countries reached $2119 million.

It is often pointed out that credit availability plays an important role in promoting trade with the Eastern countries that suffer from chronic hard currency shortages. The development of trade between Japan and Eastern countries was not an exception to this general trend. To finance the export growth that far exceeded the increase in imports from Eastern countries, export credits were widely used. Export credit is particularly important to finance the exports of plant and equipment which require substantially long gestation periods between the export contracts and actual operation.

The Japanese interest in promoting an economic relationship with Eastern countries was not limited to expanding export markets, but also included working out co-operation projects in natural resources development, to diversify the sources of supply of raw materials. In particular, the development of the Soviet Far Eastern region which has a rich endowment of natural resources is considered to have great potential for promoting trade. Although it can hardly be said that this potential has been fully exploited, due to economic as well as political reasons, five projects are currently being carried out. An agreement was reached in 1974 to enable the use of bank loans to carry out such co-operation projects between Japan and the USSR. Until then, supplier's credit negotiated for each export contract was the only possible means of financing exports to Eastern countries. But from 1975, exports of large plant and equipment that cost more than $100 million were financed by bank loans and supplier's credits were applied to medium-sized plants of around $50 million to $80 million.[8] The availability of bank loans in financing exports contributed to the expansion of trade with Eastern countries, particularly promoting exports of plant and equipment in 1976. In 1976, as much as 29.7 per cent of total plant and equipment exported from Japan was shipped to Eastern countries.[9]

In contrast to the increased indebtedness of other Eastern countries, the Chinese foreign debt position remained virtually unchanged until the end of the 1970s. Until very recently, China's foreign trade policy was characterised by extreme autarky, taking a very sceptical view of the introduction of foreign capital after the breaking up of economic ties with the USSR. When the trade deficit increased, China tried to recover the balance by curtailing imports. But reductions of imports meant fewer capital goods available for carrying out modernisation and industrialisation.

The primary reason for the changes in Chinese trade policy toward an 'outward-looking' one from the former autarky, was the urgent need for foreign technologies that became important to attain the goal of modernisation on four fronts, namely, agriculture, manufacture, defence and science and technology. Among the ten major goals set in the Three Year Economic Plan 1979 to 1981, which was made public in June 1979, the importance of the introduction of advanced technology, use of foreign funds and expansion of exports are stressed. When Prime Minister Ohira visited Peking towards the end of 1979, Japan offered a government loan amounting to 50 billion yen, untied and unredeemable for ten years and allowing twenty years for redemption, carrying a 3 per cent interest rate. Preceding this government loan, the Export Import Bank of Japan agreed to finance 42 billion yen for the development of oil and exporting it to Japan at extremely favourable terms, 6.25 per cent interest rate and a repayment period of fifteen years.[10] In view of the recent changes in Chinese economic policies, the introduction of foreign capital particularly from Japan is expected to increase.

As for the general import barriers, Japan does not have special discriminatory trade practices against Eastern countries. Preferential rates are applied to imports from Romania and Bulgaria and will also be offered to Chinese imports from 1980.[11] As for Bulgaria, Czechoslovakia, Hungary, Romania and Poland, countries that participated in the recent MTN agreements, they will automatically enjoy the low Japanese tariff rates in the 1980s. For the USSR, which exports primarily raw materials to Japan, there are almost no trade barriers since Japanese domestic supply of raw materials is extremely limited and tariffs imposed on such products are virtually nil. However, if Eastern countries wish to expand their manufactured exports to Japan, they will encounter two types of difficulties. One is the severe competition with the Western countries, particularly the newly industrialising countries, and the other is the non-tariff barriers including institutional factors such as the much talked of distribution network, commercial customs and the business practice of preferring stable domestic supply over imports. Competition with the newly industrialising countries is expected to be severe in the fields of labour-intensive light manufacturing products where these countries have recently gained substantial competitive strength. In order to overcome the difficulties of entering the Japanese market and getting helpful information about the consumer's tastes, it may be helpful for Eastern countries to find suitable Japanese firms as trading partners. The industrial co-operation between Japan and Eastern countries is presently restricted to the field of natural resource development. Also the number of industrial co-operation agreements between Japan and Eastern countries was quite limited as of the mid-1970s. According to the sample survey covering 207 cases of industrial co-operation between Eastern and Western industrial countries in mid-1975, Japan only took 6.3 per cent of the total, appreciably lower than 27 per cent in both West Germany and France.[12]

Since joint ventures are a promising way of increasing capital inflow as well as technological and managerial know-how, an increasing number of joint ventures with the participation of Western firms is being reported in Eastern countries. But for Japanese firms, only one case, in Romania, is reported thus far.[13] Several reasons can be pointed out for the reluctance of Japanese firms to invest in Eastern countries. Besides the great geographic distance between the Eastern European countries and Japan, there are differences in social and economic regimes. Also the fact that Japanese firms found ample investment opportunities in the neighbouring Asian new industrialising countries in the 1970s adversely affected investment in Eastern Europe.[14] The emergence of new industrialising countries in the Asian region meant more investment opportunities in these countries, and by setting up subsidiary plants, Japanese firms were able to save on labour costs that were rising rapidly on the domestic market. The imports of parts from these subsidiaries increased in the late 1970s and contributed to the expansion of manufactured imports from these countries.[15] Industrial co-operation and joint ventures in manufacturing seem to be a promising way of promoting trade between Eastern countries and Japan in the future.

III POSSIBLE POLICY MEASURES

Relations between Japan and the USSR

Since Japan concluded the first trade agreement with the USSR in 1957, the trade between the two has continued to grow. Japan became increasingly dependent on natural resources imported from the USSR and found the Soviet Union a promising export market for plant and equipment as well as iron and steel. Presently, the USSR ranks sixth among the major importing countries for Japanese goods. As for the USSR, Japan is the third largest supplier among Western industrialised countries that export primarily capital goods. The mutual interdependence is magnified when we look at major commodities traded between the two. For Japan, by the late 1970s, the USSR provided the largest market for such commodities as steel pipe, heating and cooling equipment, construction and mining. And in 1976, Japan relied on the USSR for 11.8 per cent of its total imports of wood, 14.1 per cent of raw cotton and 10.3 per cent of non-ferrous metals.

To enjoy mutual benefit by exploiting the rich natural resources in the Soviet Far East, five projects are currently being carried out. The standard procedure of co-operation projects is that Japan offers loans to finance machinery and other capital equipment needed for the exploitation of natural resources and the Soviet Union uses the end-products developed in the projects to repay the loans. Among the projects that are worked out, two are related to the development of timber resources and the others concern the exploitation of mineral resources.[16] Thus far only two projects on timber resources have reached the stage of exporting the end-products to Japan. This is one of the reasons why the trade balance between the two countries currently shows a substantial surplus for Japan. When other natural resources developed by the projects start to be shipped to Japan, the imbalance may be reduced since they will counterbalance the capital equipment imports to the USSR. Also the excessively high proportion of timber imports which accounted for as much as 38 per cent of total imports to Japan in 1977 may be reduced after co-operation projects in other natural resources make some progress.

There is no doubt that the recent tension in international politics will have an adverse impact on the development of Japanese-USSR relations. However, in the past ten years interdependence between the two countries has become closer, and mutual gains in the development of the Soviet Far East seem to be great for both countries. Although the actual outcome of the projects in the past was rather slow, both gained some experience in working out the co-operation projects. The USSR will need substantial amounts of capital and technology transfers to develop the Far Eastern region and this will provide vast markets for Japanese exports of plant and equipment. Increased imports of natural resources from the USSR will help Japan to diversify the sources of supply of oil and natural gas and also assure the supply needed for industries.

As Japan has built up huge industrial installations that consume a substantial amount of raw materials and mineral fuels, despite a poor domestic supply of these natural resources, economic co-operation with resource-rich countries continues to be important to sustain industrial growth in the coming years. For Japan, co-operation with the USSR, that has not yet fully utilised rich natural resources, will remain important in the future.

Possibilities for industrial co-operation between Japan and the USSR in the 1980s may not be limited to natural resource development. In view of the widening trade imbalance in recent years, Soviet officials have expressed more interest in developing processing industries such as, for example, pulp and paper in the Soviet Far East and Sakhalin.[17] The success of such industrial co-operation depends on whether it is possible to develop infrastructures in these regions. It will require a substantial amount of investment for regional development. After the development of manufacturing industries in these regions, new types of trade relations between Japan and the

USSR may emerge. But for the coming decade or so, it seems more probable that the present commodity composition will remain unchanged, with only moderate changes foreseen toward the end of the 1980s.

Relations between Japan and Eastern European Countries

The expansion of trade between Japan and Eastern European countries in the 1970s almost matched the growth of trade between Japan and the USSR. However, trade with Eastern European countries still accounts for less than 1 per cent of total Japanese trade. The Eastern European countries are an unexplored market for Japanese businessmen and their products are unknown to the Japanese people. This rather poor perception on the part of Japan may be attributed to their geographical location, but also to the lack of enthusiasm in both parties to develop close economic ties based on the exchange of manufactured goods. The increase in Japanese exports to Eastern European countries which took place in 1973 and 1974 was not matched by the increase in imports from them and left a substantial amount of trade deficit in Eastern European countries. Currently, Japanese exports exceed imports by three times in the GDR and Bulgaria, as much as 4.2 times in Poland, and 3.7 times in Romania. This large imbalance in bilateral trade accounts, together with the overall deterioration of the foreign debt position of Eastern European countries, limited the further expansion of exports from Japan in the latter part of the 1970s.

Unavailability of export credit was not the only factor that limited Japanese exports to Eastern European countries. In fact, a substantial portion of loan agreements between Japan and these countries remained unused in 1977 and 1978. In the case of the $330 million loan agreement to Romania, only 45 per cent of the total was used even after the extension for another year, and also $280 million to Bulgaria and $200 million to Hungary were hardly used as of March 1979.[18] This shows that export promotion of Eastern European countries to Japan as well as to other countries is the key to the further expansion of mutual trade.

The Eastern European countries will face two types of difficulties when they try to expand their manufactured exports to Japan. The first one is the severe competition of newly industrialising countries that are increasing their competitive strength in labour-intensive manufactures as well as in other types of products. The other is the difficulties that confront the newcomer who tries to set up distribution channels in Japan. When Eastern European countries try to export their manufactured goods, they may meet a general protectionistic movement in Western industrialised countries faced with high unemployment rates after the oil crisis. The real trade barrier in the case of Japan will not be so much these general protectionistic movements but rather non-tariff barriers of an institutional character. There are many complaints made by other industrialised countries about the non-tariff barriers limiting the possibilities of expansion of manufactured exports to Japan. Among the complaints are complex distribution channels, import systems, government procurement and others. [19]

It will be necessary for Eastern European countries to put more sales effort into getting into Japanese distribution channels and to get more information on Japanese consumers' tastes in order to increase their exports to Japan. On Japan's side, it seems important that Japanese businessmen who until recently were excessively export-oriented should shift their efforts to increasing imports from Eastern European countries and helping these countries to expand their exports to other regions as well. The joint ventures will be a promising way to overcome such trade imbalances since they will provide managerial and technological skills to Eastern European countries that will eventually help them to expand exports and increase foreign exchange earnings. Thus far, there is only one case of joint venture set up between Japan and Romania, to produce and to distribute man-made protein for animal feed. [20]

The policy measures to promote trade with Eastern European countries in the 1970s seem to have relied too much on offering export credit and this was particularly true in the case of Japan. For the future expansion of trade between the two, various policy efforts on both sides, including the opening up of the domestic market by trying to eliminate the remaining non-tariff barriers on the part of Japan and intensifying the sales effort for promoting exports on the part of Eastern European countries seem very important. The opportunities for industrial co-operation in various fields as well as in many regions of the world have to be sought. And through these efforts, there seem to be ample opportunities open to build a fruitful interdependent relationship between Japan and Eastern European countries in the 1980s.

Relations between Japan and China

By the end of the 1970s, China had become Japan's most important trading partner among Eastern countries. The importance of Japan to China, in turn, as a source of supply for imports and as an export market for earning hard currencies, is even greater. Presently, 30 per cent of Chinese imports come from Japan and 20 per cent of Chinese exports are directed to Japan. In other words, more than half of the total Chinese trade with Western industrial countries is with Japan.

The trade relationship between Japan and China showed a steady increase after the latter broke the economic ties with the USSR. In 1972, formal diplomatic relations were restored to open the new era of economic co-operation and trade. When the Chinese government announced that they would try to build a modernised socialist country by the end of the century, it was clear that they had to change their foreign trade policy to a more outward-looking one.

To carry out such a modernisation plan, Japan is expected to play an important role as a supplier of capital technology. In February 1978, a long-term trade agreement between China and Japan was concluded covering the period from 1978 to 1985. Under this agreement, Japan is scheduled to export $7 to 8 billion of technology and plants, $2 to 3 billion of construction materials and parts by 1982. In turn, China will ship 47 million tons of crude oil, 3.3 to 3.9 million tons of general coal and 5.1 to 5.3 million tons of coal for raw materials. [21]

Although China is still a country that relies heavily on exports of primary commodities, raw materials and foods taking about 80 per cent of total exports to Japan and 60 per cent of total exports to OECD countries, the proportion of manufactured goods is expected to increase in the future. The Chinese government is currently trying hard to increase exports of manufactured goods in order to diversify export commodities and increase foreign exchange earnings. The compensation trade which permits the use of end-products for the payment of technology and equipment is considered as a promising way of increasing manufactured exports. Another important development to increase manufactured exports is the plan to create special free-trade zones in Shenzhen, near Hong Kong and in Tianjin, near Peking. [22]

As private foreign investment helps the transfer of foreign technology, managerial skills and capital inflow at the same time, the Chinese government proposed to liberalise their attitude toward the introduction of private direct investment and the possibilities of permitting joint ventures with Western industrial countries by the end of 1978.

In July 1979, a foreign investment code was enacted and an agency for international investment and trust was established. The outcome of this latest development is yet to be seen, as the code has to deal with the difficult problem of ownership of land or a factory under a socialist regime. There are still many ambiguities in respect to the relationship between the code and general domestic legal systems such as labour law or wage negotiation regulations, so important in setting up joint ventures. Also the problems of foreign exchange systems or the possibilities of introducing capital from foreign banks are not clear. These ambiguities have made Japanese firms take rather cautious attitudes to participating in joint ventures in China.

This new development will undoubtedly benefit both parties by transferring new technology and introducing capital equipment to China and by enlarging the market and making low-wage labour available to Western industrial countries. However, success depends on whether the following obstacles can be removed.

The first is how to sustain the level of quality control so that the end-products in compensation trade or joint ventures can compete with the similar products of the neighbouring Asian countries. The second is whether Western industrialised countries are ready to keep their domestic markets open for imports despite the increasing pressure from their trade unions that are distressed by recent high levels of unemployment. Until now, negotiations on compensation trade have been concentrated in the textile industry, reflecting the fact that China has attained relatively high technological skills in this field and there is no need to worry about end-products not meeting the quality standards. But in the future it will be necessary to extend compensation trade in fields other than textiles since the textile industry faces strong competition from neighbouring countries and serious trade barriers in Western industrial countries. For example, the US imposes a quantity restriction on textile imports from China and the EEC excludes textile products from special preference rates items.

To enlarge the foreign exchange earnings necessary for industrialisation China has to find export markets and this will increase the need for Japan as well as other Western industrial countries to keep their markets open and allow the inflow of manufactured goods from China. As Chinese industrialisation will provide more market opportunities for capital goods, it will become necessary for Japan and other Western industrial countries to shift their products from former labour-intensive lines to more capital- and technology-intensive products. Positive industrial adjustment policies aimed at facilitating the shift of labour from declining industries to new industries, promoting research and development activities of firms and transferring firms to more efficient locations will become more important for Japan in the future.

IV CONCLUSIONS

Although the oil crisis and its aftermath had promoted trade relations between Japan and Eastern countries, a widening trade deficit in the latter impeded the further expansion of trade in the late 1970s. Numbers of industrial co-operation projects related to the development of natural resources started, increasing the exports of capital equipment from Japan, but not all the end-products developed by the projects had reached the stage of being shipped in return. This was part of the reason causing such a huge imbalance in bilateral trade. The situation may improve in the future, but in order to expand the trade in the 1980s, it will become more important to increase the exports to Eastern countries, not only in natural-resource-related products but in other lines.

The Japanese economy, which showed a substantial flexibility in adjusting its industrial structure and production processes to the recent rise in energy prices, can play a leading role in keeping the world market open for the increase in exports from the newcomers. The present protectionist tide in Western industrial countries is related to the difficulties that these countries face in adjusting their industries to changes in energy prices or to increases in wage cost that induce the changes in comparative advantages. It will become more important for Japan to move into new product lines by increasing research and development efforts and letting the new-comers enter into other fields.

Changes in Chinese trade policy toward the end of the 1970s will have a great impact on the East-West trade relationship in the 1980s. With nearly one billion inhabitants, it still has a wide potential open for industrialisation.

By transferring capital and technology, Japan can contribute greatly to promoting the economic development of China as well as of other Eastern countries. In turn, Japan can expect a substantial gain by helping the economic development of these countries, as they will provide more export markets and natural resources vital to sustaining the future growth of Japan.

NOTES

1. According to the estimates made by the Agency of Natural Resources and Energy in August 1979.
2. The cases are reported for aluminium industries that consume a large amount of electricity for smelting.
3. OECD, The Impact of the Newly Industrialising Countries: 1979, various tables.
4. Exports plus imports.
5. Eastern countries include the USSR, Bulgaria, Czechoslovakia, the GDR, Hungary, Poland, Romania and China.
6. The OECD countries include Australia, Austria, Belgium, Canada, Denmark, Finland, France, the Federal Republic of Germany, Greece, Iceland, Italy, Japan, Luxembourg, the Netherlands, Norway, Portugal, Spain, Sweden, Switzerland, Turkey, the UK and the USA.
7. Excluding the USSR and China.
8. 'Changes in Commodity Composition of Japan-Soviet Trade', Monthly Report of Japan Association for Trade with the Soviet Union and Socialist Countries (1978), No.1, Tables 4-1 and 4-2.
9. Ministry of International Trade and Industry, White Paper on Trade (1977), p.404.
10. Ministry of International Trade and Industry, Journal of International Trade and Industry, p.43 (February 1980); also see T. Okada, 'Chinese Economy and Japan-China Relationship in the 1980s', Sekai Keizai Hyoron (January 1980) (in Japanese).
11. According to the Journal of International Trade, op.cit.
12. Japan Association for Trade with the Soviet Union and Socialist Countries, East-West Trade in the 1970s (1977),   p.43, Table 9. Based on D. Lascelles, Comecon to 1980 (1976).
13. JETRO, White Paper on Overseas Markets (1979), p.153.
14. At the middle of the 1970s, 37.9 per cent of Japanese foreign

investment in manufacturing was in Southeast Asia; for details see S. Sekiguchi, Japanese Direct Foreign Investment (Macmillan, 1979), p.54, Table 3-1.

15. Ministry of International Trade and Industry, White Paper on Trade (1979), p.289.
16. 'Japan-USSR Economic Co-operation Projects', Summaries on East-West Trade (1979), East-West Trade News Agency, Tokyo.
17. The point was stressed in a speech on Soviet Foreign Trade, Institute for All Soviet Economic Condition, on 14 May 1979. Reproduced and translated in 'Japan-USSR Trade and Economic Relationship Today', Monthly Report of Japan Association for the Soviet Union and Socialist Countries (June 1979).
18. 'On Trade with Eastern European Countries 1978', in Summaries on East-West Trade (1979), pp.288-9, East-West Trade News Agency, Tokyo.
19. National Institute for Research and Advancement, The Japanese Non-Tariff Trade Barrier Issue: American Views and the Implications for Japan-US Trade Relations (Tokyo, 1979).
20. 'Recent Industrial Co-operation in Romania', Monthly Report of Research Institute of Overseas Investment, The Export Import Bank of Japan (August 1975), p.40, and also JETRO, White Paper on Overseas Markets (1979), p.157.
21. 'Long-term Trade Agreement between Japan and China, February, 1978', Special Issue on Chinese Economy, Monthly Report of Research Institute of Overseas Investment, The Export Import Bank of Japan (March 1978).
22. Far Eastern Economic Review, 20 April and 18 May 1979.

9 Main Issues of All-European Economic Co-operation

JÓZSEF NYILAS

Karl Marx University, Budapest

I THE PRESENT DEVELOPMENT OF THE PRODUCTIVE FORCES.

In the past fifteen years intensive foreign-trade, capital and technical-scientific relations have been established between East and West.
In the years 1966-70 the Western trade of the CMEA countries
increased at an average annual rate of 10.9 per cent, while in the
1971-75 period it rose by 27.6 per cent annually. The extremely high
rate in the latter period already reflects the abnormally steep price
rises of the years 1972, 1973 and 1974. Nevertheless, growth in the
two five-year periods was extremely fast, exceeding the growth rate
of world trade as a whole. The number of technical-scientific
agreements and co-operative production schemes in the countries
concerned also rose rapidly and had already risen to 1200 by the mid-
1970s.

The widening and deepening of East-West relations and their
extension to new areas in the CMEA countries were and are considered as a necessary and normal phenomenon. This is because the
development of the productive forces goes hand in hand with an
increase in their social character and internationalisation. Accordingly, world economic relations were first established in trading and
financial spheres to extend, with capital export, industrial co-
operation agreements, tourism and the new forms of technical-
scientific contacts intensifying since the Second World War, to the
spheres of production (including research and development), consumption, education, etc. The process of the expansion and deepening of
the international division of labour and of the internationalisation of
production is necessarily also a process of the growing connectedness
of different nations, and of decreasing national isolationism. With the
emergence of international industrial co-operation and regional economic integration arrangements, this process has come in our age to a

historic turning-point. The development in economic relations among the industrialised countries reflects the fact that the utilisation of the most up-to-date means of production does not bear the restraints that national segregation imposed on it until now.

The gradual elimination, within the framework of international economic integration, of the institutional systems accompanying national isolationism and regulating world economic relations first took place necessarily in the small and medium-sized countries with developed productive forces. For reasons connected with the given developmental level of the productive forces and the existence of the two social systems, they assumed in our age the form of regional integration arrangements. But the development of productive forces cannot be stopped, and thus the establishment and expansion of relations between regional integration organisations and international co-operation on a continental and in many fields on a world scale can now be regarded as an objective necessity.

The assurance of the above-outlined consequences of the development of productive forces is in the interest not only of the CMEA countries but also of all developed capitalist and developing countries. With the widening and deepening of the international division of labour, the development of productive forces may become faster and, given adequate social conditions, the living standards of the population may improve. At the same time, the expansion of economic relations may also provide the basis for an increase in mutual trust among nations and for improving the political climate.

II   THE EXPANSION OF ALL-EUROPEAN CO-OPERATION -
A TIMELY NECESSITY

The increasing utilisation of the opportunities offered by the international division of labour is an especially important necessity in the world's industrially most developed continent, Europe. It is a well-known fact that today many common interests call for the expansion of all-European co-operation. The CMEA countries stood, and are standing, for economic co-operation on a worldwide scale and within it on an increasingly all-European scale to allow thereby the most rational development of the productive forces of the continent. Exposed to the technical-scientific superiority of the United States, to its growing political and economic pressure and also to the competition of fast-expanding Japan, the Western European countries, heavily dependent on external trade, are likely to find it harder to place their products on the markets of the other developed capitalist countries as they themselves are in search of such markets. Nor can, for various reasons, the markets of the developing countries provide sufficient scope for this expansion drive. The planned economies of the CMEA countries and their expanding markets may offer the capitalist countries in question - as they did in the past - substantial additional assistance on the basis of mutual advantages to mitigate their economic troubles and to develop their economies. This would also be the most economical solution for the further development of both groups of countries because of the following facts:

(i) The developmental levels of the productive forces of the CMEA and Western European countries are, for historical reasons, still different in several sectors. Therefore, the latter countries - where the technologies concerned are more developed - may find ready markets in the CMEA countries. Thus, as regards the degree of development, the productive forces of the two groups of countries are in many respects of a complementary and not of a competitive nature.

(ii) With the levels of development coming closer to one another, the benefits deriving from complementarity may change into the advantages deriving from economies of scale. These advantages may jointly be realised in the steadily expanding markets of the CMEA countries with their combined population of 450 million and in the markets of third countries. Thus their productive forces may be prevented from becoming harmfully competitive.

(iii) The products representing different development levels of the CMEA and Western European countries may constitute in several cases an appropriate combination of the productive equipment mostly sought for at present in a number of developing countries.

(iv) Widening co-operation provides a solid basis for expanding the range of consumer goods and meeting special demands in both groups of countries - and, in addition, more cheaply than would be possible without such co-operation.

(v) Western Europe may find substantial raw material and energy sources in the CMEA countries. This fact is increasingly gaining importance as a large proportion of the world's raw material and energy reserves is concentrated in the CMEA countries, primarily in the USSR.

(vi) Wage-level differences between the two groups of countries may provide a basis for mutually advantageous co-operation for a relatively long period of time.

(vii) Finally, the geographical closeness of the two groups of countries makes the expansion of co-operation advantageous owing to low transportation costs, to the traditionally good acquaintance with local conditions, and to the possibility of establishing direct personal contacts.

But efficient co-operation in production is inconceivable today without the simultaneous improvement of technical-scientific co-operation. Large-scale production and trade co-operation agreements may provide excellent bases for mutually beneficial and fruitful technical-scientific co-operation, which in turn would accelerate technical progress in both groups of countries. The CMEA countries have repeatedly declared their readiness to put into effect such a programme, constituting an organic part of their foreign and economic policy.

Rationality and territorial neighbourhoods require perhaps still more urgent solutions in other technical-scientific fields for the co-operation of the two groups of countries in harmonising and unifying the present-day isolated technical-scientific efforts in Europe. The joint development of energy systems, the construction of a uniform waterway network, the further standardisation of land transport and of production, the harmonisation of the regulations and efforts of human and veterinary medicine, the prevention of the further pollution of land, air and water - all these processes are a common European-scale task for the peoples of the continent.

Despite these common interests and tasks, technical-scientific efforts are still largely of a national nature in present-day Europe. Thus, the drafting, not to speak of the implementation, of the multilateral recommendations for technical-scientific co-operation begun in the past decade mainly in the various UN agencies, and mainly within the framework of the Economic Commission for Europe, is extremely slow.

Undoubtedly, economic and technical-scientific co-operation between the two parts of Europe - despite the significant development achieved in the past fifteen years - lags far behind the possibilities and the increasingly urgent requirements.

In the decade preceding the mid-1970s, the initiatives of the Soviet Union and the other CMEA countries and then the strengthening of realistic political forces in certain countries in Western Europe appreciably improved the conditions and prospects for the development of all-European co-operation. The acceleration of economic and technical-scientific co-operation was made possible by the fact that the European countries belonging to the two systems substantially improved their political relations. It is commonly known that the international division of labour is usually intensified in countries which succeed in co-ordinating not only their economic but also their political interests. This recognition has gained increasing acceptance also in the Western part of Europe, making it possible to bring the German issue to a settlement, to convene and successfully conclude the Conference on Security and Co-operation in Europe with the acceptance of the Final Act. This highly important document provides a firm political basis, a starting point for the solution of the comprehensive problems affecting European nations, of European security and, in its framework, also for a considerable expansion of all-European economic and technical-scientific co-operation.

The further development of all-European co-operation based on equality and mutual advantages may also promote the mobilisation and utilisation of Europe's immense human and material resources in the interest of the urgent solution of the so-called global problems facing humanity. Europe would be able, by joint efforts, to contribute to averting the harmful world economic processes threatening mankind with serious economic and political dangers - and indeed undermining its ultimate survival - by working out and implementing as soon as possible a worldwide strategy.

The prospects for all-European co-operation are great. Of especially great importance for Hungary - just to mention a few examples - are such projects, proposed by the Soviet Union, as the electric grid connecting Kursk with Laufenberg in Switzerland, which, by making use of differences in the peak-load times, would ensure a saving of about 10 per cent for the participating countries. Similarly, great interests are also attached to building a uniform European road and waterway network as the Danube-Main-Rhine canal would make it possible for Hungary to have a direct access by water to Rotterdam, the world's largest port. Some of the motorways built or planned may extend the transcontinental road E-5, London-Brussels-Cologne-Vienna, through Budapest and Szeged as far as Yugoslavia. The conditions are also good for co-operation evolving in the field of human and veterinary medicine. In addition, Hungary is very much interested in preventing, by joint efforts, the further pollution and exploitation of the Danube.

The fact that Europe is divided into two groups of countries with different social systems need not be an obstacle to establishing economic co-operation on the basis of equality and mutual advantage and within the framework of an institutionalised security system. Security based on weapons, on the arms race, is becoming not only more and more anachronistic and harmful, but, as long as it exists, it also involves the danger of a new war which, in view of Europe's situation in the world, would inevitably be a world war with apocalyptic consequences. The argument, often referred to by European reactionary circles, that with the expansion of all-European co-operation - especially in energy supply - Western Europe would come into a dependent position vis-à-vis the CMEA countries, cannot stand a thorough analysis, as the problem could be solved in conformity with the proposals made by the Brussels-based International Commission for European Security and Co-operation and incorporated in the formula 'mutual dependence - without dependence'. The essence of these proposals is that the vital products exported by the Eastern European countries to Western Europe would be offset by the continued export of similarly highly important products by the latter, and thus the problem of security would be nullified by an equivalent mutual dependence.

Incidentally, the possibility of comprehensive co-operation between countries with different social systems is today no longer a matter of mere speculation as the CMEA countries transact 47 per cent of their foreign trade with countries of a different social system, among them the OECD countries.

III   NEW UNFAVOURABLE DEVELOPMENTS IN THE
       SECOND HALF OF THE 1970s

In the second half of the 1970s, however, unfavourable processes began to emerge in East-West and, within it, in all-European co-operation. This manifested itself, first of all, in the fact that the growth rate of reciprocal trade slowed down, and the rate of the export counterbalance for Western imports by the CMEA countries suffered a deterioration. Thus the volume of East-West trade rose at current prices by 10.3 per cent in 1976, by 4.4 per cent in 1977 and by 12.1 per cent in 1978. The volume of the Western exports of the CMEA countries fell during the 1974-75 period (by 5 per cent in 1974 and by 2 per cent in 1975) while it rose again by 8 per cent in 1976, 1 per cent in 1977 and 8 per cent in 1978. The imports of CMEA countries from the West, however, rose in the 1974-75 period and later, until 1978, much faster than their exports (also computed in terms of volume), namely by 11 per cent in 1974, by 21 per cent in 1975, by 10 per cent in 1976, by 8 per cent in 1977 and by 8 per cent in 1978. Their trade underwent similar changes with the Western European countries, too. In the years 1966-70, the OECD exports of the CMEA countries still accounted for 107.6 per cent of their imports, and in the years 1970-75 only for 82.1 per cent and in 1978 for 74.2 per cent, thus for hardly three-fourths of their imports. This development resulted in a significant increase of their indebtedness.

The basic cause of this increased indebtedness was the fact that the export opportunities of the CMEA countries suffered a set-back in their principal market, Western Europe, in the second half of the 1970s. This may be accounted for partly by objective, partly by subjective, more exactly, by political factors. As regards the objective factors, they are mainly of a cyclical and of a structural character. They are as follows:

(i)   Since the world capitalist economic crisis in 1974-75, Western Europe has been the most slowly developing area of the capitalist world. The average annual increase in output has reached about 2.5 per cent in recent years, and thus demand has remained rather slack in general. This has also aggravated the export situation of the CMEA countries. At the same time, a considerable part of the developed capitalist countries have got into balance of payments difficulties, which their active balances with the CMEA countries have helped to mitigate or eliminate.

(ii)   Unemployment has not only remained unchanged following the crisis but has even increased. It rose from an annual 5.2 million in 1975 to 7 million in 1978. The situation is further aggravated by the fact that many of the unemployed are young, mainly professional people. In Italy, for example, out of 1.52 million unemployed in 1978, 75 per cent were people under 29 years of age, and 41 per cent of the latter were people with higher education.[1] This situation is the hotbed of increasing juvenile delinquency, various ultra-left and new-left organisations and growing terrorism.

Large-scale chronic unemployment in the Western European countries raises specific, new problems, which in turn also curb the development of East-West relations, mainly of joint co-operation ventures. Western Europe reached in the second half of the 1970s a level of productivity - as a result of a kind of overcapitalisation - at which it was capable, by using less labour inputs, of turning out more products than before. It has appeared that the Western European countries are unable, in the given institutional structure and under the prevailing working-day regulations and labour law, to eliminate large-scale unemployment. The trade unions in Western Europe now have the task of ensuring not only higher incomes for the working people and that their incomes keep up with inflation, but also that job opportunities are preserved or assured for their fellow workers ousted from production.

(iii) In the second half of the 1970s, serious structural problems also emerged. The various industries one after the other got into a difficult situation both in the light and the heavy industrial sector. Thus shipbuilding, steel-making and petrochemical industries have come to be faced with difficulties, though the large capacities being built into these branches have not yet entered into the developing stage. This and the presumably still further growing unemployment induce certain governments to apply protectionistic measures, which adversely affect the CMEA countries.

Along with these cyclical and structural causes, mention must also be made of causes of a political nature curbing all-European co-operation. They are as follows:

(i) The negotiations aimed at settling relations between the EEC and the CMEA countries have made no progress and even came to a deadlock early in 1980. Undoubtedly, their successful conclusion would give a new important boost to all-European co-operation.

(ii) With its common agricultural policy, the EEC has almost completely withdrawn behind the walls of protectionism. Western Europe has reached a high degree of self-sufficiency in agricultural products, as a result of which some of the smaller CMEA countries, for example Hungary and Bulgaria, have lesser chances to place their products on the EEC market.

(iii) The CMEA countries are faced with difficulties in selling the products of their textile and other light industries, mainly because similar products from the developing countries have appeared in large volumes in the EEC market. By the end of the 1970s, the EEC countries had concluded preferential agreements with as many as 113 countries. Although the GATT-member CMEA countries are also assured of the most-favoured-nation treatment, the advantage of the preferential agreements over the latter is beneficial to the developing countries.

(iv) The partial maintenance of the 'strategic' embargo and indeed the recent attempts to extend it have hardly promoted the development of co-operation.

(v) And, finally, the same may be said of the large-scale 'Chinese opening', especially where it also extends to military supplies.

Mainly for the reasons just listed, one may venture the statement that in the second half of the 1970s the economic policies of a large number of Western European governments rather neglected the objectives formulated and accepted in the second 'basket' of the Final Act of the Helsinki Conference. These objectives envisaged, among others, the promotion of the expansion of economic and technical-scientific relations between the two groups of countries.

But what would constitute the most serious threat to the cause of all-European co-operation is that the Western European countries could get involved in the cold-war campaign against détente, which has already achieved considerable results. Serious damage has already been done in general, and the climate of economic co-operation has deteriorated due to the fact that the European NATO countries have joined in the new armament wave enforced by the US military-industrial complex and have approved, with a few exceptions, the deployment of new American missiles in their own countries aimed at the 'Europeanisation' of a possible atomic war.

IV   PROSPECTS FOR THE 1980s

The CMEA countries have been developing since the second half of the 1970s, with respect to their Western counterparts, under more complicated and to a certain extent under more difficult conditions than before. This also applies to détente. The smaller CMEA countries are in a more difficult economic situation. The new NATO armament wave has increased the economic burdens of all CMEA countries. At the same time they have increasingly embarked in the 1970s - leaving behind the extensive way of development - upon the road of intensive development. This requires a general increase in economic efficiency and the large-scale application of the latest technology in Eastern economies. This calls, as is commonly known, for very great human and material efforts in which the widening of all-European co-operation might play a great role and would also promote economic prosperity in Western Europe.

Under such conditions, the all-out attack of the representatives of the interests of the military-industrial complex against détente, the renewal of the armaments race, the repeated deployment of the embargo weapon, which has already proved inefficient and, in addition, the hysterical declaration of a psychological war, appear to be a new large-scale attempt to curb, or possibly to reverse, the historical course of progress which had registered an acceleration in the past decades. This is similar to the case when, at the time of the building of the world socialist system, the weapons of the cold and even of hot war, among them the weapon of economic warfare, were already deployed against the forces of socialism. Now, in a radically different historical situation, when a hot war could annihilate even its initiators - when the CMEA countries, standing on the basis of mutual advantages and in accordance with their constantly declared principles, have opened economically towards the capitalist world - the differentiated use of unequivocally economic weapons has come, on the part of the USA, to the foreground. Fortunately for humanity, not every developed capitalist country has done or is doing the same.

It is a well-known fact that the cold-war embargo of the 1950s failed completely because it could not stop or hold back the development of the CMEA countries. It might be illuminating even for the adherents of the embargoes of the 1970s and 1980s to bear in mind the following statements of J. Wilczynski, the well-known Western specialist of Eastern European economic affairs:

Trade embargoes in the past never achieved their expected results. Similarly, Western strategic export controls have not visibly weakened the military potential of the socialist countries. Nor have these countries been deterred from pursuing policies they had committed themselves to. Far from being intimidated, their attitudes often hardened. The détente in East-West relations . . . in recent years is not a product of the tightening up of trade controls by the West, but rather of their relaxation. [2]

The embargoes of the 1970s and 1980s will hardly fare better. The reason why these embargoes are doomed to failure is the simple truth that it is impossible to convince either people or states to act against their own interests.

I hold the view that the real interests of the other developed capitalist countries and of mankind in general, and the fact that the Carter administration has gone too far (for the sake of temporary factors and of political election interests) in exciting and overdoing the present-day tension, will eventually promote the pursuance of détente and of co-operation. One hardly needs to recall that the measures of the Carter administration designed to increase tension have all missed their objectives. The measures taken by US leadership with a view to stepping up political tension found little or no approval with many governments of the other developed capitalist countries. It seems unlikely that most of the American steps taken in 1980 in that direction will meet a different fate.

The heads of state and government of many Western European countries are fully aware that no basic change has taken place in power relations and interests. They know only too well that they need co-operation with the CMEA countries, their markets and some of their products, and that the other side also has its need for their own technologies and other products and credits - not for charity, but merely for business considerations. They also know that no changes have occurred in the economic field either, changes that would justify the great turn-round that the US leadership would like to impose on the Western European economies. It is absolutely logical that, particularly at the present time, when Western Europe is faced with serious unemployment and its economic growth is extremely slow, the capitalist governments too would want not only to maintain but possibly also to expand their business relations. This is shown, for instance, by the fact that in recent years West Germany and France have significantly increased their trade with the Soviet Union and also with several smaller CMEA member countries, despite the fact that most of the latter have been compelled partly to cut their imports from the West.

The recognition is spreading in Western Europe - and this is a promising fact - that the CMEA countries, Western Europe and the developing countries ought to embark upon a comprehensive development plan. This would be needed to boost mutual trade, to prevent parallel capacities, which have already been, and are still being, brought about in the steel and petrochemical industries and other branches.

As far as the CMEA countries are concerned, I am convinced that the policy they are pursuing - namely that they stand for co-operation and are doing everything in their power to maintain good relations, and are trying, with this end in view, to create the necessary favourable conditions in their own countries - is the only correct and feasible policy. It is also true that CMEA integration and intra-CMEA trade will experience further strengthening until, by joint efforts, the new agreements, organisational forms and methods which are designed to improve the present conditions of East-West trade and co-operation are achieved and put into effect. It also stands to reason that the forms and methods now in use may still provide ample opportunity to further all-European co-operation.

NOTES

1. Mirovaia ekonomika i mezhdunarodnie otnosheniia (1978), No.7, pp. 150f.
2. J. Wilczynski, The Economics and Politics of East-West Trade (London: Macmillan, 1969), p. 288.

10 The Role of the UN Economic Commission for Europe

FRED PARKINSON
University College, London

At a time when the question of détente in Europe is both topical and controversial, the United Nations Economic Commission for Europe - traditional pivot of détente, as well as centre of tensions - straddling the ideological divides of Europe, is a suitable subject of investigation.

I GENESIS

The United Nations Economic Commission for Europe was the heir of the United Nations Relief and Rehabilitation Agency (UNRRA), which was terminated in 1946, and of the three so-called 'E' organisations (emergency organisations) operating under the aegis of Supreme Headquarters Allied Expeditionary Forces of Europe (SHAEF). The latter consisted of (i) the European Coal Organisation (London); (ii) the European Central Inland Transport Organisation (Paris); and (iii) the Emergency Economic Committee for Europe (London). Of these three, only the second had East European participation, but all three were concerned with conditions in the liberated areas of Europe, with a view to promote reconstruction within them. SHAEF could not handle those taks, and a roof organisation was therefore required to deal with them, having a broad base of membership.

The Temporary Sub-Commission on Devastated Areas rendered its report to the General Assembly in 1946, and in December of that year the latter body took the decision to create a suitably constituted Commission to assume the tasks previously discharged by the three 'E' organisations, as well as to promote the process of reconstruction in the devastated areas generally. Europe and Asia were selected as appropriate areas, and Economic Commissions created for both of these. The Two Commissions absorbed the Temporary Sub-

Commission on Devastated Areas, and the Economic Commission for Europe also absorbed the three 'E' organisations. [1]

The actual decision to create these two Commissions was taken by the United Nations Economic and Social Council (ECOSOC) on 28 March 1947. As the first Executive Secretary of the Economic Commission for Europe, Gunnar Myrdal, was to comment: 'This may have been the last moment when such a decision could have been taken', [2] because the general political situation in Europe was deteriorating fast. While the diplomatic energies of the Powers were fully engaged in acrimonious exchanges at the Paris peace conference on the fate of the minor Axis powers, the Terms of Reference were being quietly drawn up for the European and Asian Economic Commissions in 1946. ECOSOC's launching session took place against the background of the failing Moscow Conference of Foreign Ministers in March 1947.

II LEGAL SIGNIFICANCE

The idea of economic regionalism seems never to have been seriously entertained at the San Francisco conference of 1945 or before. [3] The United Nations Economic Commission for Europe (afterwards referred to simply as the Commission) was established by ECOSOC in conformity with Art. 68 of the Charter of the United Nations, and not by Treaty, as were most international economic institutions. It is through ECOSOC also that the Commission is linked to the United Nations system in general. The legal roots of the Commission may be found in the Charter's Preamble in which members set out their 'determination', inter alia, 'to employ international machinery for the promotion of the economic and social advancement of all peoples', and 'to ... live together in peace with one another as good neighbours'. In Art. 1 (3), furthermore, of the Charter one of the purposes of the United Nations is stated as being 'to achieve international co-operation in solving international problems of an economic, social, cultural or humanitarian character'.

The nature of the powers granted by the member States of the United Nations to carry out these purposes is stated in Ch. IX, which deals in detail with 'International Economic and Social Co-operation'. In it the United Nations Organisation is authorised to promote, inter alia, 'higher standards of living, full employment and conditions of economic and social progress and development'.

The modus procedendi is indicated in two Articles. Thus Art. 13 (1.b) bestows upon the General Assembly the task of (a) initiating studies and (b) making recommendations for the purpose of 'promoting international co-operation in the economic and social ... fields', while Art. 60 states that 'responsibility for the discharge of the functions set forth in this Ch. (IX) shall be vested in the General Assembly and, under the authority of the General Assembly, in the Economic and Social Council'.

The nature of the powers of the Economic and Social Council is set out in Ch. X of the United Nations Charter, Art. 62, and they include making or initiating of studies or reports in respect of international economic, social and related matters; the making of recommendations with respect to such matters to the General Assembly, the members of the United Nations and the Specialised Agencies; the preparation of draft conventions on matters falling within its competence, for submission to the General Assembly, and the calling of international conferences on matters falling within its competence.

Art. 68 of the Charter, it may be noted, provides for the setting up of subsidiary organs of the ECOSOC, thus: 'The Economic and Social Council shall set up commissions in the economic and social fields'. Art. 68 is broadly formulated, containing the qualification 'as may be required for the performance of the Economic and Social Council's functions'.

The Terms of Reference by which the Commission was set up provide for full and consultative membership. In practice, the Commission considered that all European countries should have a chance of actively participating, and that States outside the region having a special interest in its work should be able to participate also. The United States, as occupying Power in Europe, as well as - at the time - by far the single most important provider of capital, was given full membership on that understanding, while non-United Nations members, such as Switzerland and others, were for a while granted consultative status in accord with par. 11 of the Terms of Reference. Par. 8 of those Terms allows for a certain amount of flexibility, because it is the Commission itself that may determine the extent of a country's participation in its work.

Membership should, in view of what has been said, have been a simple matter. However, the Hallstein Doctrine in respect of the German Democratic Republic proved to be a considerable obstacle in the Commission's work. Membership has nonetheless expanded steadily from 1955 when it was increased from 18 to 30. The admission to full membership of the German Federal Republic in 1956, of Switzerland and the German Democratic Republic in 1972 and of Canada in 1973 brings the present membership to 34 States.[4]

At its first session the Commission decided that voting should be by majority of members present and voting. However, the Terms of Reference do not allow the Commission to take action against any country without the latter's consent. There has therefore been from the start a sensible practice towards universality and equality of voting, and the establishment of an unwritten rule according to which the decisions and resolutions of the Commission - which have identical legal effect - should be adopted by consensus, without voting and unanimously. Eventually 'even abstentions were no longer recorded, and the unanimous vote is now customarily taken by acclamation'.[5] This is an absolutely essential practice in a region in which the concept of majority and minority could have a deeply divisive effect. It could perhaps, in certain circumstances, give the West European States, which have a numerical majority, the edge over the East European States in a critical situation in which they could use the threat of a formal vote as a last resort to force an issue. Though always implicit, such a threat has never materialised.

Though the Commission is a direct subsidiary of the ECOSOC, its Terms of Reference are wide enough to give it considerable autonomy in practice. The fact that the Commission's headquarters are in Geneva has meant that detailed supervision from New York is impracticable. The Terms emphasise not deliberative functions but the initiation of and participation in measures for facilitating concerted action for economic progress. Par. 4 of the Terms of Reference states that 'The Commission is empowered to make recommendations on any matter within its competence directly to its member governments'. It is also empowered to make recommendations to the ECOSOC on matters of universal, as distinct from regional import. It is to be noted that the Commissions differ from other subsidiary organs set up by the ECOSOC in being able to address recommendations directly to their member States. They remain nonetheless under the authority of the ECOSOC which may, theoretically, terminate their existence at a moment's notice, alter their Terms of Reference and monitor their mode of application.

The Commission is furthermore empowered by its Terms of Reference to draw up its own Rules of Procedure; to elect the Chairman of its sessions; and to set up such subsidiary bodies as are deemed necessary to carry out its functions. In return it must, again according to the Terms, submit to the ECOSOC a full report of its activities and plans, including those of any subsidiary bodies, once a year, and shall make interim reports at each regular Session of the ECOSOC. Those subsidiary bodies, known as the Commission's 'Principal Subsidiary Bodies' (it has minor ones also) were seen to be at the hub of the Commission's technical work.

The Commission's Secretariat forms part of the United Nations Secretariat. The Executive Secretary is appointed by the Secretary General of the United Nations. Though at all times acting on behalf of the latter, the Executive Secretary reports to the Director General for economic co-operation at the United Nations, as well as to its Secretary General. The policy directives the Executive Secretary receives from time to time from the Secretary General tend to give him fairly wide discretion. Similarly,

annual budget estimates prepared by the Executive Secretary for regional Secretariat operations, while subject to formal approval by the United Nations Controller and incorporated into the overall United Nations budget, are seldom modified appreciably by the Secretary General before submission to the General Assembly. In theory, the Executive Secretary is administratively responsible to the Secretary General, but in fact he can make basic operations decisions within the terms of his budget.[6]

The important thing to notice in the powers conferred on the Commission by the Terms of Reference [7] is the essentially preliminary nature of the functions it is permitted to fulfil in relation to economic progress. The powers which go with these functions are powers of recommendation. It may be interesting to note in this connection that the United Nations Economic Commission for Africa, which was created in 1958, was entitled by its Terms of Reference to initiate and participate in measures for facilitating concerted action for economic development, including its social aspects. This power was not conferred on Commissions set up before that date. It was subsequently conferred on the Commissions for Latin America and Asia and the Far East respectively, in a paragraph which instructed them to 'deal as appropriate with the social aspects of economic development and the inter-relationship between economic and social factors'. This provision was not introduced into the Economic Commission for Europe on the ground that the practice established in that Commission made such an act unnecessary. [8]

III THE COMMISSION IN THE 'COLD WAR'

Almost from the start, the Commission was involved in the 'cold war' and found that in the circumstances created by it, self-interest tended to be interpreted by the States far more in political and, above all, military than in economic terms. Yet, the tensions which paralysed many of the Commission's opportunities were at the same time important in keeping it in existence. The Soviet Union at any rate viewed the Commission with suspicion, but both sides in Europe wanted it to act as a bridge between them. [9] At one point at the height of the 'cold war', the Commission ran the real risk of becoming a de facto Western preserve.

The introduction of strategic controls as part of 'cold war' measures taken by the West played an important part in restricting trade between the two parts of Europe, and the Secretariat could not remain unaffected by those developments. In selecting his staff, even among Europeans, the Executive Secretary is obliged to pay some attention to 'geographical distribution' within the United Nations Secretariat as a whole. During the first decade of its existence, East European interest in the Commission was relatively slight, and as a result, West Europeans were for some years in excess of that quota, and the Soviets below theirs. It was only in 1959 that the gap was closed, and only in the mid-1960s that the Secretariat was from that point of view fully representative. In 1976 one prominent Swiss newspaper claimed with considerable exaggeration that 'der Ostwind weht' in the Commission. [10]

To get some idea of the problems with which the Executive Secretary was faced during the 'cold war' it is useful to review briefly the political tactics pursued by the Powers during that period. The main Soviet tactic seems to have been to propose all-European bodies to do the work of the subregional institutions created under the aegis of the Marshall Plan and to insist that the Commission would be more effective in dealing with specific European problems than would be the Specialised Agencies of the United Nations.

A role for the Commission was cast by the Soviet Union as early as January 1954. In April 1959 the pattern was spelt out under the heading of a proposed 'European Trade Organisation' (Doc E/ECE/348) as involving the creation of an all-European regional trade organ- isation within the Commission; long-term trade agreements and other economic agreements; the calling of a conference of Ministers of Foreign Trade of the members of the Commission; and the exchange of scientific and technological information.

The West tried to counter these tactics by claiming that new organs of the nature proposed by the Soviet government would only serve to duplicate the work of the Specialised Agencies. The West was ominously silent on its own duplication of this kind within Western Europe. From about 1958 onwards a significant new tactical element was injected by the newly self-conscious neutralism prac- tised by Yugoslavia, which was soon, in 1961, to host the first fully- fledged conference of non-aligned countries. At the 14th session of the Commission in May 1959, Yugoslavia formally introduced an important resolution calling for co-operation between 'sub-regional' economic groupings. The Resolution,[11] which was endorsed by the Commission without opposition but with the East European countries abstaining, called for (a) the resumption of trade between Eastern and Western Europe on the basis of existing subregional organisations; (b) a positive role for the Commission in Europe; and (c) the examination of the economic consequences of subregional economic integration on the European economy as a whole.

At first the Commission and the subregional organisations in both parts of Europe were loath to have any substantive dealings with each other. The Commission, in particular, viewed the subregionals as symbolising the division of Europe. Eventually, however, the Com- mission had to accept the need for an all-European co-ordination which takes them fully into account. As a result there has been a marked growth over the years of participation at the Commission's meetings, as well as a certain amount of co-operation in the Commission's programmes by officials of the secretariats or staffs of subregional organisations. In 1975 the European Economic Community (EEC), the Council for Mutual Economic Assistance (CMEA) and the European Commission for the Danube were all granted consultative status within the United Nations Economic Commission for Europe.[12]

IV THE POLITICAL ROLE OF THE EXECUTIVE SECRETARY

The drift into the 'cold war' which threatened to break up Europe into two water-tight political and economic units compelled the Executive Secretary of the Commission to adopt a political line of his own and launch various political initiatives in accord with it.

Like every head of an international organisation, Executive Secretaries of the Commission inevitably, and especially at times of crisis, tend to bring part of their own preconceived political, diplomatic and economic ideas to bear on their administrative assignment. Some leave an imprint on the subsequent general mode of thinking in the organisation. It is however only very rarely that an Executive Secretary succeeds in imposing a complete set of his own ideas as fully on a regional economic commission as has been the case with Raúl Prebisch, of the United Nations Economic Commission for Latin America, whose vigorously normative approach affected the entire outlook of the latter deeply, as it was to do eventually in the case of the United Nations Conference on Trade and Development (UNCTAD) whose first Secretary he became soon after his turn at ECLA had expired.[13] In the case of Gunnar Myrdal,[14] first Executive Secretary of the United Nations Economic Commission for Europe (1947-57) one was dealing with a social scientist of a severely realistic and basically sceptical turn of mind who had been engaged in studies in the theory of political economy and the welfare State, but had only a heavily qualified optimism to offer regarding the prospects of international economic institutions. State sovereignty was seen by him as the pillar of international society, and one moreover which would not be surrendered by individual States. The welfare State, the typical unit of European international society, was the most determined upholder of State sovereignty, and expectations of an international economic integration that relied for its success on a modification of State sovereignty were therefore totally illusory.[15] Yet international economic integration was, in his view, essential if the principle of welfare was to be taken from the plane of the State to that of the region. The only way to achieve this was to encourage the intergovernmental co-ordination of policies involving no loss of State sovereignty. This co-ordination had to be the result of deliberate political decisions. It would not be brought about automatically through free trade.[16] Nothing short of the adoption of international economic planning was needed for any progress to be registered.

It is not surprising, therefore, that Myrdal approached his task of Executive Secretary of the Commission by regarding the latter as the perfect instrument through which to promote regional economic co-ordination, and that he saw in the 'cold war' the potential frustration of this task.[17] Regarding it as his foremost duty to obstruct the progress of the 'cold war' by any means at his disposal, Myrdal soon found himself engaged in taking politically hazardous initiatives. The latter fell into two categories: those taken indirectly but openly, by administrative manipulation, and those taken directly but discreetly, through the pursuit of a markedly 'coexistentialist' diplomacy. Both were based on an extensive interpretation of his mandate as Executive Secretary, and both took him to the brink of being ultra vires.

Administrative Initiatives

One way of opposing the currents of the 'cold war' used by Myrdal was to provide a stream of data 'exposing the real cost of policies which tended to weaken or destroy the economic interdependence of Europe'.[18] He also put forward proposals he could withdraw without damaging the prestige of any government, and secured the deletion of programmes which governments might be reluctant to suggest for fear of laying themselves open to the charge of being unco-operative.[19] As Myrdal was to explain many years later:[20] 'The Secretariat took upon itself the responsibility for cancelling meetings from which no useful results were likely to emerge' and likewise refused to carry out useless studies. This veto power, which was of questionable legality, was never challenged by any government. As Myrdal admitted, during those difficult years the documentation of committees went unpublished, and not even summary records were kept; 'procedural questions were shunned; and committees, as well as sub-committees and working parties functioned without any formal rules of procedure'.[21] At the very end of his mandate, at long last, Myrdal noted, he was able to do justice to the Terms of Reference, when the Commission became 'an effective and stable organisation with full participation of all governments in the East, as well as in the West of Europe'.[22]

Diplomatic Initiatives

Myrdal took 'coexistentialist' nitiatives of a diplomatic kind in the field of international trade at a time when these were not generally popular. This he tried to achieve by depoliticising problems related to European trade, and by establishing or re-establishing trade between the European antagonists in the 'cold war', acting at all times as an 'honest broker'[23] and maintaining secrecy when establishing trade contacts between States having no diplomatic relations with each other between 1953 and 1954.[24] In so doing he sometimes availed himself of high-level contacts, by-passing lower-level representa-tives, for which he was promptly criticised.[25]

Furthermore, 'in the early nineteen-fifties, the whole structure of the United Nations' - and this included to a large extent the Sec-retariat - 'was undergoing deep modifications with the more or less avowed aim of turning the United Nations into a weapon to be used by the majority in the struggle opposing it to the small pro-Soviet minority'. Myrdal opposed this tendency, and by his efforts may have saved the day for the Commission.[26] On the other hand, he warned the East European States not to stand aside, but to become actively engaged in the work of the Commission. 'These urgings and warnings were publicly expressed at Commission sessions, and privately to the governments', Myrdal was to reveal many years later.[27] The Com-mission survived the 'cold war'. What Myrdal could not prevent was that, as the split in Europe widened, most significant decisions were taken in the subregional organisations. This was the problem his three successors inherited from him.[28]

V THE TECHNICAL ACTIVITIES

Par. 5 of the Terms of Reference empowers the Commission, 'after discussion with any Specialised Agency functioning in the same general field,' and with the approval of the ECOSOC, to establish such 'subsidiary bodies' as it deems appropriate for facilitating the carrying out of its responsibilities. Over a dozen Principal Subsidiary Bodies have been established in this way over the years. The first twelve deal with various technical sectors, and the steady growth in its numbers bears witness to the broadening of the scope of the Commission's activities. Even at a time when Eastern Europe would not take any part in their work, they managed to perform useful work, though they have also been charged with an atmosphere of political tension.

While the tensions of the 'cold war' persisted, the practical work of the Commission, discharged through those Principal Subsidiary Bodies, was of a generally technocratic nature. With the waning of the 'cold war' the Commission began to tackle problems of policy with the object of enabling governments to anticipate developments, a task which is normally regarded as that of a proper civil service. This involved long-term projections - now a permanent feature of its work - and other studies, undertaken in the hope that it might be possible within the European region to envisage a certain degree of harmonisation of economic policies. Seminal in this respect was the creation of three more Principal Subsidiary Bodies, composed of Senior Advisers to Governments of the Commission, in the three vital fields of (i) economics; (ii) science and technology; and (iii) environmental problems after 1969. Here was a direct connection between the technical work of the Commission and the inter-sectoral concerns of member governments, which added an element of realism to what otherwise might have been regarded as semi-academic exercises.

To focus the technical work of the Commission as much as possible, the Executive Secretary, acting under instructions, has for the past decade been preparing for each session of the Commission an annual report enabling it to concentrate its discussion on a priority theme. It is useful to enumerate some of these themes, as they would seem to reflect fairly faithfully the altering economic priorities of the Commission, itself - since the institution of Senior Advisers to Governments at any rate - reflecting the changing economic preoccupations within the area of the Commission:[29]

1971 : structural trends in European industry;
1972 : problems of the development of trade;
1973 : long-term perspectives for the European economy;

1974 : the role of technology in the economic development of the European region.

It may also be useful, at this stage of the paper, to present some thumbnail sketches of the work done in the main areas in which the Principal Subsidiary Bodies have operated.

VI PLANNING AND RESEARCH

There has been a bias in favour of planning from the beginning. However, various types of economic planning came gradually to be accepted by governments even in Western Europe. For this reason governments were ready to co-operate with the Commission in the field of economic planning through the institution of Senior Economic Advisers, in which the governments of East and West Europe collaborated, and which concerned itself not only with economic planning, but with macroeconomic problems generally. As for the role of Soviet advisers and members of technical staffs, Professor Sharp had this to say in 1961:

> How to utilise them has created something of a problem. It has proved difficult to use them on economic policy research because of their rigid ideological orientation. Soviet statisticians and specialists in specific industries (e.g. steel) have apparently adapted themselves more easily to the requirements of objective analysis.[30]

In the sphere of research, the Commission has consistently made use, through its research division, of its two official publications for which, under the Terms of Reference of the Commission, it is obliged to assume responsibility. These are (i) the Economic Survey of Europe, which has formed the basis of broad debate at the annual sessions of the Commission, and (ii) the Economic Bulletin for Europe, which is mainly devoted to the discussion of developments and problems in the field of trade. On the whole, the research division of the Commission has regarded it as its major task to focus its work in such a way as to encourage the development of links between Western and Eastern Europe. The objective nature of the research has been doubted by few.[31]

VII TRADE AND TRANSPORT

Trade has been instrumental in easing 'cold war' tensions. Yet basic political problems remained, the snag[32] with the expansion of trade between Eastern and Western Europe being that the former merely wants to earn enough foreign exchange to cover its planned imports, while the latter is interested in exporting to Eastern Europe only when its economy is in recession and manufacturing industries are working below capacity. There has been little specialisation in the composition of trade or export orientation so far, mainly because neither side has wished to be dependent on the other. No amount of trying on the part of the present Executive Secretary, Janez Stanovnik, has succeeded in completely breaking down this immobilisme, although the rapid growth of specialisation in recent years through long-term industrial co-operation agreements is a noteworthy development.

The experience of the so-called 'van Platen Group' ad hoc, created by the Commission in 1963 to study problems of East-West trade is a case in point. Having to deal with the technical peculiarities of trade between market economies and centrally directed economies the Group recommended two kinds of measures to get trade flowing: (i) market economies should remove quantitative restrictions limiting imports; and (ii) the centrally directed economies should confirm their intention 'to use their best endeavours to avoid price disturbances in their domestic markets'. The ad hoc Group furthermore suggested (i) better application of the most-favoured-nation device; and (ii) the multilateralisation of trade and payments. For its pains the Group was criticised as having gone too far. [33]

This has left the Commission with a mixture of largely 'pedagogical' and highly practical functions, particularly in the field of the facilitation of trade relations. There was, for instance, the preparation of a European convention on international commercial arbitration, which took six years to negotiate, and provided a mechanism whereby arbitrators may be designated in cases where the parties themselves did not succeed in agreeing to such a designation. [34] There was also the rationalisation and harmonisation of trade documents and procedures. [35]

The Commission scored some considerable successes in the field of inland transport, proceeding far on the road from the task of redistributing rolling stock just after the war to the long-range integration of transport in Europe. In 1975 the Commission, in conjunction with the United Nations Development Programme, undertook the preparation of studies for linking motorways running through the Baltic to Bulgaria, the Middle East and Western Asia. The Commission will also serve as the Executing Agency for UNDP support to studies for the further development of the electric power transmission systems of Bulgaria, Greece, Romania, Turkey and Yugoslavia. [36] As regards inland water transport, a Commission study on the Rhine-Main-Danube connection was completed in 1969. Construction is to be completed in 1985.

VIII ENERGY AND WATER RESOURCES

In the field of energy the Commission had to cope with growing demand and the increasing complexity of supplies. Thus, between 1947-58 the dramatic change from coal-based to a coal- and oil-based economy had to be dealt with. From the late 1950s to the early 1970s complex substitution problems arose from the relative abundance of hydrocarbons; while from the mid-1970s onwards, on the contrary, greater economies and efficiencies had to be introduced in the face of growing scarcity of oil.

In the sphere of electric power, similarly, there was a problem of growing demand. The multilateral 'Yugel-export' project proved largely successful. [37]

Rising demand for water prompted the Commission to turn to the tackling of problems of integrated water management, the results of which found expression in its report on The Role of the Commission in the Field of the Rational Utilisation of Water Resources in Europe (E/ECE/472 of 1963). The Commission's ad hoc Group of Experts was transformed into the Committee on Water Problems and granted the status of a Principal Subsidiary Organ in 1969.

IX   INDUSTRIAL CO-OPERATION AND SCIENCE AND TECHNOLOGY

The 1970s were the heyday of agreements on industrial co-operation between the two parts of Europe. As Executive Secretary Janez Stanovnik noted in a report in 1976[38] the number of those agreements had risen from a mere hundred to a thousand within ten years. From 1977 the number of new agreements of this kind has shown a tendency to fall. [39]

This was a sphere in which the Commission was supremely well fitted in rendering technical assistance. In the first place it accorded well with its underlying philosophy of acting as the bridge between the two politically diverse parts of Europe; and secondly, because this was an area par excellence in which there was no risk of political controversy. The Secretariat therefore showed some enthusiasm in fostering these agreements, both at government and at enterprise level. The Commission completed several reports, and also its Committee on the Development of Trade prepared a guide for facilitating the drawing up of international contracts on industrial co-operation. The limits of this type of co-operation were, however, shown when at the 26th session of that Committee proposals for a new ad hoc institution in this field, such as a European Industrial Co-operation Development Fund, as well as a Bank for Industrial Co-operation, failed to be accepted. Once again, the Commission had come up against definite political barriers.[40] Nonetheless, the typology of agreements elaborated by the Commission must have proved useful: six types of agreements were distinguished as follows: (i) grant of licences, paid by goods produced under those licences; (ii) delivery of whole plants, payment to be made from their products; (iii) specialisation in the production of parts or different types and quantities of the end-products; (iv) subcontracting; (v) common processes of production, whether in respect of sales, research or development; and (vi) common delivery offer for plants, machinery or equipment to customers in third countries.[41]

In the field of science and technology the 1970s, again, presented an area in which interest was growing fast. Since April 1971 - though several Principal Subsidiary Bodies continued to be substantially involved - the overall field, and the development of closer 'cross-sectoral' co-operation among European countries has been entrusted to a new body of Senior Advisers to Commission Governments on Science and Technology.[42]

X INDUSTRY AND ENVIRONMENT

In various branches of industrial activity, the Commission has been operative. Its work has been perhaps particularly fruitful in the steel industry, which is such as to call for a high degree of international co-operation, and the chemical industry, the fastest growing industry. The engineering industry has not escaped the attentions of the Commission either. A working party on automation was set up in 1970.

In the latter half of the 1960s concern was beginning to be felt about the pollution of water and the air. Consequently, the Commission created a new Principal Subsidiary Body, the Senior Advisers to Commission Governments on Environmental Problems, in 1971. When the United Nations Environmental Programme was launched in 1973, close co-operation developed between the Commission and that new UN body. There was a general recognition that environmental matters must be made an integral part of economic planning.

The present survey cannot pretend to do justice to the full range of technical activities of the Commission. Yet it is clear that the nature of its assignment has changed beyond recognition over time, from a mere temporary institution concerned with reconstruction of the area, to one deeply involved in the entire gamut of economic and technical activities of the European area.

XI NEW FUNCTIONS

Implementing the New Economic Order

The Commission was originally created to benefit the European area in the economic sphere. It so happened, however, that the United States formed part of it from the start, and Canada from 1972 onwards, and that consequently - leaving apart Australasia, South Africa and Japan - it contains all the world's developed countries.[43] In the measure in which the 'cold war' in its acute form faded, the problem of the economic development of the underdeveloped regions of the world became prominent, and growing pressure was put on the developed countries to promote that development actively.

It would have been entirely absurd to expect the Commission to turn a blind eye to extra-European economic affairs. Nor was that ever the intention. Par. 4 of its Terms of Reference enjoins the Commission 'to submit for the Economic and Social Council's prior consideration any of its proposals for activities that would have important effects on the economy of the world as a whole'. Almost by definition, any act of the Commission was, in the circumstances, bound to affect the underdeveloped world, whose regions are all represented, through ECOSOC, in the economic system of the United Nations by equivalent regional economic commissions.

The Commission has no explicit co-ordinating authority, but its broad Terms of Reference have tended to give it a position of some influence over the Specialised Agencies of the United Nations. As if to confirm this, the ECOSOC at its 54th session in the spring of 1973 reaffirmed in Resolution 1756 (LIV) that 'the regional economic commissions, in their respective regions, are the main general economic and social development centres within the United Nations system'. The wording of the Resolution makes it clear that the regional economic commissions other than that for Europe were in ECOSOC's mind, since Europe (plus the United States and Canada) is an already near-fully developed area.

Not that the Commission needed a great deal of prompting in assisting in the task of developing the underdeveloped regions of the world. It had collaborated closely with the Preparatory Commission of UNCTAD from the beginning, and the entire ethos pervading the Secretariat of the United Nations Economic Commission for Europe had predisposed it towards taking a most sympathetic attitude in this question. There was a perfect meeting of minds between Raúl Prebisch, the architect of UNCTAD and progenitor of its underlying economic philosophy - developmentalism - and the officials in the Secretariat.[44] All regional economic commissions were in addition directed by the ECOSOC in Resolution 2043 (LXI) of 5 August 1976 to work out programmes and priorities for the underdeveloped countries.

To keep in touch with the other regional economic commissions of the United Nations has been a permanent feature in the practice of the Commission, and much valuable practical work has been accomplished to the benefit of those underdeveloped areas.[45] Yet the Commission might run the risk of becoming unduly preoccupied with this worthy cause through various programmes launched to implement the New International Economic Order,[46] to the detriment of its proper task, to attend to the economic problems of Europe. The world would therefore be better served if the Commission were to stick to its original brief instead of scattering its energies in performing tasks for which it is not pre-eminently fitted.

Implementing the Helsinki Final Act

    . . . the view that some such body as the United Nations Economic

Commission for Europe might in the long run play an important part in the machinery of a general European settlement. In particular, it might serve as a forum for the discussion and settlement of the many economic interests common to Eastern and Western Europe. (Walt W. Rostow, writing in 1949[47])

If the Commission is indeed destined to play a major role, it is surely in Europe. Once before the Commission came close to being cast in such a role. When General George Marshall, Secretary of State of the United States, made his well-known offer of aid to Europe on 5 June 1947, the State Department had already given the Commission its warm endorsement, feeling that the European continent should be dealt with as a whole.[48] When on 12 June 1947 General Marshall clarified the position regarding his offer by explaining it was comprehensive, including Eastern as well as Western Europe, he was fully supported by Senator Vandenberg, a Republican 'internationalist', who wanted to work closely with the United Nations Economic Commission for Europe.[49] That the Commission was nonetheless cold-shouldered was due in large part to the foreign ministers of Britain and France, Ernest Bevin and Georges Bidault, who seized the initiative and determined the character of the international organisation, the Organisation for European Economic Co-operation, that was to be responsible for fixing priorities on the European side. One might have had, in the circumstances, some sympathies with the defensive attitudes adopted by the Soviet foreign minister, V.M. Molotov, who walked out of the Paris conference in July 1947, claiming that the proposed mode of administering the aid constituted an intolerable infringement of the sovereignty of the Soviet Union and its allies in Eastern Europe. Yet it would have been perfectly open to Molotov to propose the United Nations Economic Commission for Europe as the properly disinterested institution for administering the aid. This might have earned him the plaudits of the United States. Major damage to the European political fabric might have been prevented if General Marshall had made his original offer conditional on the Commission being appointed as the administering agency of the aid.

Twenty-eight years were to pass before the Commission was to be given another chance. The Helsinki Conference on Security and Co-operation in Europe (CSCE) which opened in July 1973, included in its Terms of Reference guidelines for co-operation in the three fields of (i) economy, (ii) science and technology, and (iii) the environment, areas which, when they were included in the Final Act of the conference on 1 August 1975, became known as 'basket two'. ('Basket one' was concerned with political relations between States, and 'basket three' with the free exchange of information and people between Eastern and Western Europe.)

The Helsinki negotiations were meant to mark the stage of multilateralisation of the process of détente which had been a notable feature of the European diplomatic scene since about 1969. The Final Act of the Helsinki conference records the wish of the signatories 'to take advantage of the possibilities offered by the United Nations Economic Commission for Europe' to implement the pertinent provisions of the Act - contained in 'basket two' - 'multilaterally . . . also within the framework of the Commission'. The choice was an obvious one. There was a virtual identity of membership of the Conference on Security and Co-operation in Europe on the one hand, and the Commission on the other hand. Delegates of the Second Committee of the Helsinki conference often took part in the relevant meetings of the bodies of the Commission taking place during the same period.

It is to be noted, however, that the three areas designated by the conference as being suited for implementation by the Commission under 'basket two' of the Final Act had been suggested by the Commission in the first place. It is furthermore to be noted that the activities listed under 'basket two' had been gradually expanding over the years as a result of what Professor Michael Howard in a felicitous phrasing has described as 'capitalist greed and socialist need'.[50] As a leading British newspaper was to comment: 'Helsinki marked no great breakthrough in economic co-operation. It merely confirmed, and ultimately streamlined, an increasingly complex web of activity pragmatically developed within the United Nations Economic Commission for Europe over the past two decades'.[51] What had happened is that 'part of the Commission's work programme was used as basis for negotiating the Final Act because it lent itself most as areas of multilateral cooperative endeavours to be agreed upon'.[52]

The decision to involve the Commission in the multilateral implementation of the Final Act was taken at its 31st session in 1976, and constituted a compromise. The Soviet Union would have preferred to set up an institution that was part and parcel of the Conference on Security and Co-operation in Europe and would have been charged with the task of applying the provisions of the Final Act. This was opposed by the Western States who insisted on linking the Commission with the CSCE.

'Basket two' expressly named the Commission in respect of areas in which the latter has traditionally operated. These include the harmonisation of statistical nomenclatures; trade promotion, including marketing; improvements in the provisions of information in industrial co-operation, and guidance or preparation of contracts in this field; co-operation on environmental problems; the elimination of legal disparities as applied to traffic on inland waterways; and the strengthening of the Inland Transport Committee of the Commission.

In addition, the Commission has been given responsibilities in conducting studies on the creation of multilateral systems in respect of the notification of laws and regulations governing foreign trade and changes therein; in regard to the multilateral expansion of co-operation in the area of science and technology; and the development of the capacity on the parts of governments to predict adequately the environmental consequences of their economic activities and technological development.

A specially delicate matter on which a compromise was reached under 'basket two' concerned the standards of the most-favoured-nation and reciprocity respectively, the former finding favour with the centrally-directed economies and the latter with the market economies. The relevant text of the Final Act makes reference to the former by recognising 'the beneficial effects which can result for the development of trade from the application of most-favoured-nation treatment', and refers to the latter by recognising that 'co-operation with due regard for the different levels of economic development can be developed on the basis of equality and the mutual satisfaction of the partners, and of reciprocity, permitting as a whole an equitable distribution of advantages and obligations of a comparable scale, with respect to bilateral and multilateral agreements'. As Bailey-Wiebecke and Bailey rightly conclude, the goal of the East European States not parties to the General Agreement on Tariffs and Trade (GATT) - to have most-favoured-nation treatment conferred upon them without having in turn to enter into the concomitant responsibilities of GATT - was thus never achieved. [53]

The only politically controversial issue regarding the implementation of 'basket two' of the Final Act of Helsinki (1975) concerned the persistent demands by the Soviet Union for the calling of all-European congresses to deal with the problems of environment, energy and transport. It may be noted that these are all areas in which the Commission had engaged the services of Senior Advisers to Governments, acting in their capacity as members of the Commission's Principal Subsidiary Bodies. It has been noticeable that the West dislikes the wide East European interpretation given to the items in 'basket two', and that it suspects that behind Soviet references to using the 'instrumentality' of the Commission in conjunction with the projected all-European congresses there lurks the intention of cutting down the potential role of the Commission quite considerably. These Western suspicions were strengthened by Soviet offers of Moscow, instead of Geneva, as the site of those congresses. The West insisted as part of its price for consenting to the holding of those congresses in principle that they should be held within the framework of the Commission. Acrimony continued to be the keynote whenever the question of those congresses was raised, and for the first time in its history occasioned the adjournment of a Commission meeting in April 1979. [54] Nevertheless, a Convention on Long-Range Transboundary Air Pollution, albeit one containing weak legal provisions, was concluded in November 1979.

XII THE PROSPECTS

The prospects of being appointed in some ways as executive agency

of a part of the Final Act of the Helsinki conference caused a flut-
ter in the ranks of the Commission. On the eve of the conference, in
1973, the then Chairman of the session of the Commission,
Ambassador Kaufmann (Netherlands) asked the expectantly rhetorical
question: 'Is it arrogant to foresee that in the long run the Secretariat
of the Commission is the only one eligible for the executive tasks of
the Conference on Security and Co-operation in Europe?'.[55] Three
years later Executive Secretary Janez Stanovnik, in a paper drafted
for the follow-up conference, could still maintain that 'new
perspectives . . . now opening for inter-governmental co-operation'
and that 'the Commission represents the link'.[56] The point was well
made, but left the relevant points unstated. The Commission
certainly represents a link; but it is neither the only one nor even, in
the present context of world politics, an important one. That the
Commission has been immensely useful for all concerned needs no
reiteration. Yet the fortunes of the States of Europe depend on the
ups and downs of world politics, and not on the institutional
excellence of the Commission.[57] That the Commission has the
potentialities of being instrumental in promoting détente, should the
Powers desire it, can hardly be disputed. It is only when this happens
that the Commission will be in a position to extend its functions
beyond its present routine administrative and technical tasks into the
executive field.

Meanwhile, there is one role which the Commission may assume
one day, and for which it is eminently fitted, and that happens to be
one the Commission had played with success at the very beginning of
its existence. It is the supply and allocation of scarce resources on an
all-European basis in an emergency. It will be recalled that after
1947 the Commission was able to lay its hand on scarce coal
resources, and to distribute them equitably throughout the continent.
The International Energy Agency, a purely Western organisation, has
been engaged for some time in perfecting rationing schemes to meet
an emergency in the sphere of oil supplies. However, a scenario could
be envisaged in which both parts of Europe would have an overriding
common interest in ensuring a safe supply of oil. This, after all, is a
matter in which both parts of Europe may be instantly rendered
equally helpless by decisions taken outside the region, over which
neither side can hope to exercise the least control. This would call
for the laying of contingency plans, including those granting the
Commission appropriate emergency powers to cope effectively if
those circumstances arose. The first steps in this direction were
taken during the annual session of the Commission in April 1980.

NOTES

1. For details, see C.H. Alexandrowicz, 'The Economic Commission
   for Europe', 3(NS) World Affairs (1949), pp. 43-54, at pp. 46-8.

2. G. Myrdal, 'Twenty Years of the United Nations Economic Commission for Europe', pp. 55-65, at p. 55 in Asociata de Drept International, Relatii Internationale (Bucharest), special seminar on 'Le développement de la coopération entre les états européens' (1969). This will henceforth be referred to as Bucharest Seminar. UN Doc. E/3052 of 6 February 1958 summarises developments leading to the establishment of the Commission, as well as of its sister Commission, the United Nations Economic Commission for Asia and the Far East (ECAFE).
   For an interesting historical precedent of what might have resulted in a similar body, see Hervé Alphand, 'Les recommendations de la Conférence de Stresa' (for the economic restoration of Central and Eastern Europe), 10 Revue de droit international (1932), pp. 555-78 and 652-69.
3. Egypt was unsuccessful at San Francisco in pressing for the inclusion in the Charter of a formula defining regional groups of States for, inter alia, 'the development of their economic and cultural relations'.
4. See also G. Fischer, 'Participation des états non-membres aux travaux des commissions économiques régionales', 1 Annuaire français de droit international (1955), pp. 330-45.
5. See UN/E/ECE/962, Three Decades of the United Nations Economic Commission for Europe (New York: United Nations, 1978), pp. 16-17.
6. See W.R. Sharp, Field Administration in the United Nations System (London: Stevens, 1961), p. 183.
7. The easiest way to locate the Terms of Reference of the Commission is the Yearbook of the United Nations 1946-7, p. 483.
8. See ECE/E/3227, Annual Report 1958-1959, p. 40.
9. D. Wightman, Economic Cooperation in Europe. A Study of the United Nations Economic Commission for Europe (London: Stevens, 1956), p. 259.
10. Neue Zürcher Zeitung, 12 March 1976.
11. Doc. E/ECE/SR. 14/22, May 1959.
12. On those points, see Three Decades of the United Nations Economic Commission for Europe, document cited in note 5 above, p. 6.
13. For a critical appreciation of Prebisch's thesis on the international economic relations between 'centre' and 'periphery', see the chapter on 'Developmentalism and Dependencia', pp. 121-6, in F. Parkinson, The Philosophy of International Relations (London and Beverly Hills: SAGE Publications, 1977).
14. On Gunnar Myrdal, see Paul Streeten, 'Gunnar Myrdal: the cheerful pessimist', New Society, 5 December 1974, and D. Wightman, op. cit. in note 9 above, pp. 256-7.
15. On this point, see G. Myrdal, Beyond the Welfare State (London: Duckworth, 1960).
16. On this point, see G. Myrdal, Das politische Element in der

nationalökonomischen Willensbildung (1932).
17. For previous thinkers of this type, see Sir Arthur (Lord) Salter, The United States of Europe and Other Papers (London: Allen and Unwin, 1933) who argued in favour of a gradual economic rapprochement in Europe; and W.E. Rappard, United Europe (New Haven: Yale University Press, 1930), especially pp. 148 and 302.
18. Wightman, op. cit., p. 241.
19. Ibid., p. 253.
20. Bucharest Seminar (1969), p. 58.
21. Ibid., p. 57.
22. Ibid., p. 60.
23. See J. Siotis, 'The Secretariat of the United Nations Economic Commission for Europe and European Economic Integration: the first ten years', 19 International Organization (1965), pp. 177-202, at p. 196.
24. Bucharest Seminar (1969), p. 59.
25. J. Siotis, International Organization, op. cit., p. 189.
26. Ibid., p. 183.
27. Bucharest Seminar (1969), p. 56.
28. These were: Sakari Severi Tuomioja, a Finnish diplomat and statesman (1957-60), who gave up the post to enter politics; Vladimir Velebit, a Yugoslav lawyer, politician and diplomat (1960-68), who resigned on account of age; and Janez Stanovnik, the present incumbent, a Yugoslav economist of considerable experience in international economic relations, appointed in 1968.

   It may or may not be significant that the geographical shift of appointments of Executive Secretaries from the Scandinavian area to Yugoslavia coincided with (a) the commencement of an energetically 'neutralist' line by Yugoslavia, and (b) the departure of Scandinavians from the Secretary Generalship of the United Nations after 1960.
29. Data taken from UN/E/ECE/962, Three Decades of the United Nations Economic Commission for Europe (New York: United Nations, 1978).
30. W.R. Sharp, Field Administration in the United Nations System (London: Stevens, 1961), p. 136.
31. The Neue Zürcher Zeitung of 1 April 1974 criticised the Commission's Economic Survey of Europe in 1973 on the grounds that it could not afford to make any statements which would not be endorsed by 'the Communist governments'.

   In reviewing the Economic Survey of Europe in 1977, however, the same Swiss paper praised its meaningfulness ('Aussagekraft'). See Neue Zürcher Zeitung, 22 March 1978.
32. See Financial Times, 15 April 1977.
33. See J. Siotis, 'The United Nations Economic Commission for Europe and the Emerging European System', International Conciliation, No. 561, January 1967, pp. 5-72, at pp. 28-30.
34. See UN/E/ECE/962, Three Decades of the United Nations

Economic Commission for Europe (New York:United Nations, 1978), p. 37.

See also P. Benjamin, 'The Work of the United Nations Economic Commission for Europe in the Field of International Commercial Arbitration', 7 _International and Comparative Law Quarterly_ (1958), pp. 22-30.

35. UN/E/ECE/962 op. cit. in note 36 above, pp. 37-8.
36. Ibid., p. 7.
37. Ibid., pp. 75-6.
38. Doc. UN/E/ECE/GEN/20 of 21 July 1976.
39. See _Financial Times_, 15 April 1977.
40. See UN/E/ECE/962, _Three Decades of the United Nations Economic Commission for Europe_ (New York:United Nations, 1978), p. 40.
41. See A. Nussbaumer, 'Industrial Cooperation and East-West Trade', 32, _Yearbook of World Affairs 1978_, pp. 64-75, at pp. 64-5.
42. UN/E/ECE/962, _Three Decades of the United Nations Economic Commission for Europe_, op. cit., p. 46.
43. Australia and Japan participate regularly in certain technical committees and seminars, while China has done so occasionally in recent years.
44. On this point, see J. Siotis, 'The United Nations Economic Commission for Europe and the Emerging European System', _International Conciliation_, No. 561, January 1967, pp. 5-72, at p. 54.
45. On this point, see B.G. Ramcharan, 'Equality and Discrimination in International Economic Law: the United Nations Regional Economic Commissions', 32 _Yearbook of World Affairs 1978_, pp. 268-85.
46. Four Resolutions of the General Assembly form the legal basis for a long-term policy of creating a New International Economic Order: (i) the Declaration for the Establishment of a New International Economic Order (GA Resolution 3201; S-VI of 1974); (ii) the Programme of Action on the Establishment of a New International Economic Order (GA Resolution 3202; S-VI of 1974); (iii) the Charter of Economic Rights and Duties of States (GA Resolution 3281; XXIX of 1974); and (iv) Development and International Co-operation (GA Resolution 3362; S-VII of 1975).
47. See W.W. Rostow, then Assistant to the Executive Secretary of the Commission, writing on 'The Economic Commission for Europe' in 3, _International Organization_ (1949), pp. 254-69. The cited passage is to be found on p. 256.
48. See _New York Times_, 14 June 1947.
49. On the history of the Marshall offer, see D. Wightman, op. cit., Ch. 2, pp. 25-51.
50. See M. Howard, 'Helsinki Reconsidered: East-West Relations two years after the Final Act', _Round Table_ (1977), pp. 241-8, at p. 244.
51. _Financial Times_, 15 April 1977.

52. See I. Bailey-Wiebecke and P.J. Bailey, 'The United Nations Economic Commission for Europe and the Belgrade Follow-up Conference', 28 Aussenpolitik (English edition), (1977), pp. 257-73, at p. 264.
  An extensive analysis of the same topic is contained in I. Bailey-Wiebecke and P.J. Bailey, 'All-European Co-operation: the Conference on Security and Co-operation in Europe's Basket Two and the United Nations Economic Commission for Europe', 32 International Journal (1977), pp. 386-407.
53. Bailey-Wiebecke and P.J. Bailey, op. cit. in par. 1 of note 52 above, p. 260.
54. Neue Zürcher Zeitung, 11 April 1979.
55. Ibid., 10 May 1973.
56. Ibid., 12 March 1976.
57. For an analysis of the Belgrade follow-up conference of 1977-78, see R. Davy, 'No Progress at Belgrade', 34 The World Today (1978), pp. 128-34.

11 Legal Aspects of an EEC–CMEA Agreement

JOSEF MRÁZEK and ALEXEJ KOHOUT

CSSR Academy of Sciences, Prague

I INTRODUCTION

Talks between the Council of Mutual Economic Assistance (CMEA) and the European Economic Community (EEC) have been going on since 1976. They are in the centre of interest from both the political and economic points of view, because it is a matter of relations between organisations belonging to different social systems. The CMEA and EEC are the most substantial integration units in the world today and each of them has a great economic potential; CMEA alone accounts for one-third of the value of the world's industrial production. These negotiations are in the centre of attention also from the legal point of view, because of the essential differences existing between the legal concepts and institutional structures of the two entities.[1]

The first direct contact between the CMEA and EEC was established in August 1973 when the Secretary of the CMEA, N.V. Faddeev, met in Copenhagen with the Danish Minister, I. Noergaard, who was then President of the Council of European Communities. In 1974 and 1975 some exploratory contacts between the CMEA Secretariat and the Commission of the European Communities continued; nevertheless, the EEC during the same period put forward proposals to the CMEA member countries to initiate individual bilateral talks on contractual arrangements in the trade policy area (the aide-mémoire of November 1974). It was only natural that the CMEA member countries rejected these proposals, taking into account the preparations for the intended collective negotiations between the CMEA and the EEC.

An important turning point was reached by February 1976 when the then Chairman of the Executive Committee of the CMEA, the Deputy Prime Minister of the German Democratic Republic, G.

133

Weiss, handed over in Luxemburg to the then President of the Council of the European Communities, the Luxemburg Minister of Foreign Affairs, G. Thorn, a detailed proposal by the CMEA to conclude an agreement covering a formal arrangement of the mutual relations between the CMEA and the EEC, providing also for the regulation of a wide range of questions with the participation of the CMEA and EEC member countries.

In November of the same year the Dutch Ambassador to Warsaw presented to the then Chairman of the Executive Committee of the CMEA, the Deputy Prime Minister of the People's Republic of Poland, K. Olszewski, a counter-proposal of the Council of the EEC covering a substantially more limited range of questions.

In September 1977, a meeting took place in Brussels between the Chairman of the Executive Committee of the CMEA, the Deputy Prime Minister of Romania, M. Marinescu, the Belgian Minister of Foreign Affairs, H. Simonet, as Acting President of the Council of the EEC, and the Vice-President of the EEC Commission, W. Haferkamp. Questions connected with the preparation of the negotiations were discussed at this meeting.

The talks dealing with an agreement between the CMEA and the EEC were opened in May 1978 when N. Faddeev and W. Haferkamp met in Moscow to clarify the choice of questions which might become the defined objects of the agreement. Further discussions were held at the level of experts in Brussels, in July of the same year.

In November 1978, talks were held in Brussels between a delegation of the CMEA and the CMEA member countries headed by N. Faddeev, and an EEC delegation headed by W. Haferkamp. At the conclusion of the talks the EEC delegation presented the so-called first compromise EEC proposal completing the original EEC proposal with some partial clauses concerning trade.

After detailed examination, the CMEA formulated its own compromise proposal consisting in a simplification of the trade policy clauses of the original CMEA proposal; this compromise proposal was sent by the CMEA Secretary to the Vice-President of the EEC Commission in June 1979.

In November 1979 a delegation of the CMEA and of the CMEA member countries and a delegation of the EEC at the levels of N. Faddeev and W. Haferkamp met in Moscow to discuss the compromise proposals; on that occasion, the EEC delegation put forward a new revised text of its proposal containing some compromise wordings concerning the agreement clauses which were not of basic significance; further talks were planned by the parties for February/March 1980 at a level of experts and for April 1980 at a level of the delegations of the two parties.

Experts met in Geneva, March 1980. When working on the text of the agreement common wordings of several articles were achieved; the two parties, however, did not succeed in reconciling the different views regarding the determination of the most important clauses of the agreement.

It was a complete surprise when the Vice-President W. Haferkamp sent CMEA Secretary N. Faddeev a letter indicating that further high-level talks scheduled for April 1980 were not regarded as useful 'as long as indications of a substantial change in the position of the CMEA are not apparent'.[2]

In April 1980, the CMEA Executive Committee confirmed once again at its 94th meeting its readiness to continue a constructive dialogue with the EEC with the objective of elaborating mutually acceptable agreements. The CMEA countries favoured the conclusion of an agreement encouraging and assisting the development of a mutually advantageous trade and economic co-operation on an equal footing both among the CMEA and EEC member countries and between the two organisations in the spirit of the Final Act of the Conference on Security and Co-operation in Europe. This sensible CMEA approach facilitated the decision by the two sides to continue the talks at the level of experts in Geneva, July 1980.

II CHARACTER AND POWERS OF CMEA

The CMEA is an interstate organisation concerned - together with the development of a broad economic co-operation among the member countries based on the principle of the socialist international division of labour - with intensive economic relations with non-member countries[3] and also - as explicitly determined in the recently amended Charter of the CMEA (1979) - with participation in the world division of labour.[4]

These principles represent a constant part of the policy of the CMEA and were confirmed at all the sessions of the CMEA Assembly - at the level of the heads of governments - in recent years, including the June 1980 Prague session whose Communiqué has once again

> reiterated the permanent efforts of the CMEA member countries to develop a co-operation with other countries in the interest of deepening the international division of labour on an equitable, equal and mutually advantageous basis as well as the readiness of the CMEA to extend, in the interests of peace and progress, a co-operation with countries that are not members of the CMEA and with international economic organisations.[5]

Steps taken by the CMEA to normalise relations with the EEC are therefore in logical accord with its general policy.

The CMEA functions and activities cover practically the entire area of economic life and the most various forms and methods of international co-operation in industry, agriculture, transport, foreign trade, etc.[6] Moreover, the CMEA is endowed with implied powers by an explicit clause of the Charter.[7] This stipulation of the Charter has acquired a special significance with the inclusion of socialist economic integration among the objectives of the Council.[8] The importance of this objective was correctly emphasised by G. Schiavone in the context of the CMEA-EEC negotiations.[9]

Unlike the EEC, however, the CMEA is not vested with supranational powers. In the CMEA, regulations that are self-executing on the territories of the member countries are quite exceptional. The only exceptions are the CMEA technical standards whose elaboration belongs to the exclusive jurisdiction of the CMEA and where no reservations are permitted. But even this case is not an example of the supranational competence of the CMEA since a government can reject a technical CMEA standard as a whole. The CMEA jurisdiction in this field is based on a special international convention.

Even in the past, however, there were no serious doubts about the power of the CMEA to conclude international agreements, judging by prevalent opinions. It can be documented by the views of Western authors as well. Thus, for instance, A. Uschakow, when dealing with the relations of the CMEA with international organisations, stated as early as 1962: 'Um diese Aufgaben wahrnehmen zu können, besitzt der Rat die völkerrechtliche Rechtspersönlichkeit'. He concludes that the CMEA 'nicht nur mit internationalen Organisationen, sondern auch mit Staaten völkerrechtliche Vereinbarungen treffen kann'. He notes: 'Hier scheint der RGW grössere Vollmachten als die Montanunion zu haben'.[10]

Similarly, J. Caillot came to a quite clear conclusion in this respect in 1971: 'Donc, que ce soit dans les rapports avec les Etats Tiers ou les autres organisations internationales et même avec ses propres membres, on peut dire que le CAEM possède le jus contrahendi. Il possède les attributs fondamentaux d'un sujet de droit international'.[11]

The same view is shared by A. Lebahn who claims that:

... a survey of the practice of external relations of the CMEA to third countries shows that already at the time of the validity of the 1959 Charter the CMEA concluded a number of agreements in terms of international law with, in part, very different contents. This confirms the thesis that the competence (Kompetenzanweisung) to conclude international agreements constituted a sufficient basis to conclude international agreements with third countries, while specific implementation was reserved to international practice of agreement conclusion and led to different types of agreements.[12]

In 1974 the treaty-making power of the CMEA in terms of international law was explicitly confirmed by Art. III para. 2b of the Charter, stipulating that 'the CMEA may enter into international agreements with member countries, with other countries and with international organisations'.[13]

G. Schiavone once again emphasised the importance of the quoted clauses. In connection with the contractual practice of the CMEA he had already written: 'In fact, CMEA appears to be endowed with international personality, even though to a limited extent. In particular, CMEA is competent to be a party to international treaties such as co-operation agreements with other international institutions and non-member states'.[14]

Even J. Brownlie believes that the CMEA - in the same way as the UN system and the EEC - belongs to those international organisations whose international legal personality seems to be beyond any doubt.[15]

The UN General Assembly accorded to CMEA the status of a permanent observer.[16] In the same way, the CMEA has the status of an observer or a consultative status even in other UN bodies.

In the contractual practice of the CMEA several patterns and models can be found, depending on the content of this or that agreement. The agreement can be concluded by the CMEA itself following a decision of its organs, if the agreement implies only the duties and commitments of the CMEA as an international organisation within the framework of the CMEA activity proper, and if the fulfilment of these duties and commitments does not require any special involvement of the member countries as such, that is such an involvement is limited to the performance of their duties as members of an organisation. As an example we might quote the agreement between Yugoslavia and the CMEA about the participation of Yugoslav representatives at the CMEA bodies; among the agreements concluded in full form with international organisations, mention should be made of the agreements with the International Atomic Energy Agency (IAEA) and the UN Environment Programme (UNEP).

It should be noted that the agreements concluded by the CMEA with third countries and international organisations require a decision of the respective organ of the CMEA (usually the Executive Committee) with the consent of the representatives of all CMEA member countries. If, however, a CMEA country is not interested in the CMEA activity in a given field or area, the agreement concluded by the CMEA with another international organisation does not require the consent of the respective country - as an example we might quote the agreement between the CMEA and the World Health Organisation (WHO).

If the agreement creates obligations not only for the CMEA as an international organisation but also for the CMEA member countries as such, the agreement may be concluded by the CMEA only with consent and a special approval by its member countries. Under the terms of the above procedure the member countries need not necessarily be the contracting parties. This legal form is properly used if the agreement covers an activity which has been entrusted to the CMEA by the member countries (e.g. organisation of multilateral international co-operation) and if the member countries are committed to duties connected with participation in this co-operation outside the normal CMEA bodies. As an example, agreements of the

CMEA with Finland, Iraq and Mexico could be quoted, whereby the CMEA member countries were bound by duties in connection with participation in newly established mixed bodies and their activities.

Naturally, this form could be used even in cases when the agreement concluded by the CMEA on the basis of a mandate by the member countries means additional duties for them. Such an arrangement is not unknown in international law.[17]

A second possible approach is that together with the CMEA the CMEA member countries also become contracting parties to the treaty; consequently, they would assume immediate obligations. If, on the CMEA side, the contracting parties are also the CMEA member countries, there can be no question of CMEA competence, nor is it necessary to specify how the competences (and, consequently, the obligations) are divided among the organisation and its member countries. After all, such an interpretation was presented by an author[18] who is well familiar - as far as we know - with the problems concerned and whose interpretation concerning the mixed agreements concluded collectively by the EEC and its member countries with third states would be taken as representative; in similar cases each of the participants is supposed to act within the limits of its competence.

III   MAIN ISSUES IN THE NEGOTIATIONS

If we were to characterise the existing state of the negotiations and the differences of approach between the two parties, we might say that the CMEA proposes to conclude a general framework agreement forming a basis for the relations between the member countries of the two integration entities as well as between the CMEA and the EEC as organisations and, finally, for the relations between each of these organisations and the member countries of the other organisation. In CMEA's view the proposed agreement should contain the basic mandatory principles of these relations and determine the areas and the mechanism of co-operation in the field of trade and economy, environment protection, standardisation, statistics, economic forecasts and other areas.

The CMEA takes into account the existing division of competences inside the EEC, and the position and the role of the Commission in the EEC structure. In due form, it respects also the specific features of the two integration organisations. Its proposal opens large prospects for further development of relations on the basis of equality.

On the other hand, the EEC is oriented rather towards the conclusion of an agreement of a technical character whose central point would be represented by a mutual information exchange. In the EEC proposals the commerce problems are conceived, as a matter of fact, only as a confirmation of its demand that the questions concerned be solved between the EEC as a whole on the one hand and the individual CMEA member countries on the other hand. The EEC proposals omit all the problems within the competence of the EEC member countries.

In the existing negotiations and their results, a degree of progress could be noted in some of the partial problems. From the very beginning of the talks there have been no doubts that it was a matter in compliance with Art. 228 of the Treaty of Rome, that is an agreement with negotiations led by the Commission and signed by the Council of European Communities. Although this fact was presented during a certain stage of the talks as a supplementary concession by the EEC, the correctness of the mentioned qualification is confirmed ab initio mainly by the fact that the EEC proposal of November 1976 had already been presented to the CMEA by the President of the Council of the EEC; it is also well known that such a qualification had already appeared when modalities were being clarified during the talks in September 1977.[19] Specific details might be divided into the following headings.

Contracting Parties to the CMEA-EEC Agreement

The CMEA proposal provides that the contracting parties shall be both the CMEA and the EEC, and all their member countries. Such an arrangement and solution would be most appropriate, taking into account some legal problems resulting from the fact that the treaty-making power of the CMEA is extremely broad, not, however, exclusive, but rather parallel to the member countries, while the treaty-making power of the EEC is, according to the Treaty of Rome, and even following the subsequent extensive practice, considerably narrower, since it is in some areas exclusive. The substance of the phenomenon was elucidated in an interesting way by E.T. Usenko.[20]

In matters of trade development the CMEA is endowed, without any doubt, with competence which can be documented by the respective clauses of the Charter[21] and by the stipulations of the Comprehensive Programme according to which '. . . the CMEA member countries shall co-ordinate their foreign economic policy for the purpose of normalising international trade and economic relations, notably of abolishing discrimination in that field'.[22] It can also be documented by another clause stating: 'The CMEA member countries shall organise and co-ordinate their activities in the implementation of the Comprehensive Programme primarily in the CMEA'.[23] This clause cannot be interpreted in a restrictive way as done by A. Lebahn,[24] especially not in relation to the CMEA draft-proposal of the agreement which is in exact compliance with the quoted clauses; one of the main objectives is a removal of any discrimination in international trade.

On the other hand, the CMEA does not examine or deal with questions of customs duties; it has not introduced any quantitative restrictions, etc. All the questions of customs duties, import controls or import licences, etc., are solved by the member countries individually and the tools of execution would remain in any event in the hands of the member countries.

From the point of view of the CMEA the simplest solution is if its member countries are contracting parties of the agreement as well. There are other reasons for the proposed solution as far as the EEC is concerned; there the competence for the trade problem solutions is mainly in the hands of the EEC. This, however, is not without exceptions.

Even some questions relating to trade policy in the general and broad sense of the word (e.g. a series of regulations and routine practice in the non-tariff area) or which are closely connected with the trade policy (financial and credit questions) remain in the competence of the EEC member countries.[25] A number of external economic relations are left outside the competence of the EEC, whose institutions are only now trying to acquire such a competence.[26]

The EEC member countries have still in their competence practically the whole area of economic co-operation (especially industrial, but also scientific and technological co-operation) as evidenced by a large number of agreements concluded in this field among the individual EEC and individual CMEA countries,[27] and even by special clauses included in the agreements concluded by the EEC with Canada[28] and the ASEAN countries.[29]

Hence, the participation of the EEC member countries as proposed by the CMEA was legally fully justified, especially by the fact that the CMEA proposal also comprised areas in the competence of the EEC member countries (i.e. financial and credit matters and the so-called 'trade-economic co-operation'). The trade-economic co-operation signified, in the first place, the trade (competence of the EEC), as well as the economic, industrial, scientific and technological co-operation, etc., remaining mainly in the competence of the EEC member countries.

The different competence delimitation of the EEC and the CMEA in relation to their member countries was therefore the main and rational reason why the CMEA proposed that the member countries of the two organisations should be contracting parties to the proposed agreement. The participation of the CMEA and the EEC member countries is also justified and explained by the politically exceptional importance of the agreement.

The EEC refused the participation of its members in the agreement during the whole course of the talks, although in other comparable cases its practice and approach were different. Thus the EEC member countries signed together with the EEC the two Lomé Conventions (1975 and 1979) with the countries of the African-Caribbean-Pacific area (ACP) containing a detailed settlement of the trade policy questions. In the same way the new agreement with Yugoslavia was signed in 1980. Other solutions are also known from the EEC practice: in March 1980 an agreement about co-operation between the EEC and a group of member countries of the Association of South East Asian Nations (ASEAN) was signed in the Malaysian capital of Kuala Lumpur. It is a so-called framework agreement determining the forms and conditions of multilateral relations in commercial and economic co-operation, science, technology, energy, environmental protection, transport, communications, etc. The agreement itself was not signed by the EEC member countries; they have, however, signed together with the EEC a programme declaration in addition to the agreement; the Declaration was also signed on behalf of the ASEAN and of all the ASEAN member countries.

The problem of the contracting parties to a CMEA-EEC agreement, however, cannot be assessed (as is apparent from the above facts) in an isolated way, but rather in connection with the substance and character of the agreement.

The composition of the contracting parties could also have an influence on some specific problems of the agreement, for example on the clause about the preservation of rights and duties resulting from other treaties concluded by the contracting parties; the respective clause and its text have been already agreed upon by the CMEA and EEC experts as one of the partial results of the negotiations conducted so far. Its legal content and impact, however, can be conceived in a different way depending on the identity of the contracting parties to the proposed agreement.

The Trade Policy Principles

It is generally known that the original proposal by the CMEA contained a relatively detailed regulation of the trade policy relations in eight out of the total of fifteen articles of the original CMEA proposal. During the negotiations and taking into account the comments by the EEC, the CMEA replaced six of these articles by only one. In that way the total structure of the CMEA draft proposal was considerably changed.

Among other things the CMEA proposals contain two important clauses: a demand for the application of the most-favoured-nation clause on the basis of the existing bilateral and multilateral treaties and agreements as well as treaties and agreements to be concluded in the future; and a demand for a removal of all kinds of obstacles, in the first place of the discriminatory ones, barring the development of trade in different types of goods, including agricultural products as well as the development of economic co-operation.

The EEC refused to apply the treatment according to the most-favoured-nation clause in the proposed agreement. In the first stage the refusal was total, later on the EEC was willing to introduce into the agreement an unbinding stipulation whereby the treatment according to the most-favoured-nation clause would be one of the questions to be taken into account when concluding bilateral trade policy agreements between the EEC as a whole and the individual CMEA member countries, very likely in combination with the so-called principle of effective reciprocity.

The Council of the EEC declared as early as November 1974 that it offered state-trading countries the most-favoured-nation clause when practically applying the uniform customs tariff. It is difficult to guess the reasons why the same principle could not be confirmed also in the contractual form.

When approaching the problems of international trade it has to be emphasised that the most-favoured-nation clause does not include and imply a material reciprocity. In accordance with a treaty comprising the most-favoured-nation clause, the contracting parties offer one another all the tariff reductions and alleviations offered either on the basis of an agreement or de facto to any third country. According to the most-favoured-nation clause, the partners are not distinguished and the clause and treatment are, therefore, without any discrimination whatsoever. The consequence of the most-favoured-nation clause is an extension of trade liberalisation.

The principle of effective reciprocity as proposed by the EEC to some CMEA member countries distinguishes partners and is therefore discriminatory. It is based on the material reciprocity of bilateral character and is supposed to guarantee 'the equality of advantages and commitments'.

It is beyond any doubt that the principle of the most-favoured-nation clause represents the best support to efforts aiming at an extension of co-operation in the field of commerce regardless of differences in the social systems.

It may be positively evaluated that the EEC - unlike its original standpoints - agreed during the negotiations that the agreement should include a point about the two organisations encouraging and assisting expansion of trade, service exchange and preparation of favourable conditions for such a co-operation; it does not yet mean, however, any specific and binding general and collective regulation of the trade policy principles - which is the objective and target of the CMEA efforts.

On the other hand, the regulation of the trade relations exclusively according to the model 'the EEC and individual CMEA countries' is disadvantageous for the socialist countries. Thus, for instance, some Western authors claim that such a solution would in fact create a serious imbalance of power in favour of the EEC.

The objection that the CMEA countries have never before regulated such problems collectively cannot be accepted as conclusive, since the CMEA member countries cannot be denied the right to regulate their external economic and trade relations on the basis of equality.

It is obvious at the same time, that the EEC is capable of finding an adequate solution to the problems raised by collective agreements with rather heterogeneous and more loosely interconnected groups of countries than the CMEA member countries. [30]

Economic Co-operation

The above diversity of approaches is valid also in the field of economic co-operation which the EEC also refuses to include in the proposed collective agreement. In this respect the comment by T. Morganti is quite interesting; the author claims that the EEC jurisdiction in this field is still excluded and that the individual EEC countries 'have retained their sovereignty in signing bilateral co-operation treaties with third countries and especially the CMEA members'.[31] It would therefore be necessary to consider 'the hypothesis of establishing, in an EEC-CMEA agreement, the same procedure . . . adopted within the EEC for the consultation on programmes of co-operation'.[32]

In the field of economic co-operation a danger is seen from time to time for the EEC in the form of 'the principle of bilateralism' which the EEC 'is trying to remove'. It is underlined that there are no binding regulations for bilateral economic relations. The EEC and the member countries do not have any obligations in this respect with the exception of mutual information and consultation (since 1974).[33]

The EEC experts refused in Geneva, March 1980, to accept the participation of the EEC member countries in the agreement, because they claimed that the EEC proposal did not include questions concerning the competence of the member countries of the EEC and that the EEC was not intending to regulate these questions in an agreement with the CMEA.

Further Contractual Instruments

As an additional comment to the previous remarks it should be noted that it follows already from the CMEA proposal of February 1976 that, in the view of the CMEA, the agreement should have a binding, but only framework form, and that it should neither formally nor substantially replace the agreements concluded between the individual countries, members of the CMEA and the EEC, nor the agreements which are going to be concluded between the individual CMEA member countries and the EEC as a whole, or between the individual EEC member countries and the CMEA as a whole. In the Communiqué of the 87th session of the CMEA Executive Committee in autumn 1978 this principle was reaffirmed.

Such an approach by the CMEA corresponds to the basic demand of the EEC to have direct contractual relations with individual CMEA member countries in the areas of EEC competence.

Mechanism of the Execution of the Agreement and the Consultations between the Parties

The CMEA proposal includes the establishment of a joint body composed of the representatives of the two organisations and of all their member countries surveying the observance of the agreement and looking for ways how to extend the co-operation. It follows from the text of the CMEA proposal that the proposed mixed commission does not change the existence and competence of bilateral commissions already established by individual CMEA member countries and EEC member countries. The CMEA and its member countries consider that even in the future the traditional well-proven bilateral relations between the member countries of the two organisations will continue in matters of their competence.

The EEC refuses the establishment of such a mixed body, claiming it cannot imagine its real content of work. The EEC mentions its apprehension that in this way trade policy matters might be brought to a multilateral level.

The EEC, however, has a different approach to the problems of mixed bodies when dealing, for instance, with the Association of South East Asian Nations (ASEAN) and the countries of the African-Caribbean-Pacific area (ACP).

T. Morganti recommends the establishment of a Joint Commission, in order to achieve the goals established by the EEC-CMEA.[34] He also proposes the work content for the 'Joint Commission' and divides the body into five subcommissions. Concrete work content of the Joint Commission would have still to be settled in detailed talks. Its establishment, however, would be advantageous both for the CMEA and for the EEC.

The EEC did not even give approval for providing in the agreement for regular consultations between the parties, although this form is quite common in international co-operation.

The need for consultations between the parties is strongly felt even by the Western experts as can be documented by T. Morganti's idea of establishing mutual permanent missions exchanged by the EEC and the CMEA. [35]

Problem of the International Legal Recognition of the EEC by the CMEA and the CMEA Member Countries

The question of the recognition of the EEC should be mentioned in this respect; it has a special significance for the EEC. The EEC is not only an international organisation but also a supranational entity. The entities of a supranational character, however, go beyond the framework of the common international law and therefore require a special recognition.

There is no doubt that the EEC has achieved a relatively broad recognition in the world including diplomatic recognition. This recognition, however, is not complete, and the absence of recognition by the socialist countries in particular represents a serious gap. We have in mind a formal legal recognition of the EEC institutions and competence and a diplomatic recognition; on the other hand, the EEC has quite certainly achieved a recognition de facto by the CMEA and its member countries - be it in the form of explicit declarations or conclusive acts.

It was sometimes believed in the past that the CMEA and the CMEA member countries had a negative or evasive attitude towards the EEC de jure recognition,[36] but as a matter of fact, the CMEA had already expressed its willingness to recognise the EEC in its original proposal of February 1976.[37] In the course of subsequent negotiations the CMEA several times reconfirmed this willingness - when looking for an overall solution and arrangement - for instance in the presentation and evaluation of compromise formulations of those clauses which were somehow related to the EEC competence.

A satisfactory agreement between the CMEA and the EEC would therefore be a significant factor even in this area so important to the EEC, since it could lead to a general recognition of the EEC by the socialist countries and thus contribute to a universal EEC recognition. On the other hand, it may be concluded that the CMEA does not legally need recognition by the EEC or by the EEC member countries, because the CMEA is not a supranational entity and its international legal subjectivity in all its implications reflects the erga omnes principle as shown by E.T.Usenko.[38]

IV SUMMARY AND CONCLUSIONS

There are many reasons in favour of a conclusion of a CMEA-EEC agreement on the basis of equality. It is in the interests of all the participants to achieve a mutually acceptable solution. As long ago as 1976 G. Schiavone wrote:

The significant dissimilarities, both formal and substantial, between EEC and CMEA do not seem to be such as to preclude negotiations and eventually the conclusion of an agreement on mutual relations. After a rather long period of reciprocal cold-shouldering, an orderly and mutually beneficial relationship is regarded by both parties as a decisive step towards the achievement of the goals set forth in the Helsinki Summit Declaration.[39]

The idea that mutual communication, co-operation and commitment is possible and feasible only for entities that conform with each other in all respects is unrealistic in the condition of the modern world and quite certainly absurd from the point of view of peaceful coexistence.[40]

Major political significance is attributed to the proposed agreement in the West as well:

The political importance, in terms of détente and security, requires, in fact, an initial basic multilateral agreement in order to establish a general framework of principles and rules within the individual countries of the EEC and of the CMEA which are left to organize their mutual commercial transactions.

It is generally admitted that the advantage of bargaining collectively the terms of the treaty and of the future common guidelines for an external commercial policy is equally relevant for both the EEC and the CMEA.

As G. Schiavone says, in the West it is usually claimed that mutual commerce between the CMEA and EEC countries is more important for the CMEA countries. On the other hand, the advantage of mutual trade exchanges between the socialist and capitalist countries is generally recognised. For different political and economic reasons, however, the official policy of most of the capitalist countries does not lead towards a removal of the existing obstacles and barriers in East-West relations.

The exports of the socialist countries to the West are negatively influenced by strong protectionist policies and severe quantitative restrictions. But the socialist countries do have considerable possibilities of increasing their exports. The Western countries are also interested in getting energy supplies from the socialist countries.[41]

Next to this global view of the problems of trade between the two organisations it should be added that the role of the CMEA member countries in the EEC trade would be even more tangible if we analysed in more detail the structure of this trade and its proportion in individual fields and branches.

Moreover, observers notice correctly the future possibilities of a closer co-operation between the countries of Western and Eastern Europe. Thus G. Schiavone comes to the conclusion that:

> The present extent of intra-European specialization is far from being appropriate to the economic, scientific and technological potential of the countries concerned; the failure to recognize and to make full use of the complementarities existing between West and East European natural, industrial and human resources will be of benefit to neither side in the long run.[42]

Gradually, the West has begun to accept the importance of the Soviet proposals to convene all-European conferences on energy, transport and environment. 'Apart from their broader political implications, these specific proposals seem to deserve careful consideration and should not be regarded merely as an expression of the Soviet and East European pressing need to get access to Western technology'.[43]

As the experience of détente showed for a number of capitalist countries, trade and co-operation between East and West represent an important counterbalance to the chaos of the crisis and the US economic hegemonism.

The Western mass media and specialised press admit that the approach of the EEC and especially of the EEC Commission to talks with the CMEA was always conditioned by extremely complex and very often controversial legal, political and prestige considerations. On the one hand lack of competence was attributed to the CMEA, on the other hand fear was expressed about the extension of this competence.

The EEC approaches reflect quite outspoken efforts to differen-
tiate in commercial policy with individual socialist countries. A
differentiated approach is motivated mainly by political reasons; it
should contribute to an appearance of divergent tendencies inside the
CMEA. An undifferentiated trade policy is said to increase the
dependence of the smaller CMEA countries on the Soviet Union and
to prevent economic reforms in these countries.[44]

In the past we also came across statements that one of the reasons
why the EEC refuses the CMEA proposal is a different evaluation by
the EEC of the real interests of the smaller CMEA countries than is
reflected by the CMEA proposal.[45]

Such a claim, however, is not likely to be successfully defended,
since stipulations and principles like non-discrimination and an uncon-
ditional application of most-favoured-nation treatment are, in the
first place, in the interests of the smaller and medium-sized CMEA
member countries, whose diversified structure of trade with the West
requires a similar regime. The same can be said about the CMEA
proposals - very moderately worded - in the field of trade in
agricultural products.

At the same time a differentiated trade policy tends to an
acquisition or consolidation of unilateral advantages in relation to the
socialist countries and to emphasised discriminatory positions to
some of them.[46]

In the West, the necessity of a 'uniform strategy' is often talked
about in relation to socialist countries. This is valid not only for the
field of politics, but also in economy and commerce. The requirement
for a togetherness of the EEC is often quoted. In connection with the
proposed CMEA-EEC agreement, it has been noted that a
multilateral treaty with an international organisation like the CMEA
requires a good degree of integration and cohesion among the 'Nine'
in order to elaborate a successful Common Commercial Policy
towards the East, and this would be a great advantage for the EEC
institutions.

It is quite natural that the CMEA member countries, confronted
with the common commercial policy of the EEC and its efforts to
strengthen it even more, should consider it necessary to protect their
interests by a collective action and attitude which might provide
them with at least the basic standard of a commercial regime. For
that reason, the CMEA countries regard the conclusion of trade
agreements limited to the scheme 'EEC-individual CMEA countries'
as dangerous for their interests.[47]

This solution as proposed by the EEC would mean not only a
cancellation of equality in the relations between the CMEA and the
EEC, but could also be misused for political and economic pressure
against individual socialist countries. In this respect, the socialist
countries consistently apply the principle of equality to be found in
the multi- and bilateral relations between the East and West.

Progress in negotiations depends on the readiness and good will of the two parties. With good will an agreement can be reached, significantly contributing to a development of equal and advantageous relations between the two organisations and their member countries. By arranging and normalising their relations to the CMEA and its member countries the EEC and its member countries could accomplish in practice important objectives emphasised in the preamble to the Treaty of Rome: to remove barriers dividing Europe as well as restrictions in foreign exchanges.

At the press conference about the results of the XXXIV meeting of the Assembly of the CMEA in Prague, June 1980, the CMEA Secretary, N. Faddeev, stated it was not the responsibility of the CMEA that no agreement had been concluded on co-operation in basic trade, political and economic questions. He added that the EEC would like to conclude agreements with individual CMEA member countries but had refused under various formal pretexts the conclusion of an agreement with the CMEA as an entity, although the EEC had concluded agreements of this kind with the ASEAN and similar economic groupings. But such an approach could not be accepted because it would mean a violation of the principle of equality and an exposure of the CMEA countries to discrimination. Instead of that the EEC offered agreements in the fields of statistics and standardisation which, after all, do not represent the most significant aspects of co-operation between the integration groupings. On that occasion N. Faddeev declared that the CMEA was ready to conclude an agreement on co-operation in areas of basic importance.[48]

It can be only hoped that the EEC will also show a similar constructive approach; the Vice-President of the Commission of the EEC in his letter of March 1980 addressed to the Secretary of the CMEA, where he proposed to delay the high-level negotiations scheduled for April 1980, appreciated positively the work of the experts of the two sides during a drafting meeting in Geneva, March 1980, and confirmed in the conclusion of his letter the willingness of the EEC to sign an agreement whose significance had been already emphasised by the two parties and which should, as W. Haferkamp underlined, facilitate new prospects of co-operation.[49]

The countries of the CMEA are highly interested in détente, they are deeply devoted to the idea of peaceful coexistence and co-operation and they are also ready to do all they can for its implementation. It can be hardly expected, however, that these countries would intend to 'conclude an agreement at any cost' or that they could accept clauses giving unilateral advantage to the other partner or even worsening the existing trade-political position of the CMEA member countries.[50]

NOTES

1. A detailed legal comparison is presented by V.I. Kuznetsov, SEV i

'Obshchii rynok' (Moscow 1978).

2. Le Monde, 30 - 31 March 1980, p. 16. Also Neue Zürcher Zeitung, 2 April 1980, p. 10.

3. In the preamble to the CMEA Charter the member countries declare explicitly: '. . . reaffirming their readiness to enter into economic relations with all countries, irrespective of their social and political systems on the basis of equality, mutual advantage and noninterference in internal affairs . . . '. Charter of the Council for Mutual Economic Assistance (as amended by Protocols of 21 June 1974 and 28 June 1979), CMEA Secretariat, Moscow, 1980.
   Similarly, in an important document drafted by the XV meeting of the Assembly of the CMEA (1961) and approved by the June 1962 Summit of the CMEA member countries, it is stated that 'the International Socialist Division of Labour is shaped with an eye to the world-wide division of labour'. Basic Principles of International Socialist Division of Labour, CMEA Secretariat, Moscow 1962, p. 9.
   In the same way it is established among the fundamental principles of the socialist integration: 'In accordance with their policy of peaceful co-existence, and in the interests of social progress, and also because the international socialist division of labour is effected with due account taken of the world division of labour, the CMEA member countries shall continue to develop economic, scientific and technological ties with other countries irrespective of their social and political system, on principles of equality, mutual advantage and respect for sovereignty'. Comprehensive Programme for Further Extension and Improvement of Co-operation and Development of Socialist Economic Integration by the CMEA member countries, CMEA Secretariat, Moscow 1971, Chapter I, para. 3, p. 15.

4. Article III, para. 1 (b) of the Charter reads: 'the Council for Mutual Economic Assistance shall . . . promote the improvement of the international socialist division of labour by . . . specialisation and co-operation in production between member countries of the CMEA with due regard for the world division of labour'.

5. Rudé Právo, 20 June 1980.

6. See Charter of the CMEA, Art. III, para. 1.

7. Charter of the CMEA, Art. II para. 1 (f): 'the taking of such other actions as may be required in pursuit of the purposes of the CMEA'.

8. Charter of the CMEA, Art. 1, para. 1.

9. G. Schiavone, 'The EEC-COMECON Dialogue: Towards a Recognition of Realities in Europe?', La Comunità Internazionale, No. 2, 1976, pp. 311-20.

10. A. Uschakow, Der Rat für Gegenseitige Wirtschaftshilfe (Köln, 1962) p. 55.

11. J. Caillot, Le C.A.E.M. - Aspects juridiques et formes de coopération économique entre les pays socialistes (Paris, 1971)

p. 118.
12. A. Lebahn, Sozialistische Wirtschaftsintegration und Ost-West-Handel im sowjetischen internationalen Recht (Berlin (West), 1976) pp. 380-1.
13. Art. III was completed in this way by the Protocol signed in Sofia, 21 June 1974. See also the CMEA Charter, Moscow, 1980.
14. G. Schiavone, 'The EEC-COMECON Dialogue', op. cit., p. 315.
15. J. Brownlie, Principles of Public International Law (Russian Edn.), Part 2 (Moscow 1977) p. 411.
16. Resolution No. 3209 (XXIX).
17. See J. Brownlie, Principles of Public International Law (Russian Edn.), Part 2 (Moscow 1977) pp. 424-5; P. Pescatore, 'Les relations extérieures des Communautés Européennes', 103 Hague Recueil 1961, II, pp. 112-14; H. de Fiumel, 'On the scope of intended agreement between the CMEA and the EEC', Państwo i prawo (English Summary), Warsaw, No. 11, 1978; E.T. Usenko, 'O dogovornoi kompetentsii SEV', Sovetskoe gosudarstvo i pravo, Moscow, No. 6, 1979.
18. P. Pescatore, Le droit de l'intégration (Leyden-Geneva, 1972) p. 47.
19. See A. Kohout, 'On the verge of talks between the CMEA and EEC', Zahraniční obchod, Prague, No. 1, 1979 (Czech text).
20. E.T. Usenko, op.cit., p. 105.
21. Charter of the CMEA, Art. III, para. 1 (d): '. . . (the CMEA) shall . . . assist the member countries . . . in the expansion of commodity trade and exchange of services among the member countries and between them and other countries'.
22. Comprehensive Programme, Chapter I, Sect. 1, para. 3.
23. Comprehensive Programme, Chapter IV, Sect. 16, para. 2.
24. A. Lebahn, Sozialistische Wirtschaftsintegration, op.cit., p. 385.
25. See for a more detailed analysis: V.I. Kuznetsov, 'SEV-EES: vozmozhnosti sotrudnichestva', Sovetskoe gosudarstvo i pravo, No. 4, 1978.
26. See for instance V.I. Kuznetsov, SEV i 'Obshchii rynok', op.cit., especially p. 175 and the following pages.
27. See A. Kohout, 'Efforts for an arrangement between the CMEA and the EEC continue', Zahraniční obchod, Prague, No. 7, 1978 (Czech text).
28. Art. III, para. 4.
29. Art. 3, para. 3.
30. See: 'About the negotiations concerning a regulation of relations between the CMEA and EEC', Zahranicni obchod, Prague, No. 4, 1980 (Czech text).
31. T. Morganti, 'Blueprint for an EEC-CMEA Framework Agreement', in this volume, p. 156.
32. Ibid., p. 156.
33. F. Franzmeyer, 'Zum Stand der wirtschaftspolitischen Beziehungen zwischen RGW and EG', Europa Archiv, 1, 1977.

34. T. Morganti, op.cit., pp. 165-7.
35. 'The EEC and the CMEA could agree on the exchange of permanent representatives with their offices at the Commission of the EEC in Brussels and at the CMEA Secretariat in Moscow. This would create a permanent basis for direct consultations between the two organisations'. T. Morganti, op.cit., p. 162. Some of Morganti's other ideas concerning mutual participation in the sessions of some of the CMEA or EEC bodies go too far and from the point of view of the two parties concerned are not likely to be regarded as realistic and useful.
36. Thus, for instance, F. Franzmeyer, op.cit., p. 12, says: '. . . die Vertragsexegeten in Brüssel meinen die RGW-Länder wollten einmal mehr die Annerkennungs frage umgehen and nur die Realität einse losen Zusammenschlusses von Staaten gelten lassen'.
37. Art. 1 provides: Le présent Accord établit des relations officielles entre le CAEM et la CEE. (Quoted from an unofficial translation.)
38. E.T. Usenko, op.cit., pp. 100-1.
39. G. Schiavone, 'The EEC-COMECON Dialogue', op.cit., p. 320.
40. A. Kohout, 'On proposals to arrange mutual relations between the CMEA and the EEC', Zahraniční obchod, Prague, No. 7, 1976 (Czech text).
41. G. Schiavone, 'The Implications of Economic Reforms in Eastern Europe for the Future of East-West Relations', in Economic Reforms in Eastern Europe and Prospects for the 1980s (Oxford: Pergamon Press, 1981) pp. 287, 290-1.
42. Ibid., p. 288.
43. Ibid., p. 292.
44. See, for instance, A. Lebahn, 'RGW und EG - Faktoren des Ost-West-Handels', Aussenpolitik, No. 2, 1978, pp. 126, 129; F. Franz-meyer, op.cit., p. 16.
45. See F. Franzmeyer, op.cit., p. 12: '. . . Es dürfte zweitens aus der Rüchsichtnahme auf die kleineren RGW-Länder resultieren, deren wirkliche Interessenanlage die Gemeinschaft anders einschätzt als sie durch den Vertragsentwurf vertreten wird'.
46. See F. Franzmeyer, op.cit., pp. 12-15.
47. See O. Bogomolov, 'Ekonomicheskie svyazi mezhdu sotsialisticheskimi i kapitalisticheskimi stranami', Mirovaia ekonomika i mezhdunarodnye otnoshenia, No. 3, 1980, p. 50.
48. Rudé Právo, 21 June 1980, p. 1.
49. See: 'On negotiations about the arrangement of relations between the CMEA and EEC', Zahraniční obchod, Prague, No. 4, 1980 (Czech text).
50. For instance Czechoslovakia has been from the very beginning a full contracting party to GATT; other CMEA member countries joined GATT later on. A number of member countries have arranged their trade-political principles in bilateral agreements with Western countries. Such an agreement - and this has to be

correctly understood - would be unacceptable not only for economic reasons and for basic political principles, but because it would damage a genuine expansion of trade and other forms of peaceful economic relations.

12 Blueprint for an EEC–CMEA Framework Agreement

TULLIO MORGANTI

Doctor of Law, Milan

The purpose of this study is that of defining the basis on which an EEC-CMEA agreement can be signed in order to establish successfully a multilateral framework of rules among East and West European countries in the fields of trade and co-operation. The aim is not, however, that of describing the historical evolution of the EEC-CMEA negotiations; on the contrary, the draft of a formal treaty, which the EEC and the CMEA could conceivably sign together, will be introduced.

The existence of a certain degree of institutional asymmetry between the EEC and the CMEA can be considered as the primary source of obstacles to the final achievement of a formal treaty on trade and co-operation. As a matter of fact the conclusion of a formal agreement mainly depends on a clear definition of the treaty-making power with which both the EEC and the CMEA are endowed. In view of drafting a framework agreement it will be necessary to consider some institutional improvements which the CMEA especially must undertake. In this respect it will be indispensable to reinforce the procedures of implementation of the CMEA resolutions and to further the implementation of those mechanisms of integration that the CMEA has recently adopted. It will also be necessary, on the EEC side, to provide the Commission with more effective powers of control in the field of economic co-operation. These preliminary measures for the formation of an EEC-CMEA framework agreement must not be based on the introduction of radical reforms which could disrupt the economic and political equilibria existing within both the EEC and the CMEA.

I THE EEC TREATY-MAKING POWER

The progressive adoption of institutional and economic mechanisms, aimed at creating an Economic Union among the EEC countries, has provided the European Community with a high degree of integration. This becomes a particularly relevant element as far as the EEC treaty-making power is concerned. A concrete framework of economic relations is in fact required for the successful achievement of commercial agreements with any third international subject. As a result of this reality, Articles 19 and 113 of the Treaty of Rome become fully effective in granting to the EEC a common external commercial policy on behalf of its member countries.

As a direct consequence of the creation of a Customs Union and in view of the setting of measures of Common Commercial Policy (CCP) the EEC has adopted a Common External Tariff (CET) which results from the arithmetical average of duties applied in the four customs territories of the Community.[1] Against the definition of the CET as a device aimed at reinforcing the trade-discriminating and protective character of the EEC it is possible to oppose the analysis of the norms of GATT. The existence of a CET among the 'Nine' is not contrasting with Article XXIV of GATT since no other barriers but tariffs (negotiable) have been erected between the Community and third countries.[2] In addition, the flows of traded goods between the Community and third parties can be increased, in quantitative terms, and qualitatively improved by the fact that the CET provides a level of tariffs no higher than the general incidence of the national tariffs of the 'Nine'.[3] Finally, the possibility of having reduced rates for selected goods or at least duty-free imports for individual members of the Community and in particular circumstances, indicates a high degree of flexibility.

The feared protective results that such a mechanism could entail are less than could be expected. On the contrary, the CET provides easier conditions for the conduct of negotiations on tariff reduction between a multilateral unit like the Community and other trading partners. The EEC in this respect has full jurisdiction in negotiating the terms of the CET and referring to it in an eventual agreement with the CMEA.

On the ground of the common link represented by the CET the 'Nine' can easily co-ordinate, through the EEC Commission, a Common Commercial Policy toward third countries or international organisations. As a result of the setting of this supranational mechanism the Commission has been provided with the full competence of negotiating the terms of the CCP on behalf of the 'Nine'. The treaty with the CMEA is certainly feasible in light of this competence of the EEC institutions. According to Article 113 of the Treaty of Rome the treaty-making power of the Community, vis-à-vis an agreement with the CMEA, will allow the EEC Commission to establish measures of trade liberalisation for imports from the CMEA area, for the progressive reduction of trade tariffs on East European imports and for the control against the disruptive effects of dumping and exports subsidisation which frequently affect East-West trade.

One of the fields in which the EEC-CMEA agreement could give satisfactory results for both the contracting organisations is that of trade in the agricultural sector. The Common Agricultural Policy (CAP) of the EEC is the most effective instrument of sectorial integration in the hands of the Community. It is also true that a very high degree of protectionism is behind the mechanism of the CAP. The existence of compensatory duties and quantitative restrictions which particularly affect the imports of agricultural goods from the CMEA area could confirm the presence of an actual trade discrimination operated by the EEC. The framework agreement will aim at working out the proper measures which can meet the requirements of the export-oriented policies of the CMEA members in the agricultural sector and the protectionist policy of the EEC. The EEC is vested with the full competence of negotiating the terms of the CAP on behalf of its members. In the eventuality of an EEC-CMEA agreement this will become possible if the CMEA is able to reciprocate any liberalisation with well-co-ordinated measures of prices policy for the agricultural goods which are to be exported.

The elaboration of a Common Industrial Policy (CIP) of the EEC is still, unfortunately, a goal to achieve rather than an effective instrument of economic integration. The several branches into which the industrial sector is subdivided, and the conflicting interests of the 'Nine', make difficult the co-ordination of common measures for regulating imports and exports of manufactured goods. The main goal of an EEC-CMEA agreement is that of reducing the quantitative restrictions which, in both groups, hinder the flow of industrial goods, and of securing an acceptable base of prices and quality for the East European products. Several problems, however, adversely affect the elaboration of common policies and effective intergovernmental rules in this field of trade. The difficult comparison between the EEC and the CMEA prices for industrial goods, the structural economic changes that in both areas would be required for more liberalised flows of trade, and, finally, the practice of countertrade which is secretly, or openly, part of the East-West co-operation programmes, represent obstacles against which the EEC and the CMEA have to struggle by reinforcing their own areas of competence. The EEC, after undertaking the exclusive jurisdiction of the ECSC, is theoretically fully competent for negotiating measures of industrial policy with the CMEA.

Besides the limits of the EEC competences which are listed in Article 113 of the Treaty of Rome, there are other fields in which the EEC can operate with full jurisdiction.[4] The export-credit policy is one of these fields according to the interpretation of the Court of Justice of the EC. The Community can, in fact, regulate the individual states' credit policies, co-ordinate a common policy in this field and negotiate it with third countries. It is true that the effective implementation of these measures is dependent on how the EEC competence will prevail over the resistance of the 'Nine' which are competing among themselves for extending to third countries the most advantageous credits, in spite of the 1977 guidelines adopted by the EC Council. The possibility is not excluded, therefore, that the Commission will be able to include in its negotiations with the CMEA some rules which will introduce a regulation in the EEC credit policy towards the CMEA countries.

A delicate question, practically relevant, is that concerning the EEC competence in concluding co-operation agreements with third international subjects. The EEC jurisdiction in this field is still excluded and the individual EEC countries have retained their sovereignty in signing bilateral co-operation treaties with third countries and especially the CMEA members. In 1975 the EEC Council of Ministers adopted an information and consultation procedure according to which the Commission and the 'Nine' inform each other, through periodical consultations, about the commitments and measures planned in the framework of the signed bilateral treaties. The objectives of such a procedure are to make sure that the co-operation agreements conform to the CCP, to co-ordinate the actions of the member states and to assess the value of measures that the Community might adopt to encourage further co-operation.[5] It is not unusual for these intergovernmental agreements to be frequently geared to circumvent the EEC CCP by including real external trade concessions.[6] It is, therefore, necessary to consider the hypothesis of establishing, in an EEC-CMEA agreement, the same procedure which is adopted within the EEC for the consultation on programmes of co-operation. This would not automatically extend the full competence, in this matter, to the EEC but could create a framework of contacts in which the development of co-operation would become multilaterally well co-ordinated.

II THE CMEA TREATY-MAKING POWER

It is difficult to define, in precise terms, the limits of the treaty-making power of the CMEA. It is therefore important to try to outline such a competence from the experience of the intergovernmental activity of the entire organisation. For this purpose it is necessary to avoid relying on any type of comparative analysis of the CMEA with other similar existing international organisations. The CMEA is not provided with any mechanism of integration resembling the multilateral CCP of the Community. In addition, the system of bilateral relations is still prevailing over multilateralism among the East European countries. The Charter of the CMEA, then, does not define the matters with which the organisation can deal in the case of international talks or agreements. The exclusive competence of the CMEA countries in conducting foreign commercial relations and the double procedure of recommendation and ratification of the resolutions, adopted by the organisation, make the eventual agreement signed by the CMEA not bound to have a uniform implementation by all the member countries. All these apparent obstacles create some pessimism on the side of the European Community. This, however, does not exclude for the CMEA the possibility of signing international agreements on trade and co-operation. The existence, within the CMEA framework, of mechanisms and instruments, aimed at developing the powers of this organisation, indirectly provides the limits of the CMEA jurisdiction in its treaty-making activity.

The process of economic integration, which has been undertaken by the CMEA countries, is mainly based on the principles of co-ordination of economic plans and intergovernmental co-operation.[7] As a consequence the CMEA countries are acting as sovereign political entities, and as exclusive owners of their nationalised means of production, in the conduct of international/bilateral or inter-regional/multilateral trade relations.[8] Through this activity of co-ordination the CMEA determines the general conditions leading to a progressive integration of the socialist economies. In this context the CMEA can only negotiate, with third countries, the possibility of creating propitious conditions for the establishment of those structural and economic measures which would allow the creation of effective interregional/multilateral trade relations. In other words it is unjustifiable to expect that the CMEA will be a fully competent partner in negotiating tariff reductions, payment policies, price policies or other measures on a basis of strict reciprocity with the EEC. The CMEA can, however, commit itself to securing the adoption of institutional adjustments which can give, within the limits imposed by the socialist economic system, a satisfactory margin of reciprocity to the commercial advantages extended by the EEC. It is possible to define the limits of competence of the CMEA from what is stated by Article III of the CMEA Charter which confers on the organisation the tasks of:

(i)   organisation of programmes of technical and scientific co-operation in view of more rational allocation of resources;
(ii) improvement of the international socialist division of labour through the co-ordination of economic plans;
(iii) co-ordination of common programmes in the agricultural, industrial and transportation sectors and improvement of the exchanges of goods and commodities among the CMEA countries and between these and third countries outside the CMEA.

This indicates the primary role which physical plans, and their co-ordination, play in the strategy of integration of the CPEs, among which any measure of trade liberalisation entails the quantitative balancing of imports/exports planned quotas with little consideration for any form of tariff reductions. As a consequence of this the EEC-CMEA negotiations will be essentially concentrated on the balanced reduction of tariffs (on the EEC side) versus the reduction of quantitative restrictions (on the CMEA side).

The accomplishment of the tasks indicated by Article III of the CMEA Charter will bring as a result a more rational allocation of resources and a clearer multilateral view on the planned individual priorities and needs, in terms of imports and exports, of the CMEA countries. Through a comprehensive scheme of the harmonised foreign commercial policies of the CMEA members it will be possible for the EEC to negotiate the terms of its trade liberalisation programmes with the CMEA area. The goal of granting diversified and increasing imports from the EEC can be attained by the CMEA only through the implementation of the measures indicated by the 'Comprehensive Programme' of 1971. This will be essential for the extension by the EEC to the CMEA area of the Most-Favoured-Nation (MFN) treatment as it already exists for some of the East European countries which are members of GATT.

In view of its international activity the CMEA has started, in the last decade, an important programme of reforms and improvements which have, consequently, strengthened its internal efficiency and organisational framework. The idea of a more co-ordinated policy, achievable through a clear programme of co-operation, lies at the origins of the principles contained in the 'Comprehensive Programme'.

In particular the 'Programme' has proposed that the CMEA members undertake to co-ordinate their long-term and five-year plans more carefully; that they elaborate joint prognoses on major economic aggregates; that they actually engage in joint planning for the production and consumption of selected products; and that they conduct regular exchanges of information on the nature of economic reforms in their respective countries.[9]

Several changes in the CMEA have promoted the attainment of the 'Programme'. The International Investment Bank (IIB) had begun its operations with the purpose of financing investments of interest of more than one CMEA member and of financing large CMEA-wide investment projects connected with the 'Programme'.[10] Several committees on co-operation have been set up and it is important to note the role which could be played by the CMEA 'Co-operation Committee on Planning' and the 'Co-operation Committee on Science and Technology'. According to the CMEA Charter, the committees can assign tasks to the Standing Commissions as well as submit proposals to the Assembly and to the Executive Committee.[11] A new 'Co-operation Committee on Material and Technical Supply' was added in 1974 in order to improve the CMEA framework. In 1972 the Executive Committee approved the 'Organisational, methodological, economic and legal principles concerning the technical-scientific co-operation among the members of the CMEA and its organs'.[12] This important document (158 articles) is mainly aimed at regulating the different aspects of technical-scientific co-operation with the purpose of eliminating the prevailing role played by bilateralism.[13] This is an important step toward a new flexible multilateral framework of relations among the CMEA countries and, eventually, other economic areas. The Executive Committee of the CMEA then approved the 'Standard Rules on the Conditions for the Establishment and Activity of the International Economic Organisations in the CMEA countries'.[14] This document is aimed at regulating the activity of the so-called 'multinationals' of the socialist bloc.

The Executive Committee has also reviewed the principles and general conditions of external trade and has begun to set new rules concerning this matter. Substantial reforms, of a predominantly normative character, have also been implemented through the revision of the Charter in 1974. In order to reinforce the institutional framework of the CMEA, and to extend its range of competences, the 1974 amendments of the Charter modified Article III(b), para. 2, which states that the CMEA can sign international agreements with its member countries, third countries and international organisations. Article XII (formerly Article XI) states, then, that the CMEA can have direct diplomatic relations with the organs of the UN and its specialised international organisations.[15] According to the new Article XI the CMEA can invite non-member countries to participate in the activity of the organisation and sign agreements with it. It is possible therefore to consider the hypothesis of applying this norm also to future EEC-CMEA relations.

In light of the above mentioned reforms, and of the not completely implemented programmatic rules of the Charter and of the 'Programme', it is possible to state that, as far as the CMEA is concerned, there is, in principle, a strong legal possibility of reaching an agreement signed by the CMEA countries, within the framework of the CMEA and through its diplomatic mediation, with the EEC. In order to translate such a theoretical possibility into reality, some details must be settled and some additional reforms must be accomplished. This would entail a meeting of the formal and substantial requirements necessary to induce a partner, like the EEC, to accept the CMEA as an equal counterpart. At least it is possible to say that the CMEA has already met the majority of the requirements necessary to conclude agreements with any of the international subjects. What will remain for the CMEA is to give a more concrete base to such an open possibility by using the existing common and intergovernmental institutions and implementing the economic and political programmes of integration.

III THE EEC-CMEA FRAMEWORK AGREEMENT

Previous experience of the EEC and CMEA in concluding international agreements with third countries indicates that these two organisations have a general inclination to sign different types of treaties. While the EEC has a tendency to conclude exclusively commercial agreements, with the only exceptions of the Lomé Convention and the EEC-Yugoslavia agreement, which include clauses on co-operation, the CMEA always prefers to sign co-operation pacts. The final EEC-CMEA treaty could be a mixed type of agreement in which commercial and co-operation issues could be equally included. The final document, then, should be based on a policy of 'non-strict' reciprocity[16] according to which the EEC negotiators should not insist on full reverse liberalisation measures, on the side of the CMEA countries, because of the structural bottlenecks created by the system of central planning. Stricter reciprocity will be expected as a consequence of economic reforms within the CMEA countries, of organisational reforms within the CMEA framework and of the eventual collective participation of the CMEA members in GATT. The EEC-CMEA agreement should grant the extension of the MFN treatment, on the side of the EEC, against the planned increase of imports coming from the EEC area. There should be no claim by the state-trading countries to the tariff reductions granted by the EEC to free trade or other existing preferential agreements. The treaty should not be aimed at creating any free trade area, but only .at establishing a regime of progressive trade liberalisation between East and West Europe. Finally the EEC-CMEA agreement should contain a so-called 'evolving-clause' which should allow both the EEC and the CMEA to develop economic co-operation as a complementary element of the commercial relations between the two integrated economic areas.

The final EEC-CMEA treaty should be a protocol which should define the 'framework' of rules and principles within which the individual countries of the two organisations would act while conducting their commercial transactions or programmes of co-operation. Given the general character of such a framework of rules, the 'Nine' and the CMEA member countries would be given the possibility of signing bilateral or multilateral commercial agreements strictly respecting the general guidelines of the 'framework agreement'. The binding character of the rules of such a treaty should derive from the expressed ratification of the protocol by the individual CMEA and EEC countries. The legal effects of the treaty should regard neither the negotiating parties (the EEC and the CMEA) nor the signing parties (the EEC on behalf of its members and the CMEA countries) but exclusively those parties (basically the individual countries) which will be interested in the agreement as a consequence of the ratification of the multilateral protocol which has been signed.

In order to provide the CMEA with a more definite basis for representing the goals and interests of its own member countries it will be necessary to establish a sort of 'temporary mandate' extended by the CMEA members to the Secretariat in order to negotiate and to draft the contents of the agreement with the EEC. Such a temporary mandate will define, also, the fields of competence of the CMEA for the exclusive case of the EEC-CMEA agreement. The mandate will, then, expire when the final framework agreement has been signed and it will be expressly renewed only when new EEC-CMEA direct negotiations are required.

It is necessary, then, to improve the present situation of informal talks and lack of mutual formal recognition between the EEC and the CMEA, through the adoption of an 'agreement on recognition' in which the EEC and the CMEA will mutually acknowledge their political and economic realities. In the 'Protocol' the two organisations will establish the rules and procedures of consultation between the EC Commission and the CMEA Secretariat in view of a formal framework agreement on trade and co-operation. In the same document the setting up of a Mixed Commission, in charge of studying the technical problems which characterise EEC-CMEA relations, will be considered. It will be the task of the Mixed Commission to elaborate a preliminary draft of the EEC-CMEA agreement which will be based on the results of the studies performed by the new provisional interorganisational body. During their periodical consultations the EEC and the CMEA will compare and study new improvements concerning their institutional frameworks in view of future and easier multilateral trade relations.

It is necessary, at this point, to introduce a tentative draft of the eventual EEC-CMEA framework agreement on trade and co-operation.

The Goals

The EEC and the CMEA, on behalf of their member countries, agree to develop direct relations for the purpose of (i) improving the conditions of economic and commercial co-operation between the EEC and the CMEA countries; (ii) standardisation; (iii) environment; (iv) statistics; and (v) economic forecasts in the fields of production and consumption concerning agreed types of goods and commodities. The goal of the EEC and CMEA through this treaty is that of improving and stimulating mutually advantageous trade relations and co-operation programmes in view of economic growth and development for the Eastern and Western European countries.

Information

The basic grounds on which economic relations can be built between the EEC and the CMEA are the exchange of information concerning the economic life of the two areas, and joint study of the problems which have been mentioned above. The exchange of information between the EEC and the CMEA will concern the main tendencies and current activities of the two bodies and their member countries in the economic field. The two contracting parties shall exchange information on any problems that may arise with regard to their trade and shall open consultations with the intention of promoting trade. Any measure, undertaken by one party, in prejudice of the agreed implementation of regular trade exchanges, will be communicated to the other contracting party and to all of its interested member countries. A regular system of exchange of statistical data, elaborated by the statistical services of the two organisations, will be transmitted to the Joint Commission which will be created within the framework of the EEC-CMEA agreement.

Representatives

The EEC and the CMEA undertake to make efforts to induce their member countries to modify their domestic legislations with a view to reducing the existing administrative restrictions affecting the free circulation of persons, groups and delegations from economic, industrial and commercial circles. These measures will be taken on the basis of reciprocity and within the limits indicated by eventual further arrangements negotiated by the EEC and the CMEA. The provisions of the present item should not affect persons or institutions of the countries linked to the EEC or the CMEA by particular agreements. The EEC and the CMEA will also undertake the task of improving, within their geographic areas, the administrative measures necessary to allow the establishment of permanent offices of representatives of firms, or foreign trade organisations, engaged in trade or co-operation programmes in countries belonging to the EEC or to the CMEA areas. Finally the EEC and the CMEA could agree on the exchange of permanent representatives with their offices at the Commission of the EEC in Brussels and at the CMEA Secretariat in Moscow. This would create a permanent basis for direct consultations between the two organisations. The CMEA representatives could be allowed to participate in meetings of the Council of the Ministers of Foreign Affairs and of Foreign Trade, and in the working meetings of the External Relations Committee of the European Parliament (EP). On the other hand, the EEC delegation could participate in the CMEA Executive Committee sessions, in the 'CMEA Committee on Planning', in particular cases, or at least could be kept regularly informed of the working activity of the CMEA ordinary and extraordinary sessions. Regular information from the Standing Commissions on Foreign Trade and for Economic and Statistical Problems should be provided to the EEC delegation permanently based in Moscow. The Statistical Services of the EEC and the External Relations department of the EC Commission should provide information to the permanent delegation of the CMEA based in Brussels.

MFN Treatment

The CMEA and the EEC should reach an agreement under which the two major contracting parties undertake the task of providing a general basis for adopting the MFN treatment in the bilateral transactions of their respective member countries. The two parties, the EEC and the CMEA, should establish the basis for MFN treatment in all matters relating to customs duties and charges on all kinds of imports and exports, including charges made at the time of importation or exportation or levied on international transfers of funds intended for the settlement of imports or exports. The already existing agreements (so-called technical arrangements) signed with some of the CMEA countries by the EEC within the framework of GATT, or selected imports, cannot be used as a basis for the setting of this new multilateral MFN treatment. The parties will also agree to implement the MFN treatment in matters regarding (i) regulations, procedures and formalities concerning customs clearance, transit, warehousing and transhipment of imported or exported products; and (ii) administrative formalities for the issue of import or export licences. The implementation of these last provisions, certainly, entails a strong preliminary agreement among the CMEA countries in order to improve their administrative instruments in this specific area. The MFN treatment will be mutually granted between the EEC and the CMEA members when the CMEA provides the European Community with precise information concerning import-export plans of the individual CMEA countries and lists of projected imports in the fields of industrial goods produced by the EEC members. Indicative lists of the projected exports of agricultural and industrial goods of the CMEA area to the EEC and periodically increasing imports from the EEC countries are expected in order to reciprocate the EEC tariff reductions granted to the CMEA area. The MFN treatment should not apply in the cases of (i) advantages accorded by either contracting party to states which are members of a customs union or free trade area; (ii) advantages accorded by either contracting party to neighbouring countries for the purpose of facilitating border trade; and (iii) measures which either contracting party may take in order to meet its obligations under international commodity agreements. The specific duties established in this field, like those fixed for the Multifibres Agreement between the EEC and Romania, cannot provide the basis for the establishment of the general guidelines for a multilateral MFN treatment between the EEC and CMEA economic areas.

Trade Liberalisation

The EEC and the CMEA should agree to undertake the task of improving their internal administrative instruments, and organisational mechanisms, with a view to achieving better results in the field of trade liberalisation. In this respect the CMEA should agree to improve its mechanisms of long-term planning and plan co-ordination, intergovernmental co-operation and economic integration in order to secure regular flows of imports and exports to, and from, the EEC area. The EEC, on the other hand, should strive for a more open reworking of its CAP, especially toward the CMEA countries, and for the elaboration of basic guidelines for an effective ICP. This will entail an increasing liberalisation of imports from the CMEA area, reflected in increasing country-to-country trade relations. The EEC, in response to the eventual organisational improvements of the CMEA, will be able to extend the list of products coming from the CMEA countries, and for which import limitations are still applied. The EEC-CMEA Joint Commission will encourage the adoption of all those measures which will reduce quantitative restrictions in both the East and West economic areas.

Maritime Transportation

The CMEA and the EEC will concentrate their efforts in order to find a solution to the problems of unfair competition, and market disruption, in the field of maritime transportation. In this respect, it is advisable for the shipping companies of the CMEA members to find a multilateral agreement, within the CMEA framework, on the pricing system in the field of freights. For an acceptable solution freights should be determined on the basis of averaged world market prices subject to periodic adjustments. Stricter co-operation should be established between the EEC and the CMEA in this field. The Joint Commission would, then, be assigned the task of controlling the cases of dumping in this matter and promoting multilateral negotiations in order to obtain an additional EEC-CMEA 'Protocol on Maritime Freights'.

Fishing

The EEC and the CMEA should agree to define their fishing rights and the limits of their respective exclusive fishing zones. In this respect the two organisations should exactly determine the geographic limits of their own 'two-hundred-miles' fishing areas. Within the general framework of this norm, bilateral or multilateral agreements between the members of the two organisations should take place.

Prices

The CMEA and the EEC should reach an agreement on the prices referred to goods and commodities traded between the EEC and the CMEA member countries. The most acceptable solution would be that of price determination (for the CMEA countries) based on the averages[17] of world market prices renewable every one or two years. The CMEA by signing the agreement with the EEC would honour this provision on prices through the supply of accurate descriptions of the single members' pricing mechanisms, and by discouraging the practice of price equalisation as far as possible. The EEC would also reduce the practice of price distortion through compensatory duties as it is adopted for agricultural products. The EEC-CMEA Joint Commission should, then, undertake the task of studying the question of prices and elaborating new measures.

Payments and Credits

Given the limitations on the convertibility of the CMEA currencies, and until different conditions affect those currencies, it is possible to think that the EEC and the CMEA will agree to make payments in any of the free convertible currencies of the EEC members or in other 'hard' currency.

The CMEA will make efforts to induce its member countries to reduce the obstacles imposed by 'commodity inconvertibility'. This will help the formation of larger quotas of goods destined to expand trade with the European Community. The EEC, then, on the basis of a decision of the Council of Ministers (4 April 1978) will agree with the CMEA to induce its members to apply the EEC general guidelines for export credits equally to third countries. The export credits in question are those which have the support of the public authorities and which cover a period of two years or more. These guidelines should fix:

(i)   the minimum payments made up to delivery, including those made on delivery in relation to the per capita GNP figure for the country receiving the goods;
(ii) the minimum interest rate;
(iii) the maximum duration of the credit.[18]

This type of measure will ease the commercial relations between the EEC and the CMEA areas with the consequent result of not increasing the burden of debts to the West which affect the socialist economies.

The Joint Commission

In order to achieve the goals established by the EEC-CMEA agreement a Joint Commission will be created. The main tasks of the Commission will be those of:

(i)   co-ordinating and studying the information gained from the single countries of the EEC and CMEA and by the offices of the organisations themselves;
(ii) elaborating plans for the development of trade and sectorial co-operation;
(iii) stimulating and co-ordinating programmes of co-operation;
(iv) providing the EEC and the CMEA with indications concerning eventual institutional adjustments in accordance with the improvement of East-West relations in the field of finance, trade and co-operation.

The Joint Commission will monitor the functioning of the treaty and will provide itself with the necessary instruments for its own working activity in order to become an autonomous body. The 'Commission' will recommend to the members of the EEC, and of the CMEA, the resolutions which it will adopt in order to attain the goals of the 'Framework Agreement'. For those countries which will accept and ratify the recommendations of the Joint Commission the accepted recommendation will have the value of an international treaty. In order to improve its functional competences the Joint Commission will be subdivided into several subcommissions. They will be established as follows:

(i)   subcommission on trade, economic and financial problems;
(ii)   subcommission on statistics;
(iii) anti-dumping and anti-trade discrimination subcommission;
(iv)   subcommission on co-operation;
(v)   subcommission on arbitration.

The first of the five subcommissions will study mainly the opportunities for developing trade and finding possible solutions to the major problems which hinder regular flows of East-West trade. This subcommission will be in charge of elaborating plans and projects and will operate in close relation with the EC Council of Ministers, the EC Commission on External Relations of the EP, the CMEA Co-operation Committee on Planning, the Executive Committee and the Secretariat of the CMEA, the Standing Commissions on Standardisation, External Trade, Economic and Statistical Problems, Financial and Monetary Problems and Transport. The Joint Commission representatives will participate in, and will be informed on, the bilateral and multilateral agreements signed between the EEC members and the CMEA countries. The subcommission on statistics will receive information from the EEC and the CMEA and from their respective members. It will analyse the data received and will study the opportunities for trade and co-operation in light of the resulting information. It will work with the EC Statistical Service, the CMEA Standing Commission on Economic and Statistical problems and the CMEA International Centre for Technical-Scientific Information.

The subcommission dealing with the study and elimination of 'dumping' and trade discrimination will be mainly involved in analysing the supposed, or actual, cases of 'dumping' and quantitative restrictions for goods which should be granted a regime of import/export liberalisation. The subcommission should, therefore, address recommendations to the countries which operate 'dumping' in order to eliminate, or avoid, any restrictive or disruptive commercial practices.

In order to co-ordinate and improve future bilateral programmes of co-operation between either the EEC members and the CMEA countries, or the two organisations, the subcommission on co-operation will provide the necessary guidelines and instruments. This subcommission will be composed of members of the governments of the EEC and the CMEA areas, representatives of the EC Commission and of the European Investments Bank on the one hand, and representatives of the CMEA Executive Committee, the Committee on Scientific-Technical Co-operation and of the IIB, on the other. This subcommission will be committed mainly to the exchange of information dealing with programmes of bilateral co-operation and of future multilateral co-operation. Further, it will seek the combination of co-operation programmes, elaborated by the CMEA long-term plans, with West European initiatives. Indicative guidelines for future common co-operation policies between East and West will be drafted by the subcommission. The subcommission on co-operation will always be part of any bilateral or multilateral agreement on co-operation signed between members of the EEC and of the CMEA.

Finally, the subcommission on arbitration will be vested with jurisdiction on all legal problems arising from the implementation of the EEC-CMEA agreement and the problems arising from trade and co-operation other than 'dumping' and non-tariff discrimination. The Joint Commission will meet periodically during the year and at the beginning of the first month of implementation of every new five-year plan. The Joint Commission will be informed on the drafting of the one-year plans and of the five-year plans in order to resolve eventual conflicts arising from the application of the EEC-CMEA framework agreement among the East and West European countries which are already undertaking policies of integration and multilateral co-operation.

Safety Clause

The EEC and the CMEA and their respective member countries will agree never to adopt political measures against each other which entail embargoes, boycotts or any type of economic sanction during the time of validity of the treaty. The adoption of such measures will take place only after the denunciation of the treaty according to the rules of international law.

Duration

The treaty between the EEC and the CMEA should last not less than five years and should be tacitly renewable every year. The rules of the denunciation of the treaty should be those usually adopted for equivalent international commercial agreements. The treaty should be signed by the EEC, the CMEA and the CMEA governments. The consequent process of ratification undertaken by the interested countries - members of the EEC and the CMEA - will make it executive exclusively for the ratifying countries.

IV CONCLUSIONS

The conclusion of a formal commercial agreement between the EEC and the CMEA, and its legal effectiveness between the two contracting parties, mainly depends on the powers and legal competences of the two organisations in the fields of trade and co-operation. In order to achieve this result the organs of the two bodies have to be provided with the necessary legal authority to enact and to implement, after having negotiated, the rules of the EEC-CMEA treaty. For the moment the Community's jurisdiction is exclusively limited to the field of trade. Eventual internal reforms within the EEC framework affecting the Community competences in the field of economic co-operation, will certainly expand the legal capacity of the organisation so that the EEC-CMEA agreement on trade and co-operation will be possible. On the CMEA side the intergovernmental character of the organisation strongly affects the CMEA treaty-making competence. In theory, according to the rules of the Charter, which have been recently amended, the CMEA can stipulate international agreements with third countries and international organisations. In order, then, to give the signed agreement the necessary legal force to be successfully implemented within the CMEA area, it is necessary that the CMEA members give a mandate to the organisation to sign this particular 'framework agreement'.

In light of these indications, it is possible to conclude that the EEC and the CMEA are given the possibility of signing a commercial agreement which can establish the general guidelines for the conduct of trade between East and West Europe. It is also possible that, as happened for the EEC-Yugoslavia agreement, a special section on economic co-operation will be included. The basic content of the EEC-CMEA agreement will concern the exchange of information and of representatives, the concession of MFN treatment, trade liberalisation, credits and payments, anti-dumping measures in the field of maritime transportation and the creation of a Joint Commission.

The final EEC-CMEA treaty should be a framework of rules and principles negotiated by the EEC and the CMEA, signed by the EEC, the CMEA and its members, with the possibility, left to the single countries belonging to the two organisations, of concluding bilateral or multilateral arrangements which should be linked to the framework agreement signed by the EEC and the CMEA. The binding character of this set of rules and principles should derive from the process of treaty ratification by the individual member countries of the EEC and the CMEA.

NOTES

1. W.J. Feld, The European Community in World Affairs (Port Washington, New York:Alfred Publ.Co., 1976), p. 23.
2. B. Tomsa, La Politique Commerciale Commune de la CEE et les Pays de l'Europe de l'Est (Brussels:Bruylant, 1977), pp. 14-18.
3. W.J. Feld, op. cit., p. 24.

4. Bulletin EC No. 6 - 1977 point 2.2.27.
5. European Parliament, Report on the state of relations between the EEC and East-European state-trading countries of Comecon. Rapporteur: M. Schmidt. EP Working Documents 1978/1979, doc. 89/78, 11 May 1978, p. 11.
6. Ibid., p. 12.
7. A. Wasilkowski, 'Aspects juridiques de l'intégration économique socialiste', The Hague Academy of International Law, Colloquium, 1971, p. 285.
8. Ibid., p. 289.
9. H.A. Hewett, 'Recent developments in East-West European economic relations and their implications for U.S.-East economic relations', United States Congress, 95th Congress 1st Session, Joint Economic Committee, 25 August 1977, East European Economies post-Helsinki, p. 187.
10. A. Belicenko, 'International Investment Bank: What it does to facilitate Socialist Economic Integration', Foreign Trade, No. 3 (1980), p. 15.
11. G. Schiavone, The Institutions of Comecon (London: Macmillan, 1981), pp. 116-18.
12. Ibid., p. 35.
13. Ibid., p. 35.
14. Ibid., p. 35.
15. Ibid., p. 62; A. Lebahn, 'RGW und EG - Faktoren des Ost-West-Handels', Aussenpolitik, No. 2 (1978), pp. 135-6.
16. W.J. Feld, op. cit., p. 124.
17. This mechanism of price determination which has been adopted for intra-CMEA trade since 1975 could be improved and linked to the eventual extra-CMEA international trade relations.
18. Europe Information - External Relations, 12/78, July 1978, 'The European Community and the Countries of Eastern Europe', p. 5.

13 Soviet–Western Technological Co-operation*

PHILIP HANSON
University of Birmingham

I INTRODUCTION

In early 1980 the prospects for East-West technological co-operation in the decade that is just beginning can hardly be said to be bright. It is only to be hoped, however, that the political setting for such co-operation will improve rather than deteriorate further. Let us, at all events, make that assumption for the purposes of the present discussion. Let us, in other words, focus on the economic factors affecting the extent of that co-operation in the near future. In considering some of these, I shall concentrate on the particular case of Soviet-Western technological co-operation.

The particular influence with which this paper will be concerned is both a familiar and a fundamental one: the influence of financial constraints. More precisely, it is the nature and the importance of the limitations imposed by the Soviet hard currency balance of payments that I wish to consider here.

The justification for treating this as a constraint of fundamental importance may be briefly summarised. Technological know-how, and products embodying new technology, cross national boundaries in numerous ways. Some of the channels of international .technology transfer are not of a 'commercial' kind: travel by scientists and technologists, scientific exchanges, the reading of foreign technological literature, industrial espionage, and so on. It is widely agreed by students of the innovation process, however, that commercial transactions provide major channels of transfer. The sale of products (especially machinery and other capital goods) embodying technology not otherwise available in the importing nation; the sale of licences and know-how; training, technical assistance, joint R and D design work - all these occur predominantly within the framework of commercial transactions. Scientific and technological contacts and

170

'exchanges' within the framework of intergovernmental agreements may facilitate later technology transfers, but it has been found that transfers of productive technology scarcely feature in such exchange arrangements.[1] In general, those international flows of technology which are mediated through measurable international dealings, and which are subject to the influence of government policies in both the 'transmitting' and the 'receiving' country are of a commercial kind. (Which is not to say that they are the only important kind.)

Moreover the important channel of direct foreign investment, which mediates some of the technology flows among Western countries and from Western to Third World countries, is not legally available so far as the transmission of Western technology to the USSR is concerned. It is true that Soviet direct investment in the Western world is of some importance, but this appears to be directed primarily to the marketing of Soviet products rather than to the transfer of technology in either embodied or disembodied form.[2]

The consequence of these circumstances is that a large part of the technological interaction between the USSR and the West depends on transactions on which the Soviet hard currency balance of payments - - and the current account in particular - exercises an extremely strong influence. This is, of course, a commonplace observation. What is perhaps less widely appreciated is the tightness of the constraints which this consideration appears recently to have been imposing on Soviet technology imports. If we take the rate of Soviet ordering of Western machinery as an indicator of the rate of technology import-ation, we find the following picture (see Table 13.1).[3]

Table 13.1   Reported Soviet Orders for Machinery from
Multilateral Trading Partners (million dollars)

1974	1975	1976	1977	1978	1979 (prelim.)
4300	4650	6000	2500-3800	2000-2800	1800

Sources :
1974-76 and higher figures for 1977 and 1978: P.G. Ericson and R.S. Miller, 'Soviet Foreign Economic Behaviour: a Balance of Payments Perspective' in US Congress JEC, Soviet Economy in a Time of Change, vol. 2 (Washington, 1979), pp. 208-44, Appendix I. The lower figures for 1977 and 1978, and the preliminary figure for 1979 are derived from the author's own compilation. (My total for 1976 coincides with the Ericson-Miller figure.) Both series are approximate and are compiled from Western press reports.

The reasons for this marked cutback in ordering lie, I believe, in the exigencies of the Soviet hard currency balance of payments as perceived by Soviet policy-makers. The precise nature of the balance of payments constraints, however, is hard to assess. As Table 13.2

Table 13.2   USSR Hard-currency Balance of Payments (million dollars)

	1970	1971	1972	1973	1974	1975	1976	1977	1978*
A. Current account balance	22	160	-587	1151	2014	-4714	-2931	2	467
Balance on sales and purchases of goods and services	77	217	-521	1234	2115	-4616	-2824	127	612
Balance on merchandise trade	-500	-313	-1356	-1757	-978	-6422	-5595	-3300	-3794
Exports, f.o.b.	2201	2630	2801	4790	7470	7835	9721	11345	13157
Imports, f.o.b.	-2701	-2943	-4157	-6547	-8448	14257	15316	14647	16951
Sales of nonmonetary gold	0	79	380	900	1178	725	1369	1618	2673
Receipts from military sales	100	87	122	1345	1000	793	1108	1500	1644
Net income from services	477	364	333	746	915	288	294	309	89
Net income from tourism	43	45	53	116	117	136	150	175	200
Merchandise freight balance	397	257	220	480	570	390	470	590	560
Income	400	260	250	640	640	520	640	710	700
Outlays	-3	-3	-30	-160	-70	-130	-170	-120	-140
Net income from other transportation	120	110	120	230	330	330	390	390	410
Investment income balance	-83	-48	-60	-80	-102	-568	-716	-846	-1081
Income from direct investment abroad	0	0	0	0	1	2	8	2	3
Interest on outstanding assets in Western banks	-83	87	110	252	405	234	288	292	685
Interest paid on outstanding debt	-83	-135	-170	-332	-508	-804	-1012	-1140	-1769
Government transfer outlays	-55	-57	-66	-83	-101	-98	-107	-125	-145
To the U.N.	-44	-46	-54	-59	-88	-98	-107	-125	-145
Settlement of lend-lease debt	-11	-11	-12	-24	-24	0	0	0	0
B. Capital account balance	266	227	-77	522	386	5694	2952	1917	173
Direct investment abroad	0	-6	0	-9	-11	-3	-31	0	0
Borrowing from abroad	291	288	602	1340	1426	5402	4694	1777	1785
Not backed by Western credit guarantees			452	1183	746	4160	2720	191	458
Backed by Western credit guarantees	291	288	150	157	680	1242	1554	686	1041
East European loans for Orenburg							420	900	286
Lending to other countries	-25	-55	-679	-809	-1029	295	-1711	140	-1612
Net increase in Soviet assets held in Western commercial banks			-629	-729	-939	395	-1611	240	-1512
Net increase in outstanding supplier credits	-25	-55	-50	-80	-90	-100	-100	-100	-100
C. Net errors and omissions	-288	-387	664	-1673	-2400	-980	21	-1919	-640

* Preliminary estimates.

Note: Since with complete and accurate accounting net receipts (net outlays) on the current account would be offset by net outlays (net receipts) on the capital account, net errors and omissions (C) can be found by the following identity: C = -(A+B), where A = the current account balance and B = the capital account balance.

Source: P.G. Ericson and R.S. Miller, op.cit., p.212. The figures are US calculations from Soviet and other data.

indicates, the Soviet merchandise trade balance on hard currency account was negative in 1970-78. The overall current account, however, is estimated by US analysts to have been in deficit (in this period) only in 1972, 1975 and 1976. The sharp movement into deficit in the two latter years, associated with a rising (though not, by international standards, high) hard currency debt-service ratio, may have prompted some retrenchment in the key area of machinery ordering, which accounts for about a third to two-fifths of hard currency imports (with a one-year lag between order and delivery, on average). Even so, given the modest Soviet debt-service ratio and the absence (according to the data of Table 13.2) of a chronic hard currency current-account deficit, it is not clear why the retrenchment has been so sharp.

The rest of this paper consists of an analysis of the pressures and constraints on Soviet technology imports, and tests a simple hypothesis about the financial determination of rates of importation of Western machinery into the USSR. The analysis tends to confirm the implication of the previous paragraph that there is a large element of discretionary behaviour in Soviet policy-makers' identification of financial limits to their purchasing of Western capital goods. I conclude that the absence both of official Soviet balance of payments data and of any substantive Soviet public discussion of the relevant planning criteria generates an undesirable degree of unpredictability about this major segment of East-West trade. Improved information should benefit both the USSR and the West.

II   CONSTRAINTS ON SOVIET-WESTERN TECHNOLOGICAL CO-OPERATION

It is often argued that a centrally-administered economy such as that of the USSR will exhibit a certain built-in aversion to foreign trade in comparison with a market economy of the same economic size, resource-endowment and development level. A firm in a market economy has no greater administrative leverage over other firms in the same economy than it has over foreign firms. To that extent, transactions with foreign firms are not inherently riskier than transactions with firms in the home market. There may be special costs attached to entering foreign markets, and costs of legal actions against foreign business partners may be higher than for equivalent actions against fellow-nationals, but these are separate issues.

In a centrally-administered economy, however (the argument goes), decision-makers will tend to be relatively averse to foreign transactions because they entail a special degree of uncertainty. The administrative control over both customer and supplier enterprise, which is available to the central authorities in the domestic economy, is not available in foreign transactions. In the latter, only one side of the deal is under the direct administrative control of the central planners and policy-makers. Therefore, it is argued, there is a systemic trade aversion of a kind not present in market economies.[4]

Franklyn Holzman has recently developed a somewhat different line of argument about the trade-planning process in centrally-administered economies.[5] He seeks to account for what he believes to be a chronic tendency to hard currency trade deficits in the USSR and Eastern Europe by reference to what he calls the 'saleability illusion'. His hypothesis is carefully elaborated and I shall not attempt to restate it here. It should suffice for our purposes to note that Holzman posits that rates of hard currency importation are planned ahead on the basis of expected hard currency earnings (allowing for credits, etc.), but that the latter expectations are persistently underfulfilled primarily because of systemic weaknesses in marketing and in technological development on the part of centrally-administered economies.

Both these lines of argument are quite persuasive. I believe, however, that the 'systemic trade aversion' argument should be modified to take account of the complexities of actual Soviet (and probably East European) foreign-trade decision-making. The source of trade aversion just described may well operate at the central-planning level: that is, among top policy-makers and in USSR Gosplan. But Soviet planning is in large part a process of responding to pressures from lower levels: from branch ministries and, ulti-mately, from enterprises. A fundamental experience of Soviet enter-prises is that supplies of inputs from other Soviet enterprises are highly unreliable, since the initial plans for interdependent activities contain many internal inconsistencies and are, in addition, often poorly implemented with respect to product-mix and timing. One response to the chronic supply problem is for each enterprise to attempt as far as possible to make its own components, tooling, etc. But it is likely that in those industries where imports are perceived as a feasible option there will also be another response: to seek allocations of imports of producer goods from the West in preference to domestic supplies. Western suppliers are subject to effective penalties for late delivery, after all, and are in general relatively reliable. Such a preference could be predicted on grounds of supply uncertainty' alone, even if the domestic products were perfect substitutes for the imports.

Branch ministries share the interests of their subordinate enter-prises in securing favourable conditions for plan fulfilment. And under present Soviet arrangements they are not normally required to earn, by exporting, the hard currency to pay for imports acquired for their use. One would expect, therefore, that Soviet branch minis-tries, far from being trade-averse, would be trade-biased with respect to imports of producer goods.

At enterprise and branch-ministry levels, however, there is evi-dently considerable trade aversion with respect to exports, especially hard currency exports. Supplies to domestic civilian customers require as a rule only modest quality standards; delivery deadlines are not strongly enforced; requirements of spares and technical assistance can often be ignored. Special payments are needed to cover the extra costs of supplying more demanding customers, and indeed certain export incentive payments do exist. Their effects on Soviet enterprises' readiness to produce for export appear however to be weak; indeed, production for export is often regarded as a laborious and ill-rewarded task to be avoided, since the extra costs tend to outweigh the limited special incentives. [6]

The Soviet central planners and policy-makers are therefore likely to be faced with bids for import allocations which exceed proposals for export supply, at least as far as hard currency is concerned. They must contain this (hypothesised) pressure towards a hard currency trade deficit in various ways. First, there is the procedural screening through which bids for licences and machinery imports (for example) are required to go. Second, the central authorities apply pressure to elicit hard currency exports in excess of proposals. Third, they apply a cut-off to a list of priority-ranked import proposals (or so we may reasonably suppose) in the light of known and expected hard currency availability.

These methods can be supplemented by a tying of branch hard currency allocations to branch hard currency earnings. One way of doing this with respect to capital goods imports is to insist on, or give priority to, product payback deals. In these the Western partner arranges to be paid for (e.g.) a turnkey project by means of a contractual undertaking to purchase the product resulting from the completed project. Another way of tying imports to exports is to allow branch (or even enterprise) retention of a portion of hard currency export earnings. This latter method has not been formally and generally used in the Soviet Union, though it may be employed in a limited and informal way.[7] The obvious limitation to any such branch-by-branch tying of imports and exports is that a pattern of trade that was balanced by branch would almost certainly be far removed from the economically most efficient levels and commodity-composition of imports and exports.[8] It would also impose certain costs on the Soviet economy by shifting the terms of trade against the USSR in comparison with trade arising from the same plant imports without product payback arrangements. This is because in a product payback deal the Soviet partner is shifting the burden of uncertainty-bearing to the Western partner. A charge will generally be exacted for this service, in the form of contractual prices for the payback products that are less than the expected value of the product prices in non-payback deals.

It seems highly likely, therefore, that the 'demand' for Western machinery and know-how that is communicated by Soviet branch ministries to Soviet central planners substantially exceeds the 'demand' which the latter allows to become effective in world markets. The corollary of this is that effective demand for Western technology is likely to appear to Soviet central planners to be perpetually constrained by the hard currency balance of payments.[9] No doubt bids for hard currency allocations, like all resource bids from below, will be known to be in some degree exaggerated. But information on the cost effectiveness of various import proposals, in relation to the resource costs of exports, will be patchy because of the insulation of domestic from world price ratios and the non-scarcity nature of domestic prices. So the precise extent to which the apparent demand is exaggerated, in comparison with that demand which it would be economically efficient to implement, is probably unknown.

In general there seems to be a great deal of scope for discretionary behaviour by Soviet branch-level administrators in shaping the demands for Western technology. Competitive pressures do not compel a Soviet enterprise or ministry to be forever in search of least-cost technological solutions. The processes by which a Soviet ministry may either succumb to or resist demands from customer ministries for new products are probably better accounted for by reference to so-called 'bureaucratic politics' than by reference to demand and costs.

The Ministry of the Chemical Industry, for example, under pressure to supply more nitrogenous fertilisers to agriculture, polyester film to insulate electric motors, and many other items, has bought large quantities of Western equipment and know-how for these purposes; the Ministry of Ferrous Metallurgy, under pressure to incorporate series production of 24-metre lengths of large-diameter pipe in its 1976-80 plan, apparently refused to do so.[10] It appears to have resisted such pressures for a long time without importing the relevant technology. The status of individual ministers and their varying 'access' and 'influence' probably have a great deal to do with such differences in response. By the same token the influence of different branch R and D and design organisations in either hindering or promoting technology-import proposals is likely to vary for non-economic reasons.[11]

There is also a great deal of scope for discretionary behaviour by the top-level administrators when it comes to setting ceilings on the demand for Western technology that is actually embodied in foreign-trade plans. In particular, the determination of what constitutes the overall hard currency balance of payments constraint has rested in the 1970s on the perceptions and preferences of Soviet policy-makers. The precise terms on which (for example) medium-term Eurocurrency loans have been available to the Soviet authorities from Western banks have varied, but the willingness of Western banks and governments to extend credit to the USSR has generally exceeded Soviet willingness to contract new debts. In international finance, as in many other fields, Soviet policy-makers have been impeccable conservatives. The hard currency debt-service ratio (calculated in relation to non-arms, hard currency merchandise exports) has so far remained below 30 per cent.[12] The status of the USSR as the world's second largest gold producer, its excellent record of debt repayment and the system's known capability to control the import bill by direct administrative decision - all these considerations combine to give the USSR a high credit rating. This could have been exploited by borrowing more than has (up to 1980) been borrowed, and thus supporting higher rates of import of Western machinery and know-how.

The above remarks are intended as a modification of the 'systemic trade aversion' hypothesis. They are not necessarily inconsistent with Holzman's 'saleability illusion' hypothesis. I would draw attention, however, to two difficulties about the 'saleability illusion' with respect specifically to the USSR and to Soviet imports of capital goods from multilateral-settlement trade partners. (The thesis of a 'saleability illusion' effect may work well for other East-West trade flows.)

The first difficulty is that - if the Ericson-Miller estimates in Table 13.2 are correct - the USSR has simply not had a chronic hard currency shortage that requires explanation. That is to say, more often than not, in the 1970s, it had a hard currency current account surplus. This was probably not the case for most of the other CMEA countries, but for the USSR the difference between the hard currency merchandise trade balance as usually measured (excluding arms and gold exports) and the overall hard currency current account balance is so considerable (according to Western calculations) that the latter exhibits no chronic hard currency shortage.

This is not to say that Soviet planners would not have wished to see a more dynamic hard currency export performance; nor is it to say that rates of importation have not had to be held down by perceived financial constraints. But it does mean that ex post the observed import flows have not been self-evidently 'too high'. If the planners focused (as would be sensible) on the current account as a whole, it would be hard to contend that hard currency exports have turned out ex post to be 'too low' relatively to imports.

The second difficulty is less amenable to documentation. It is more a matter of speculation about the character of the Soviet foreign trade planning process in recent years. We know that on average observed machinery import flows reflect contracts of about twelve months earlier and therefore reflect import decisions of at least twelve months earlier still.[13] We also know that world trade conditions in the 1970s were volatile and hard to predict. We can be fairly sure, finally, that Soviet import and export decisions affecting East-West trade are in general of a short-run character and are not strongly determined in any binding way by, for example, five-year-plan decisions. (Recent Soviet five-year-plan pronouncements, for both the Ninth and the Tenth five-year-plans, gave vague and minimal information on non-CMEA trade plans, and what could be inferred from them was nothing like what has actually transpired.)

Source notes :

Column A: Exports, f.o.b., of SITC 7 goods, from the 14 major OECD countries to the USSR. The only OECD exporter of machinery on more than a negligible scale to the USSR that is omitted is Finland (see text). From OECD, Statistics of Foreign Trade, Series B and C.

Column B: Weighted average of various national price series, with adjustments for parity changes; weights (altered as between four subperiods) reflect country shares in SITC 7 sales to USSR. For 1970-78, the index is based on the export price index series for machinery and transport equipment for Japan, FRG, US and Sweden only, from UN Monthly Bulletin of Statistics, May 1979, weighted by 1975 shares.

Column C: Conversion rates pivot on a modified 'Boretsky' ruble-dollar conversion rate for 1964, adjusted annually in line with Column B.

Column D: Column C as a percentage of a 1969-ruble-estimate series derived from Narkhoz (various years) for total gross investment in machinery and equipment. For the 1970s this series incorporates adjustments to 1 January 1973 wholesale machinery prices. (Narkhoz, 1977, pp. 341, 349). The differences between 1969 and 1973 valuation appear to be small.

What is surprising, in fact, is how closely Soviet rates of machinery buying have so far conformed to an extremely simple pattern. In fact, tolerably good predictions of the rate of Soviet buying can be made for 1974-77 with a very crude model in which machinery imports respond with a one-year lag to export earnings in the West and grain imports from the West, and other influences are ignored.

In an earlier study I tested for the period 1955-72 such a crude 'explanation' of the level of Soviet imports of Western machinery in any one year (Mk). It was posited that these would be positively influenced by the level of merchandise exports to the West (X), as a proxy for hard currency earnings, and negatively influenced by grain imports from the West (MG), representing a major competing claim on hard currency resources.   Straight-line least squares regressions of the form:

$$Mk = A + bX - cMG$$

worked well statistically. Various time-lags were applied to X and MG. The R^2s were around or above 0.9 and the t statistics for the b and c coefficients were significant at 5 per cent.

The strong upward trends over time in both Mk and X, however, were an obvious source of correlation that was to some extent extraneous, and which gave an exaggerated impression of a very simple set of Soviet decision-making rules. (The exponential trend rates, estimated by least-squares, were 14.1 per cent per annum for Mk and 10.3 for X.) Removing the trends from these series and relating deviations from trend in Mk to deviations from trend in X and to MG sharply reduced the R^2s. Time-lags of zero, one and two years were tested for MG and X (separately and together), and a one-year lag in both gave the best fit. Detrended, then, the following 'explanation' still had moderate force (in million dollars at current prices):

$$Mk_t + 38.17 + 0.76X_{t-1} - 0.27 MG_{t-1}$$
$$(1.823) (2.475) (-2.689)$$

Here the R^2 was 0.544 and the (bracketed) t statistics indicated that the coefficients were significant at 5 per cent.

Except for the tumultuous year of 1973, an extrapolation of this relationship from 1972 through 1977 yields 'predictions' of Soviet machinery imports that are better than might be expected from such a crude mode, as Table 13.4 shows.

Table 13.4 Actual and 'Predicted' Soviet Imports of Western Machinery (Mk) 1973-1977 (million dollars)

Year	Actual Mk	Predicted Mk	Error as % actual
1973	1574	1036	34.2
1974	2094	2415	15.3
1975	4184	4821	15.2
1976	4259	4664	9.5
1977	4571	4703	2.9

Source: Actual, Table 13.3. Predicted, see text.

The predicted import levels in Table 13.4 are derived by:

(a)   extrapolating the 1955-71 trend growth rate of X (10.3 per cent p.a.) through 1976;
(b)   predicting each year's deviation from the extrapolated 1955-72 trend of Mk by applying the coefficients estimated for 1955-72 to the previous year's deviation from trend of X and previous year's MG;
(c)   adding the predicted deviation of Mk to the extrapolated trend series of Mk.

III   CONCLUSIONS

Many factors not allowed for in this extrapolation should in logic be capable of influencing machinery import levels: hard currency earnings from services; hard currency merchandise earnings in the Third World; the gold price and Soviet gold reserves; Western interest and inflation rates. Arithmetically, however, their combined influence seems from this exercise not to have been very great, except in 1973.

Thus a crude and oversimplified account of balance of payments influences on Soviet machinery buying works tolerably well amid the rapid changes of the mid-1970s. Does it therefore correspond to a crude, and even somewhat irrational, 'rule of thumb' that does in fact guide Soviet planners' behaviour? One possibility is that the apparently weak influence of other factors may be a statistical illusion. In any case, considerable scope undoubtedly exists for policy shifts at Soviet policy-makers' discretion. Nonetheless Table 13.4 suggests that the Soviet approach to deciding what volume of machinery imports can be 'afforded', may have remained fairly constant through the Khrushchev and Brezhnev eras.

Can it therefore be used to project future rates of Western machinery sales to the USSR? This would surely be rash since there is no obvious necessity for this approach to be adhered to in future. We are, as I have suggested above, observing what must be classified as discretionary behaviour on the part of Soviet foreign trade planners and Soviet central policy-makers, and we cannot be sure that our regressions have picked up a real behavioural pattern, let alone a real behavioural pattern that can be expected to persist. There are in fact two grounds for believing that a recovery in the rate of Soviet importation of Western machinery in the near future is feasible. First, the perceived financial constraints that have so far (apparently) been observed seem to be perceived from a standpoint of considerable caution with respect to acceptable levels of hard currency indebtedness; and such perceptions could change. Second, the cutbacks in ordering, as well as other factors, have assisted in a return to a favourable current account hard currency balance (it is believed) in 1977-79, and to some reduction of outstanding hard currency debt.

The practical problem underlying these uncertainties is one that is important for Western firms and governments and for Soviet policy-makers alike. It is that future East-West aggregate trade flows are harder to predict than they need be, because of two information gaps. First, there are no published official Soviet data on the Soviet balance of payments except for merchandise trade. Second, there is hardly any authoritative Soviet information on the substance of Soviet non-CMEA trade planning methods or on the short-term or medium-term targets for non-CMEA trade. It would surely be in the interests both of Western governments and industry and of Soviet policy-makers themselves if these information gaps were filled.

NOTES

* Part of this text appears in Dr Hanson's Trade and Technology in Soviet-Western Relations (London: Macmillan, 1981).

1. Loren Graham, 'How Valuable are Scientific Exchanges with the Soviet Union?', Science, 201, No. 4366 (27 October 1978).

2. Carl H. McMillan, 'Soviet Investment in the Industrialized Western Economies and in the Developing Economies of the Third World', in US Congress JEC, Soviet Economy in a Time of Change, vol. 2 (Washington, 1979) pp. 625-48.

3. This is not unreasonable, since what Mansfield has termed 'design transfer' and 'capacity transfer' will be facilitated - in so far as it is mediated by commercial transactions at all - by flows of capital goods embodying technology new to the recipient and by licence and know-how sales. It is evident that most Soviet know-how and licence purchases from Western suppliers are closely associated with machinery purchases (e.g. in turnkey projects).

4. See F.D. Holzman, Foreign Trade under Central Planning (Cambridge, Mass.: Harvard University Press, 1974), pp. 8-9, 140.

5. F.D. Holzman, 'Some Theories of the Hard Currency Shortages of Centrally Planned Economies', US Congress JEC, op. cit., pp. 297-317.

6. N. Smelyakov, 'Delovye vstrechi', Novyi mir, 1973, No. 12, pp. 203-40, refers (pp. 219-80) to 'some' engineering enterprises regarding export assignments as 'a form of punishment', and discusses the reasons for this. G.A. Kulagin, 'Moi partnery, nachal'stvo i pravila igry', EKO 1975, No. 2, pp. 82-96, discusses the reasons (at pp. 84-5) in more detail.

7. See Dzh. Gvishiani in C.T. Saunders (ed.), Industrial Policies and Technology Transfers between East and West (Vienna: Springer, 1977), pp. 209-11.

8. Such branchwise balancing would not correspond to so-called intra-industry trading (two-way flows, between trade partners, of products of the same industry). What would be entailed would be a balancing of branch outputs with branch inputs; many of the latter would be products of other industries.

9. Periods during which intense chauvinism, backed by terror, may have inhibited officials from expressing any preference for Western supplies, are probably confined to the Stalin era.

10. V. Barvinskii in Sotsialisticheskaia industriia, 23 December 1975.

11. An emigré Soviet scientist, M. Perakh ('Utilization of Western Technological Advances in Soviet Industry', in NATO Economic Directorate, East-West Technological Co-operation (Brussels: NATO, 1976), pp. 177-97 argues persuasively that many Soviet R and D organisations will often resist proposals to import Western machinery and know-how because this would reveal the extent to

which their own work, which has been 'sold' to their superior ministry as original, has in fact been based on plagiarising Western ideas.

12. According to CIA calculations, 24 per cent in 1977 and only 19 per cent in relation to all hard currency earnings. US CIA, Simulations of Soviet Growth Options to 1985, ER 79-10131 (March 1979), p. 8. 'All hard currency earnings' would include receipts from sales of gold and arms for hard currency, as well as revenue from tourism and shipping.

13. Ericson and Miller, op. cit., in note to Table 13.2.

14. X and MG derived from Soviet Vneshtorg data. See Hanson, 'The Import of Western Technology', in A. Brown and M.C. Kaser (eds.), The Soviet Union Since the Fall of Khrushchev (London: Macmillan, 2nd edn., 1978), pp. 16-49, and Table 13.3 of this paper. Full details of the regression analysis are given in Appendix A of Hanson, 'External Influences on the Soviet Economy since 1955: The Import of Western Technology', CREES Discussion Paper RC B/7 (1974).

14 East–West Co-operation in the Field of Environment

MARIO GUTTIERES

International Juridical Organisation, Rome

I INTRODUCTION

Environment protection is an area where international co-operation on global, regional and bilateral levels is imperative. Pollution, particularly of air and water, knows no boundaries; nor for that matter, does it discriminate on the basis of ideologies or politics.

In the last few decades there has been an ever increasing global recognition of the need for national action and international co-operation towards the preservation and improvement of the human environment for the benefit of all people and for their posterity.

The present paper examines such co-operation in the East-West context beginning with a discussion of the United Nations Economic Commission for Europe (ECE) which, including countries of both Eastern and Western Europe, as well as the United States of America and Canada, is the international organisation playing the most significant role in the environment. Along with this is presented a brief discussion of other international organisations, primarily UNEP, CMEA, EEC and OECD. Attention is also given to the various levels of East-West environmental co-operation, both within and without the ECE framework, ranging from discussions and meetings, to formulations of declarations, recommendations and guidelines and, finally, relevant bilateral and multilateral agreements and their precedent proposals. Particular emphasis is placed upon the Stockholm Conference of 1972, the Final Act of the Helsinki Conference of 1975 and the 1979 High-Level Meeting of the ECE States and the resulting ECE Convention on Long-Range Transboundary Air Pollution.

There follows a brief discussion of the important legal issues of liability, equal access and monitoring, the concluding paragraphs considering prospects for the 1980s.

II THE UN ECONOMIC COMMISSION FOR EUROPE

Including among its members the countries of both Eastern and Western Europe,[1] the United Nations Economic Commission for Europe (ECE) is the international organisation playing the most significant role in East-West relations generally, with questions of the environment taking on ever increasing importance within its activities and structure. In fact, of the five UN regional economic commissions, ECE has been the most active in environmental matters, working particularly on air and water pollution and urban problems.

The ECE principal subsidiary bodies most directly concerned with the environment are the Senior Advisors to ECE Governments on Environmental Problems and the Committee on Water Problems. These two bodies, together with the Committee on Housing, Building and Planning (involved in environmental as well as social and economic questions) are served by the Environment and Human Settlement Division of the ECE Office of the Executive Secretary.

Given the leading position of the ECE in matters of East-West relations, and taking into account the organic quality of ECE involvement in questions of the environment, a logical starting point for an understanding of prospects for continued East-West environmental co-operation is a review of past ECE activities in this field.

The ECE considered specific environmental problems, along with its examination of many others, in 1955 at the ad hoc meeting on Inland Waterway Problems of the Inland Transport Committee. Based on this committee's recommendation to the Eleventh Session of the Commission in 1956, a number of studies were subsequently undertaken and meetings organised under ECE auspices concerning an integrated approach to water pollution control.

In the 1960s the Commission's concern with the overall implications of water pollution led it to undertake studies and organise meetings on the broader question of the efficient utilisation of Europe's water resources. These activities were later combined with the earlier established programme on water pollution control. This led to the creation in 1967 of the ECE 'Body on Water Resources and Water Pollution Control Problems'. The name of this body, one of the Principal Subsidiary Bodies of the ECE, was changed in 1969 to the 'Committee on Water Problems'.

Since its establishment the Committee on Water Problems has, among other things:

Carried out and published studies on such questions as water management and investment choices; economic incentives in water supply and waste water disposal systems; sludge treatment, disposal and utilization; combined treatment of sewage and industrial wastes; cost evaluation of industrial effluent treatment; balances of water resources and needs; pollution of coastal and estuarial waters; rational methods of flood control planning; and the protection of inland waters against accidental pollution by oil and oil products.

Prepared and organized seminars for detailed examination of such selected problems as the protection of ground and surface waters against pollution by crude oil and oil products; river basin management; selected water problems in Southern Europe; methodology for the compilation of balances of water resources and needs; pollution of waters by agriculture and forestry; the use of computer techniques and automation for water resources systems; protection of coastal waters against pollution from land-based sources; and long-term planning of water management.

Undertaken in-depth studies of such problems as the methodology for the establishment of national and international protection standards for major water pollutants; long-term prospects for water use and supply; the application of systems analysis in water resources management; the prevention and control of water pollution, in particular of transboundary rivers and international lakes; and the protection of the marine environment from pollutants emanating from land-based sources.[2]

In the early 1960s the Coal Committee and the Inland Transport Committee, responding to an increasing international awareness of the problem of air pollution, initiated work on air pollution abatement techniques. At the same time the Commission decided on a comprehensive study of methods for dealing with air pollution from various domestic, commercial and industrial sources. The activities and meetings which followed this study led to the Commision's establishment in 1969 of a 'Working Party on Air Pollution Problems'. The early activities of the Working Party included preparation for the 1970 seminar in Geneva on the problem of desulphurisation of fuels and combustion gases. More recent developments regarding ECE activities for the control of air pollution are presented below under the discussion of the ECE Convention on Long-Range Transboundary Air Pollution.

In 1971 the Commission set up a new Principal Subsidiary Body, the 'Senior Advisors to ECE Governments on Environmental Problems', to which the Working Party on Air Pollution Problems was subordinated. This new body grew out of an increased recognition of the need for comprehensive international co-operation on protection of the environment, first proposed in the ECE context by the Czechoslovak Government in 1967. This proposal suggested the convening in Prague of an ECE Meeting of Governmental Experts on Problems Relating to the Environment in order to consider ever-increasing environmental problems from a comprehensive and long-term perspective. The Czechoslovak proposal was a forerunner of a similar proposal of the

Swedish Government to the UN General Assembly, which led to the United Nations Conference on the Human Environment in Stockholm in 1972 (discussed below), which preceded the establishment in 1973 of the United Nations Environmental Programme (UNEP).

At the time of the establishment of the Senior Advisors to ECE Governments on Environmental Problems it was also agreed that the ECE Symposium on Problems Relating to Environment, following the Czechoslovak proposal, be held in Prague in May 1971. The symposium was attended by approximately 300 participants from ECE member countries, other regions and some 40 international organisations. The symposium reviewed the state of the environment, examined the economic sectors generating pollution and nuisances, geographical regions affected and policies and strategies for protection of the environment. The participants discussed such matters as methods of planning and management; organisational and institutional arrangements; research, dissemination of knowledge, training in environmental disciplines and public education and information; costs, financing and other economic aspects of environmental protection and improvement; and the need for effective environmental information services at national and international levels. The symposium also made a series of recommendations for activities by the newly created Principal Subsidiary Body.

The main achievements of the Senior Advisers on Environmental Problems since its inception include:

Studies prepared and seminars and other meetings held to examine such subjects as environmental policy; methods of impact assessment and planning; appropriate use of natural resources and waste management technology control; and the data and information systems.

Through the Working Party on Air Pollution Problems, activities have been initiated for pollution abatement and control in the ECE region.

With the help of intergovernmental task forces, cooperation has been promoted on specific environmental problems of a technical nature, such as methods for economic assessment of environmental damage, control of noise and odours, establishment of indicators of environmental quality and control of emissions from certain heavily polluting industries.

Close cooperation has been set up with other international organizations, especially UNEP, for the implementation of projects of common interest.[3]

And, most recently, a High-Level Meeting on the Environment was convened.

Besides the Senior Advisors to ECE States on Environmental Problems and the Committee on Water Problems, environmental matters have been taken into account by other ECE Principal Subsidiary Bodies, most notably the Coal Committee, the Committee on Electric Power, the Committee on Gas and the Committee on Housing, Building and Planning.

While the great majority of East-West co-operative activities on environmental law and policy within the context of the ECE have remained on the level of discussion, study, meetings and seminars, and exchange of information, there are many notable examples of more concrete steps having been taken in the form of the drafting of declarations, recommendations and guidelines and, most recently, a convention (on Long-Range Transboundary Air Pollution). Recommendations and guidelines established have been aimed primarily at the harmonisation of legislation, policies and practices in the ECE region.

Examples of relevant declarations, resulting from efforts of the Senior Advisors on the Environment and the Water Committee include the ECE declaration of Policy on Water Pollution Control (1966) and the Declaration on Low and Non-Waste Technology and the Re-Utilization and Recycling of Wastes (1979) (discussed further below). Their recommendations have covered the abatement of emissions from the non-ferrous metallurgical industries (1974); legislative and economic measures to reduce solid wastes at the source, and on re-use of solid wastes (1976); the promotion of environmentally sound technology (1976); the abatement of emissions from the inorganic chemical industry (1977); the Protection of Ground and Surface Waters against Pollution by Oil and Oil Products (1970); Selected Water Problems in Southern Europe (1972); Pollution of Waters by Agriculture and Forestry (1974); Long-Term Planning of Water Management (1976).

Promising co-operation in the East-West context is taking place in the form of ECE development of guidelines. For example, as a follow-up to the ECE seminars on Air Pollution Problems from the Non-Ferrous Metallurgical Industries, held in Dubrovnik in 1973, a task force from eleven countries was established to draft guidelines for the abatement of pollutants from such industries. The Report of the Eighth Session of Senior Advisors to EEC Governments on Environmental Problems (18-22 February 1980) states regarding progress in the development of these guidelines:

The Senior Advisors noted that this project was near completion, as the final report and guidelines adopted by the task force had been forwarded to the secretariat by the lead country (Federal Republic of Germany) for final consideration by the Working Party on Air Pollution Problems in April 1980.[4]

The Working Party on Air Pollution also intends to draft guidelines for the control of emissions from the inorganic chemical industry, although work on this project has not yet begun. And although the Senior Advisors had established a project for the development of guidelines for the control of emissions from specific branches of the organic chemical industry, this was deleted from the work programme of their Eighth Session, February 1980.

The ECE Convention on Long-Range Transboundary Air Pollution and the Declaration on Low and Non-Waste Technology and Re-Utilization and Recycling of Wastes are discussed below.

Somewhat discouraging regarding the future development of formal agreements is the decision of the Senior Advisors on Environmental Problems at its Eighth Session to delete from its work programme the project on 'Treaties, Conventions, Agreements and International Problems of Large Areas in the ECE Region'.[5] This deletion, of course, would not necessarily exclude the possibility of agreements arising out of the Senior Advisors' individual work areas.

III OTHER INTERNATIONAL ORGANISATIONS

The primary UN bodies with which the Senior Advisors co-operate include UNEP, UNESCO, WHO, FAO, UNIDO, WMO, IMCO and IAEA. There follows a brief description of UNEP and its co-operative relationship with the ECE.

As a result of a recommendation at the Stockholm Conference (discussed below under 'Stockholm, Helsinki and Brezhnev Proposals'), UNEP was established, and held its first session at Geneva in June 1973.

The basic aims of UNEP are (1) to promote international cooperation in the environmental field; (2) to keep under review the world environmental situation in order to ensure that environmental problems of wide international significance receive appropriate consideration by governments; and (3) to promote the acquisition, assessment and exchange of environmental knowledge.

Also in 1973 a co-operative programme was established between the ECE and UNEP. One of the main objectives of the programme is to accelerate or expand specific ECE activities in accordance with the priority requirements of UNEP. A number of areas of mutual interest and concern were identified at the intersecretariat UNEP-ECE Joint Programming Meeting in 1976. Particular areas of co-operation were specified in the Memorandum of Understanding between the two secretariats drafted subsequently to this meeting and signed by the Executive Secretary of ECE and the Executive Director of UNEP. The present basis for co-operation is the contractual arrangement[6] signed by ECE and the UNEP Fund in 1978 for a further two-year period. Indications are that this relationship will certainly be renewed in 1980, given the important ECE contributions which could provide substantive input into the work of UNEP in other regions.

The general subjects covered by the UNEP and ECE cooperation include environmentally sound and appropriate technologies; techniques of environmental impact assessment; environment and resource conservation in forestry and agriculture; effects of pollution on vegetation; building materials and construction techniques for low-cost housing in developing countries; water resources management; environmental problems of ECE countries bordering the Mediterranean; environmental aspects of land-use planning; and environmental statistics. More recently, financial support has been given by UNEP to such ECE projects as the international programme for the monitoring and evaluation of the long-range transport of air pollutants, starting with sulphur dioxide; and the compendium of available knowledge on low and non-waste technology. [7]

Examples of specific co-operative activities are the contribution to the Coal Committee's Symposium on Environmental Problems Resulting from Coal Industry Activities, held in Poland in 1976 (this provided a forum for discussion of intergovernmental and inter-industry co-operation on land reclamation after open-cut extraction of coal, mining damage, treatment and utilisation of mine waters and sewage and related topics); co-operation in the preparation for the ECE Symposium on the effects of pollution on vegetation, Poland 1978. Most recently, the ECE and UNEP jointly convened the Regional Seminar on Alternative Patterns of Development and Life-styles, in Ljubljana, Yugoslavia, December 1979. UNEP also convened an interregional seminar on this subject in 1980, with the participation of the Executive Secretaries of the Regional Committees, including that of the ECE.

In 1982 it is expected that the first system-wide medium-term Environment Programme for the whole UN system, covering the period from 1984 to 1989, will be presented to the UNEP Governing Council. A new important development is the launching in March 1980 of the World Conservation Strategy simultaneously in thirty-three capital cities, including sixteen in ECE countries. This strategy was prepared by UNEP-IUCN-WWF (World Wildlife Fund), and will be briefly discussed in the section on Future Prospects.

There are other UNEP initiatives which, like the above mentioned medium-term programme and the Conservation Strategy, do not arise in the express ECE context of East-West co-operation, but, nonetheless, deserve mention since they include the active participation of representatives of both East and West countries and, at the same time, directly concern development of environmental law on national, regional and global levels. Most significant in this regard are:

1. The 'Draft Principles of Conduct in the Field of the Environment for the Guidance of States in the Conservation and Harmonious Utilization of Natural Resources Shared by Two or More States' included in the Final Report of an Intergovernmental Working Group of Experts.[8] This report was adopted by the Governing Council of UNEP by its decision 6/14 of May 1978 and later, following recognition of the principles being purely recommendatory in nature, by the UN General Assembly.

2. The work of UNEP's Working Group of Experts on Environmental Law, thus far, in its first five sessions,[9] on the establishment of conclusions on Pollution from Offshore Mining and Drilling Carried out Within the Limits of National Jurisdiction. The Group hopes to conclude its work on this topic by the end of 1980 and begin another tentatively established as 'The Improvement of Remedies Available on a National and International Basis to Victims of Pollution, Taking into Account the Concept of Non-Discrimination'.

Although the ECE maintains relations with many intergovernmental non-UN organisations, those most important in a discussion of East-West relations are the European Economic Community (EEC), including a number of states in Western Europe, and the CMEA, including a large majority of the Eastern European States.

It was only with the favourable political climate of the mid-1970s that the ECE was able to give a formal interorganisational status to the European Economic Community (EEC)[10] and the Council for Mutual Economic Assistance (CMEA)[11] at its XIII Session, in 1975.

Both the EEC and the CMEA are active in areas of environmental protection. The EEC programmes in this area fall within the jurisdiction of the Environment and Consumer Protection Service of the Commission of the European Communities. What can be considered the corresponding organ in the CMEA is the Board for the Protection and Improvement of the Environment.[12]

The primary difference between the EEC and the CMEA is that the EEC has a generally recognised legal personality and acts as a supranational body to which its member nations have agreed to be subordinate, while the CMEA remains an association of States, with no juridical personality and, therefore, unlike the EEC, not empowered to conclude treaties in its own name. It concludes treaties but the contracting parties are always the individual states, not the organisation as such.

Even though the CMEA as an organisation cannot be compared to the EEC in its structure and international competence, it has made certain valid contributions to the international development of environmental protection such as, for instance, in the preparation of the Paris Seminar of November 1976 on the Principles and on the Development of Non-Waste Technologies and Productions, when the Senior Advisors to the ECE Governments on Environmental problems asked the Secretariat of the CMEA to submit a report on the chief findings of the symposium in Dresden (March 1976) held by specialists and scientists of the CMEA countries, under the auspices of CMEA. The CMEA are stressing the need to standardise measurements and classifications, which are matters also stressed by the Geneva Convention 1979 on Long-Range Transboundary Air-Pollution.

Despite its vast powers to conclude treaties in its own name, the EEC has not really concluded much. The pending agreement with the CMEA has not been concluded because of political differences. The latest Convention, the Convention on Long-Range Transboundary Air Pollution, is therefore especially significant because the EEC signed it in its own name, and there are CMEA-member countries also signing despite this. The Community is a contracting party to the Barcelona Convention, and has adhered to the Paris Convention on the Prevention of Marine Pollution from Land-Based Sources. The Community is further negotiating accession to the Helsinki Convention on the Protection of the Marine Environment of the Baltic Sea Area. Negotiations have continued for a number of years between the EEC and the CMEA for the establishment of a co-operation agreement but, for political reasons, these negotiations have not yet moved beyond the proposal stage. What agreements exist between the two are bilateral, between individual member States.

Of value for the furthering of provisions and agreements in the field of environment can be the studies conducted by the OECD, which have had a wider application than the regional scope of this body, especially on the question of transfrontier pollution.

IV VARIOUS LEVELS OF EAST-WEST CO-OPERATION

Because water courses delineate the principal boundaries between Eastern and Western Europe, they provided a natural point of departure for East-West co-operation in the form of bilateral agreements. On the subject of transfrontier water pollution, several examples of early bilateral agreements involving a country of Eastern and a country of Western Europe can be cited: the Austro-Hungarian Danube Agreement of 1956, the Finnish-Soviet Boundary Treaty of 1960, the Austrian-Czechoslovak Boundary Waters Agreement of 1967, the Greek-Bulgarian Boundary Rivers Agreement of 1969, the 1973 Intra-German Agreement on Boundary Waters Management, the 1973 bilateral agreement between FRG and GDR on Transfrontier Emergencies and the 1974 Italian-Yugoslav Agreement on Marine Pollution Control in the Adriatic Sea.

There are also relevant East-West agreements concluded between States with no common frontier, such as the US-USSR agreement of 1972 and the US-Poland Environmental Protection Agreement of 1974, the latter of which provides among other things, for collaboration, especially in the abatement and control of atmospheric and water pollution, noise and vibration abatement and protection against the effects of ionising radiations as a pollutant. Also envisaged in the

US-Poland agreement are: joint scientific and technical research, exchange of scientific and technical information and documentation, etc. Another example is the Franco-Polish environmental collaboration which dates from 1969 and is based on the Agreement on Scientific, Technological and Cultural Co-operation. Within this framework meetings of experts are being organised (e.g. the Franco-Polish Session for the Prevention of Water Pollution, March 1975, Warsaw) and an exchange of information and experience is taking place. Also relevant to the question of environmental protection is the restriction of underground nuclear arms testing.

There are also many multilateral agreements of a global or universal character relevant to environmental protection and including signatory States of both East and West. Perfect examples of such agreements are the numerous IMCO Conventions and the agreement being negotiated at the Third UN Conference on the Law of the Sea.

The most important of the regional multilateral agreements fitting in an expressly East-West context include the Convention on the Protection of the Marine Environment of the Baltic Sea, Helsinki 1974, and its precursor Convention on Fishing and Conservation of the Living Resources in the Baltic Sea, Gdansk, 1973; the Environmental Chapter of the Final Act of the Conference on Security and Co-operation in Europe (CSCE) Helsinki, 1975; and the Convention on Long-Range Transboundary Air Pollution. Consideration here is limited to the Baltic conventions; the Final Act of the CSCE and the Transboundary Air Pollution Convention are taken up later in the paper.

The Gdansk Convention applies to the Baltic Sea and the Belts with the exclusion of internal waters and applies not only to fish but, as its title indicates, to all living resources of the sea. Included among the terms for the protection of these resources are provisions for the artificial reproduction of certain fish species.

Recognising that protection of the Baltic against pollution was necessary for, among other reasons, protection of its living resources in accordance with Gdansk, the Baltic States in March 1974 signed at Helsinki the Convention on the Protection of the Marine Environment of the Baltic Sea - a comprehensive approach to the protection of that sea. It is worth noting that among the terms agreed the States specifically undertook to adopt all necessary measures to implement the objectives of the Convention in their internal waters in order to minimise pollution from harmful substances carried by those waters. The States also agreed to develop without delay and to adopt unified standards concerning responsibility for damages caused by actions or omissions violating the provisions of the Convention. While there have in fact been delays regarding the implementation of the Convention, it can only be hoped that the efforts of the Interim Baltic Maritime Commission for the Protection of the Marine Environment will soon lead to its full implementation.

Global impetus for international co-operation in the field of the environment - which had been earlier initiated in the East-West setting by the Czechoslovak Proposal of 1967 (discussed above), the resulting 1971 Prague Symposium, and the creation of the Senior Advisors to ECE Governments on Environmental Problems - was provided by the Stockholm Conference.

In June of 1972, following a recommendation of the Government of Sweden to the UN General Assembly, delegates from 113 States gathered for the United Nations Conference on the Human Environment in Stockholm and approved a Declaration on the Human Environment, an Action Plan and a detailed proposal to the UN General Assembly to set up continuing institutional and financial means to implement the Action Plan.[13] A political consensus was reached to assess and reduce pollution levels for the protection of future generations, and the institutional and financial means - the United Nations Environment Programme (UNEP) - were created by the General Assembly in December 1972.[14] The Declaration formalised numerous global principles regarding aspects of man's natural and man-made environment, including recognition that:

> Through fuller knowledge and wiser action we can achieve for ourselves and our posterity a better life in an environment more in keeping with human needs and hopes. ... this environmental goal will demand the acceptance of responsibility by citizens and communities and by enterprises and institutions at every level, all sharing equitably in common efforts. Individuals in all walks of life as well as organizations in many fields, by their values and the sum of their actions, will shape the world environment of the future.

The introductory proclamations go on to note that:

> A growing class of environmental problems, because they are regional or global in extent or because they affect the common international realm, will require extensive cooperation among nations and action by international organizations in the common interest. The Conference calls upon Governments and peoples to exert common efforts for the preservation and improvement of the human environment, for the benefit of all the people and for their posterity.

Principles 21 and 22 of the Declaration proclaimed three principles which hold very important positions in all negotiations for further development of international environmental law:

1. States have a sovereign right to exploit their own resources pursuant to their own environmental policies.
2. States are responsible for ensuring that activities within their jurisdiction or control do not cause damage to the environment of other states, or of areas beyond the limits of national jurisdiction.

3. States are under a duty to co-operate to develop further the international law as to liability and compensation for the victims of pollution and other environmental damage caused by such activities to areas beyond national jurisdiction.

With the momentum created by Prague and Stockholm the Governments of Europe were ready to include a chapter on the environment in the Final Act of the Conference on Security and Co-operation in Europe, Helsinki 1975.

Among the topics considered in the Helsinki accords, signed by thirty-five States, are:

(i)   Questions Relating to Security in Europe (Co-operation in the Fields of Economics, Science and Technology, and the Environment);

(ii)   Questions Relating to Security and Co-operation in the Mediterranean;

(iii) Co-operation in Humanitarian and Other Fields (Human Contacts, Information, Culture, Education);

(iv)   Follow-up to the Conference.

It was at Helsinki that Leonid Brezhnev made his proposal for all European Congresses on the topics of energy, transport and environment, which has influenced consideration of High-Level Meetings in the ECE context.

The Helsinki Chapter on Environment calls for the States to:

make use of every suitable opportunity to cooperate in the field of environment, in particular within the following areas:

- Air Pollution Control;
- Water Pollution Control and Fresh Water Utilization;
- Protection of the Marine Environment;
- Land Utilization and Soils;
- Nature Conservation and Nature Reserves;
- Improvement of Environmental Conditions in Areas of Human Settlement;
- Fundamental Research Monitoring, Forecasting and Assessment of Environmental Changes.

As well as work within international organisations and the national implementation of laws which would bring into line the various conventions and bilateral agreements they had signed, the idea of meetings of heads of State and other high-level officials on environmental problems in Europe was given a major thrust at the 33rd Session of the ECE, held in Geneva in 1978.

There was passed a resolution (I XXXIII) requiring the preparation of various high-level meetings within the framework of ECE, especially on the subjects of long-range transboundary air pollution, and low and non-waste technology and reutilisation and recycling of wastes. At the same time the establishment of a body of Senior Advisors to ECE Governments on energy was proposed.

Evidently precursory was the above-mentioned proposal of Leonid Brezhnev calling for the convening of European conferences on the topics of energy, transport and environment. Much discussion took place between the making of the proposal and the actual consensus, finally reached at the 32nd Session of the ECE which adopted the proposal in Res. (I XXXIII). This Resolution established as criteria for the selection of topics:

> That the subject matter should require a high level of represen-
> tation; that such a meeting should hold promise of important
> decisions, and that the topics under consideration should be of
> concern to the region as a whole, and not lead to unnecessary
> duplication of work of other international organizations.

On request, Governments submitted commentaries on the topics they thought most suitable for treatment at high-level meetings. The answers indicated mostly: transboundary air pollution, low and non-waste technology, transboundary water pollution, control of toxic substances and toxic wastes, and protection of native flora and fauna and their habitat.

Following substantial ECE preparatory efforts, the first High-Level Meeting in the thirty-three years of the ECE was held in Geneva, 13-16 November 1979 on the subject of environmental protection. At this meeting, representatives of the ECE member countries of ministerial or equivalent rank formally adopted an ECE Convention and a Resolution on Long-Range Transboundary Air Pollution and a Declaration on Low and Non-Waste Technology and Re-Utilization and Recycling of Wastes. This High-Level Meeting additionally engaged in a general debate on other environmental problems in the ECE region.

Concern within the ECE region about long-range transboundary air pollution has grown along with the problem itself, which is often manifested in the form of 'acid rains' falling hundreds of miles from the air pollution source. As discussed above, study of techniques for limiting such pollution has been going on within ECE's Working Party on Air Pollution Problems since its preparation for the 1970 seminar on the problem of desulphurisation of fuels and combustion gases. Desulphurisation techniques have been used with some success in the region and some countries have, through national regulation, restricted the use of high-sulphur fuels and other air pollutants. While these approaches, coupled with the advent of ever-higher smokestacks, have often been effective in reducing local air pollution, the higher stacks have also had the effect of causing wider dispersion of pollutants beyond national borders.

The Convention represents a major step forward in regional (as well as East-West) co-operation following the Brezhnev proposal for all-European conferences on energy, transport and environment and the CSCE (Helsinki).

Following many bilateral agreements, this Convention represents the first multilateral agreement which addresses itself to the problem of transnational air pollution on a multilateral scale. It contains provisions on such matters as exchange of information, consultation, and research and monitoring. The parties agree to use the best available technology which is economically feasible and undertake to develop, without undue delay, policies and strategies which shall serve to combat the discharge of air pollutants.

The accompanying resolution adopted by the Meeting provides that the signatories to the Convention shall initiate as soon as possible, on an interim basis, the provisional implementation of the Convention and shall carry out the obligations arising under the Convention to the maximum extent possible pending its entry into force. The Convention and the Resolution represent an important step forward in East-West environmental co-operation and pave the way for further agreements for co-operation on other regional environmental concerns. Even given the landmark quality of the Convention, however, many observers had hoped for a stronger agreement. It should be noted particularly that the Convention contains no provision concerning the effects of violation or disregard of the provisions of the Convention.

The Declaration on Low and Non-Waste Technology and the Re-Utilization and Recycling of Wastes recommends the evaluation of the industrial application of this technology to optimise the use of raw materials and energy, recycling and economic efficiency. There is also to be an exchange of information with the ECE Working Groups. Although the Declaration does not enter upon any new ground, it does formalise the existing will of the ECE Governments in this regard and thereby provides impetus for future work.

One major issue which warrants increased attention in, among others, the East-West context is the question of responsibility for damages caused by pollution. The Baltic States undertook at Helsinki to develop and adopt unified standards concerning responsibility for damages caused by actions or omissions violating the provisions of the Convention. It is to be regretted that no agreement in this regard has been reached by the Contracting Parties and that no such provisions appear to be in preparation on a wider scale as, for instance, in the recent Convention on Long-Range Transboundary Air Pollution where the question of liability is expressly omitted.

It is significant that between States sharing frontier waters provisions are often made for compensation for damages caused by pollution. An example of this is found in the agreement between Poland and the USSR of 15 February 1961, which provides for the parties to pay damages should they fail to comply with the obligations to maintain frontier waters in a proper state. It is to be hoped that such provisions will be extended to other types of agreement, also on a multilateral scale, thereby furthering the duty undertaken at Stockholm to co-operate on establishing standards for liability and compensation.

In this regard, the International Law Commission (ILC) has studied and prepared draft articles on the question of State responsibility.

The object of the ILC is to codify the rules governing State responsibility as a general and independent topic. The work is proceeding on the basis of two decisions of the Commission: (a) not to limit its study of the topic to a particular area, such as the responsibility for injuries to the person or property of aliens, or indeed any other area; (b) in codifying the rules governing international responsibility, not to engage in the definition and codification of the 'primary' rules whose breach entails responsibility for an internationally wrongful act.[15]

Evidently, much remains to be done even after the codification by the ILC, not least to achieve universal recognition of State responsibility principles. One problem in this context which will also have to be examined is how far States are responsible for the actions of their nationals, or in the case of ships, for vessels registered under their flags, the latter being especially relevant in the case of maritime oil pollution.

Having once established the need for definite rules and policies on the questions of liability, another area requiring attention is that of which body shall have competence to decide questions of liability - should it be a national court, and if so, which nation's court; an international body, such as the International Court of Justice; an arbitrator; or any combination of these. Arbitration procedures exist under some conventions such as the Bonn Convention 1976 (binding), the 1976 Barcelona Convention (non-binding) and the London Dumping Convention, but the States often prefer to settle their differences by negotiation and other diplomatic means.

The OECD investigation on the possibility of the States having equal access to the internal judicial fora of the other signatory or member States is highly relevant in this procedural context. Not only because of its findings on the question of equal access, but also because it brings up the question of whether one should first have to exhaust the remedies available in separate States, before going to an international body (as is the case, for example, with the International Court of Justice).

Further in this regard, if there is to be a system for the international liability of States, there must also be an effective monitoring system, which is independent politically and nationally, presumably an international body. It is, however, difficult to create such a body as its activity would be considered by many states as interfering in its internal affairs.

A step in the right direction is found in the Oslo agreement of 1974 on a Cooperative Programme for the Monitoring and Evaluation of the Transmission of Air Pollutants in Europe. It was therein agreed that the Programme would be implemented under the auspices of the ECE as a part of the global monitoring system set up within the framework of UNEP. Much, however, still remains to be done for an effective monitoring system. There is a great need for further co-ordination of existing monitoring programmes under way in numerous international fora, most notably: UNEP, WHO, IOC, UNESCO, ECE, IUCN, SCOPE (Scientific Committee on Problems of the Environment), EEC and CMEA.

Hopefully, the good intentions expressed by both East and West in numerous international fora and instruments will lead to further co-operation on questions of liability, equal access and monitoring.

VI PROSPECTS FOR THE 1980s

Much has been accomplished on the arduous road of East-West environmental co-operation and agreement, and a great deal has still to be accomplished. The way agreements on environmental protection have developed, it seems that more than ever before there are chances of achieving rapid progress in the form of global, regional, subregional and bilateral agreements. Indeed, in certain areas multilateral agreements seem the only solution. It appears as if most of the multilateral co-operation between East and West will continue to occur under the auspices of the UN organs, especially the ECE. The ECE, and more particularly, the all-important Senior Advisors to ECE Governments on Environmental Protection, have a full programme for the near future.

The Senior Advisors in conjunction with the Committee on Water Problems have been invited, as far as possible, to draft the ECE Declaration of Policy on Prevention and Control of Water Pollution, including Transboundary Pollution. With the example of the Convention on Long-Range Transboundary Air Pollution concluded, it is not impossible that an international agreement on water can also be reached. Certainly, the already existing commissions (e.g. the Danube, the Rhine, the Interim Baltic) would work very closely with the ECE in this regard.

Within the activities of the ECE a topic which is steadily gaining in importance, and which is sure to advance greatly during the 1980s, is that of Environmental Impact Assessment (EIA). It is still in its infancy - the Seminar of the Senior Advisors to ECE Governments on Environmental Problems in its recommendations indicates that they are as yet in the stage of collecting for analysis, information of environmental impact procedures. They are also considering linking the study of EIA with energy problems and efforts for their resolution. EIA remains a relatively new area requiring a great deal more study.

Another area where further co-operation is foreseen is energy, which so far has not had a prominent place, but which, considering the predicted and actual energy shortages and the proposals of, among others, Leonid Brezhnev, is steadily gaining in importance. With this increased importance and recognising the need for a comprehensive, balanced approach to the development of energy sources and the conservation of natural resources and the environment in the ECE region, at its 34th Session the ECE established an ad hoc Principal Subsidiary Body, the 'Senior Advisors to ECE Governments on Energy'. Part of their mandate is set forth as:

(b) To elaborate (. . .) a programme of work subject to annual review and approval by the Commission, taking into account the need for regular cooperation and coordination with the committees on Coal, Electric Power, and Gas, and cooperation with other Principal Subsidiary Bodies concerned; (. . .).
(c) To examine problems related to a possible High-Level Meeting on Energy organized within the framework of the ECE.[16]

The activities of this new ad hoc body deserve the close attention of observers of East-West co-operation. The proposed High-Level Meeting on Energy would, indeed, accelerate the momentum established by the unprecedented November 1979 High-Level Meeting, by again bringing together ministerial level representatives of East and West to make concrete decisions and commitments for future co-operation.

Suggested topics for a conference on energy have been: long-range transmission of energy and the interlinking of energy systems in Europe; the establishment of a unified system of gas pipe-lines; rationalisation and efficiency in the production, transport and utilisation of fuels including modern refining methods and construction of fuel and energy complexes for the utilisation of black coal, brown coal and lignites.

There are several other projects and studies conducted within the ECE which should reach conclusion in the near future and lead to increased co-operation, perhaps even in the form of further multilateral conventions where appropriate.

An example of such studies is the project on the 'Economic Assessment of Environmental Damage Caused by Air Pollution', expected to be completed by 1981. This is especially important because of the new emphasis on the close relationships between development and environmental protection. There are several more specific projects, such as the one on the 'Recycling, Re-use and Recovery of Municipal and Industrial Solid Wastes', due to be completed this year. These studies have a very wide scope, cover a vast range of different topics, and certainly will be served by the co-ordination of the new ad hoc ECE Subsidiary Body on Energy.

Also important for the 1980s is the implementation of the latest convention, on Long-Range Transboundary Air Pollution, which hopefully will get early ratification, and immediate implementation in accordance with its accompanying resolution.

The work of UNEP as the UN family catalyst, watchdog and co-ordinator on environmental matters is very encouraging, particularly as it acts in co-operation with the ECE in the East-West context. Also very promising are the environmental activities of the sub-regional organisations such as the CMEA, the EEC and OECD, which are often undertaken with a view toward eventual ECE regional (East-West) co-operation.

The Stockholm principles and declarations show that nations have come to realise the important connection between development and environmental protection. What must be even more fully realised is that although individual States do have a right to their own natural resources, they are also responsible for their administration, and for their conservation for future generations. It follows that there is a duty of all States to take this into account in their policies - a responsibility for which they are answerable to the rest of the world.

Connected is, of course, the ever-present problem of monitoring and State liability - if one recognises principles of international responsibility then there must follow recognition of the need for an efficient system of monitoring.

These considerations are not only important for East-West co-operation but also for the North-South dialogue. The East-West co-operation on environmental protection is a necessary prelude to a meaningful North-South dialogue on the same theme.

Worthy of special attention in this regard is the recently released World Conservation Strategy, elaborated by IUCN,[17] UNEP and the WWF. This points out what obstacles there are to achieving conservation, such as the already discussed failure to integrate conservation with development. The strategy, as stated in the Executive Summary, is intended to stimulate a more focused approach to the management of living resources and to provide policy guidance on how this can be carried out. The guidance is for three main groups: (a) government policy-makers and their advisors; (b) conservationists and others directly concerned with living resources; and (c) development practitioners, including development agencies, industry and commerce, and trade unions.

The contributions these different groups could make to development of the Conservation Strategy vary in different countries. It is, for example, more probable that in a developed market economy it would be the industry and commerce sector, and possibly the trade unions, who would oppose conservationist policies which might jeopardise the incrementation of industrial production. In developing nations, the governments themselves might have arguments against too close a connection between environment protection, the conservation strategy and development (witness the controversial recommendation at Stockholm on measures for compensation). It is, however, to be hoped that such obstacles will be overcome, considering the importance of the World Conservation Strategy.

In conclusion, it may be said that East-West co-operation in the field of environment, despite the many halts for diverse political reasons, is conducted on different levels, the bilateral and the regional, the latter especially under the auspices of different international UN organisations. Hopefully, in a not-too-distant future, a more direct regional co-operation will be possible.

A lot of activities are planned for the future, some of which have been referred to in this paper, but despite this there is still a great need for further planning. It is therefore essential that the peoples and governments of both East and West realise that what is at stake is something which is of vastly greater importance than political differences or political and economic ideologies. It is simply the survival of man in an environment he has contributed to create. It is to be hoped that governments will continue to develop bases for meaningful co-operation on the environment, and that the temporary halt of East-West environmental co-operation following the Afghanistan events will not be allowed to continue. The efforts of concerned individuals and organisations will only be as effective as the co-operative desires of the governments of both East and West.

NOTES

1. The following thirty-four countries are members of the Economic Commission for Europe; Albania; Austria; Belgium; Bulgaria; Byelorussian Soviet Socialist Republic; Canada; Cyprus; Czechoslovakia; Denmark; Finland; France; German Democratic Republic; Germany, Federal Republic of; Greece; Hungary; Iceland; Ireland; Italy; Luxembourg; Malta; Netherlands; Norway; Poland; Portugal; Romania; Spain; Sweden; Switzerland; Turkey; Ukranian Soviet Socialist Republic; Union of Soviet Socialist Republics; United Kingdom; United States; and Yugoslavia.
2. From Three Decades of the United Nations Economic Commission for Europe, E/ECE 962, Chapter X, p. 157.
3. Ibid., p. 72.
4. Senior Advisors 8th Session ECE/ENV/33, 28 February 1980.
5. Ibid.
6. UNEP project number FP/0302/78/02 - 'Continuation of Cooperation with the U.N. Regional Commission (Europe)'.
7. From Three Decades of the United Nations Economic Commission for Europe, E/ECE 962, Appendix D, p. 224.
8. Report of the Intergovernmental Working Group of Experts on Natural Resources Shared by Two or More States, Fifth Session, UNEP/IG.12/2; 8 February 1978.

9. UNEP's Working Group of Experts on Environmental Law, Geneva
   First Session: UNEP/WG.12/3, 3 October 1977;
   Second Session: UNEP/WG.14/4, 12 April 1978;
   Third Session: UNEP/WG.24/3, 16 March 1979;
   Fourth Session: UNEP/WG.34/1, 12 October 1979.
10. Members of the EEC include Belgium, Denmark, Federal Republic
    of Germany, France, Ireland, Italy, Luxembourg, Netherlands and
    United Kingdom.
11. Members of the CMEA include Albania (an 'inactive' member
    since 1961), Bulgaria, Cuba, Czechoslovakia, German Democratic
    Republic, Hungary, Mongolia, Poland, Romania, the USSR and
    Vietnam. Yugoslavia participates under special arrangements. See
    G. Schiavone, The Institutions of Comecon (London: Macmillan,
    1981).
12. The Board for the Protection and Improvement of the Environ-
    ment undertakes the co-ordination of co-operation in solving the
    questions included in the Overall Expanded Programme of Co-
    operation, worked out by the CMEA Committee for Scientific and
    Technical Cooperation in the Field of the Protection and Im-
    provement of the Natural Environment and Related Rational Use
    of Natural Resources. The Programme was worked out for CMEA
    member-states and Yugoslavia.
13. Report of the United Nations Conference on the Human
    Environment, Stockholm, 5-16 June 1972, UN Doc.
    A/Conf./48/14/Rev.1.
14. UN General Assembly 27th Session, Resolutions number 2997
    (XXVII); 3002 (XXVII), and 3004 (XXVII).
15. Report of the ILC on the work of its Twenty-first Session, 14 May
    to 3 August 1979.
16. From 'The Resolution and Other Decisions Adopted by the Thirty-
    Fourth Session of the Economic Commission for Europe' E/ECE
    (XXXIV)/L.21.
17. The International Union for the Conservation of Nature and
    Natural Resources (IUCN) is the leading worldwide general
    conservation organisation. Although it is classified as a non-
    governmental organisation (NGO), its members include national
    governments and governmental agencies as well as national and
    international NGOs.

Index